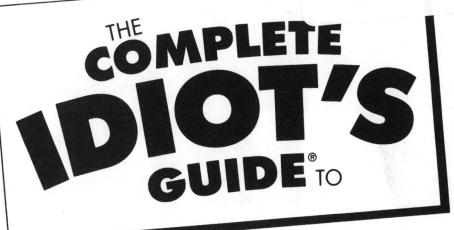

THE COMPLETE IDIOT'S GUIDE® TO

Personal Finance for Canadians

by Lori M. Bamber

Prentice
Hall
Canada

A Pearson Company
Toronto

alpha books

Canadian Cataloguing in Publication Data

Bamber, Lori M.
 The complete idiot's guide to personal finance for Canadians

New ed.
Includes index.
ISBN 0-13-089358-7

1. Finance, Personal—Canada. 2. Investments—Canada. I. Title.

HG179.B33 2000   332.024'01   C00-931440-7

ISBN 0-13-089358-7

Editorial Director, Trade Division: Andrea Crozier
Acquisitions Editor: Nicole de Montbrun
Copy Editor: Valerie Adams
Substantive Editor: Bruce McDougall
Production Editor: Lori McLellan
Art Direction: Mary Opper
Cover Image: Photodisk
Cover Design: Monica Kompter
Interior Design: Scott Cook and Amy Adams of DesignLab
Production Manager: Kathrine Pummell
Production Coordinator: Gerda Hockridge
Page Layout: B.J. Weckerle
Illustrator: Paul McCusker

1 2 3 4 5 WC 04 03 02 01 00

Printed and bound in Canada.

Visit the Prentice Hall Canada Web site! Send us your comments, browse our catalogues, and more. **www.phcanada.com**.

Prentice
Hall
Canada

A Pearson Company

Contents at a Glance

Contents

Foreword

Competition has always been in my blood. From my earliest days on skis, I can remember taking on all comers. This stubborn, competitive streak certainly served me well on the downhill tracks around the world as I aspired to become an Olympic champion.

And just how does one become a ski champion?

It starts as the pursuit of a dream. But winning gold does not happen overnight. It's achieving a series of interim targets, building patiently to the ultimate goal. It's an attitude. Learning from both mistakes and successes. Working closely with good coaches, as they offered advice and guidance. And in the end, the wealth of experience, built through dedicated effort, brought it all together in a successful game plan. As I moved closer to my ultimate goal in sport, I realized these same basic principles could help me achieve any important task.

Success is never is attained by accident. It's a combination of hard work, focusing and remaining dedicated to a plan. It is a journey of discovery, seeking out new ideas or concepts. There really is precious little separating a strategy to win a World Cup downhill race and preparing a successful investment plan.

This book provides you with your plan, your roadmap. Lori Bamber provides sound strategies and a wealth of experience to help you build a solid financial foundation. Success often can be found with outside the box thinking. For example, who would think investing time in your community would have a personal finance payback?

It's easy to extol the virtues of how to save your money. But what about how you spend your hard-earned cash? The essential building blocks of investment-RRSPs, RESPs, mutual funds and investment strategies are explained in clear, concise language. I found the tips, charts and advice, which Lori uses to illustrate the financial roadmap, both insightful and entertaining. After reading *The Complete Idiot's Guide® to Personal Finance for Canadians*, I'm ready to review my own portfolio, now that I understand the concept of asset allocation to weight a portfolio. As well, I discovered how index funds reduce my investment expenses to increase returns.

No pain, no gain is a truism in sport and the same applies to your portfolio. Good advice helps negotiate the shoals of divorce and bankruptcy, paying your taxes, or handling a mortgage.

I achieved my sport goals by investing time and energy to reach the goal of becoming a world champion. None of it would have been possible without good coaching. These dedicated individuals and their instruction, insight and experience made all the difference in realizing success. Consider this book to be your coach. It lays out the plan and the tools for achieving your personal finance goals. The rest is up to you.

Ken Read

Author, broadcaster and one of Canada's most recognized international athletes, as a member of the Crazy Canucks Ken Read became the youngest ever male to win a World Cup downhill going on to capture 5 more and represent Canada in two Olympic Winter Games. He has worked for CBC, CBS, NBC, TSN and CTV Sportsnet as well as writing regular columns in Canada, the USA and Europe. Ken currently hosts MoneySense Television as well as sitting on numerous public and charitable and amateur sport boards.

Introduction

How to Use This Book: Answering the Million Dollar Question

Money. We earn it, we spend it, we owe it, we save it. Unlike the really useful things we learned in school, like algebra and geology, personal financial planning is something we're left to master on our own. Or not. At first, it's enough that the bank will give us a debit card and we've managed to put insurance on our car—but as life blesses us with responsibilities, like a home, spouse, even children, the complication factor seems to increase. One day, or more usually, one night at about 3 a.m., we conclude that we need to get a better handle on this financial stuff. We face the million-dollar question: Are we going to be okay?

It finally dawns on us that financial well-being is similar to life in general—it is not something that happens to us, but something that we create.

You are to be congratulated—you've just picked up the tool-kit in this business of financial life management. In a world in which most financial advisors are paid based on the amount of investment products they sell us, it is integrally important to know what we want and need—and what we can be sublimely ignorant of while still attaining financial well-being. (Things like what the commodity markets are doing, and which hot stock is going to the moon, and leveraged-buy-out IPO sector plays.)

The good news is that attaining financial well-being is a simple, manageable process. If you follow this step-by-step guide, you will achieve not only a more comfortable future but a much higher quality of life today.

Part 1—Money In, Money Out

In the first section, we go over the basics—determining where we stand right now and how best to handle the daily stuff. This is where we build the foundation that is going to support us in the future. Everything that follows will only be as sound as the work we do now. Start tracking your cash flow, your expenses, and your net worth—and examine how your attitudes toward money are helping or hindering your goals.

Part 2—Hitching Your Wagon to a Star

In this section, we move a little beyond the basics. We identify what we want for the future and try to figure out how to get there. Then, we'll look at some of the pitfalls and dead-ends of credit abuse, and we'll examine some of the sources that can be of help.

Part 3—Home Sweet Home

House of belonging—home of the soul. Not only is this the place in which we spend much of our time, but it's also the place where we spend most of our money. In this section, we look at the virtues of both buying and renting and explore ways of using our hard-earned money most effectively on the home front.

Part 4—Savvy Investing

No area of financial planning captures our attention more than this business of investment. Let's face it—we do need to know this stuff, if only to know what we don't need to know. In this section, you'll read all kinds of stuff that your broker would love to tell you but can't—because it would be bad for business. Not yours—his or hers. Here you'll learn how to participate in business and the stock market in ways that make the most sense for you.

Part 5—Family Planning—The Money Kind

In this section, we look at everything from the cost of raising children and sending them on to university to how we can minimize the financial havoc caused by a marital separation.

Part 6—Retirement: Will You Be Ready?

Once upon a time, retirement was something we all looked forward to. Now, it's too often something we feel sick about whenever it crosses our mind. Stop right here, right now. Let's look at what retirement means to you, what it's going to cost, and exactly what you have to do today to prepare for tomorrow. Here's everything you need to know about RRSPs and what to do with them when you get to retirement age.

Part 7—Risk Management and Estate Planning

In this section, we look at making sure that money is the last thing we have to worry about when facing life's inevitable ups and down. From insuring your car to making sure your family gets more of your estate than Revenue Canada, this section looks at what to do once you've achieved financial well-being—how to ensure it stays that way and how to pass it on in the most effective way possible.

A Word of Warning ...

Things in the world of law, investment, and taxation are changing even as I write this sentence, so before undertaking any endeavour, double-check your data. Experts in each of the fields addressed have reviewed this book for accuracy, but before you make any decisions, go directly to the source. You can find them in Appendix A.

Extras

If you're just flipping through, you'll love the sidebars, which give you concise information in bite-sized pieces.

Beware

This is a warning, something you need to look out for and recognize if you find it in your path.

Who Knew?

Facts, figures, statistics, and bits of information you might find interesting.

Definition

Each industry has its own jargon, and the financial industry is unfortunately no different. There's a great Financial Dictionary in Appendix B, but the definition sidebars give you an idea of the terms we're using in the sections where we use them.

Tip

Helpful strategies and hints for smoother financial sailing.

Part 1

The Basics of Money In, Money Out

In this day of multimedia, tech-mania, and day trading, it's easy to look outside of ourselves for answers to our financial dilemmas.

Not so fast, my friend.

Financial well-being begins with ourselves, with issues that are within the realm of our control. Until we step up to the plate and accept this awesome responsibility, that's the bad news. Once we do, however, we quickly realize that "boldness has both power and magic in it," and that our dreams are well within our means.

It is time to take control. Over the next three chapters, I will help you do just that. We will explore your attitudes toward money, help you figure out where it comes from in your life, and explain some of the basic concepts of making, spending, and saving money.

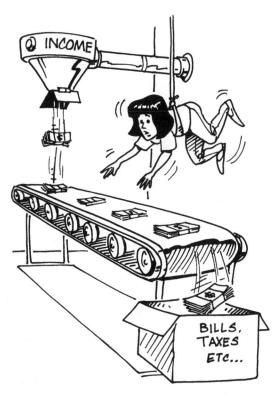

Chapter 1

Getting Rid of Paper Overflow

In This Chapter

➤ The element of attitude

➤ Some of the obstacles you'll find in your path, and ways to avoid them

➤ Reframing your beliefs to create prosperous behaviours

➤ Creating order to attract prosperity

Before we begin any journey, we have to figure out where we are. Financial planning is no different. We're also going to find some obstacles in our path along the way—so let's begin by exploring the things that may hinder us in our search for financial well-being. Then we'll move on to some fool-proof obstacle-avoidance techniques.

Attitude!

"I can never get ahead."

"Money doesn't grow on trees, you know."

Whether we're aware of it or not, we were deeply affected by the way our parents handled money when we were growing up. No matter how much we know about money management, our *behaviour* is more often determined by our unconscious belief system than it is by our intellectual knowledge, and it's our behaviour—not our know-how—that creates our financial reality. Therefore, while we know we shouldn't rack up our credit cards, we do it anyway. We know we should participate in long-term investment in order to prepare for retirement, but we keep putting it off. I don't have to say more. We all know what we do, because we then lie awake at night worrying about it.

The Chaos Effect

We tell ourselves we don't have the time. Or the energy—"I'm too tired to go through those statements tonight." On the contrary, we often don't have the time because we're operating in chaos. Creating order is a *huge* time saver, and I'm here to show you how. If you're like most Canadians, simply knowing where you are financially is going to enhance your overall feeling of well-being significantly and *immediately*.

Tip

Procrastination is almost always a by-product of fear. If you find yourself putting off important financial planning decisions, begin by addressing your anxiety through education.

Avoidance Behaviour and Procrastination

Listen, I've been there, and I know what you're thinking. You're afraid that if you put everything in order you'll find that it's every bit as bad as you imagined, or even worse. I've been there too, and in Chapter 6, we're going to talk about what to do when we hit our financial bottom. Believe me, if things are really that bad, your worry and anxiety are as acute now as they're ever going to be, and I promise you that when it's all over, you'll wonder why you didn't take the proverbial bull by the horns a long time ago.

Intimidation

It's all so complicated, isn't it? Who has the time to compare credit card fees, never mind learn about investments and RRSPs and tax planning? We're victims of information overload, most of which is not information at all, but rhetoric, dogma, conjecture, opinion, and ill-founded theories. This guide will help you separate the wheat from the chaff, so to speak, and therefore, each chapter will begin with the questions to be answered and end with the basics—that is, the minimum you need to know to succeed. In Appendix B at the end of the book, you'll find a Financial Dictionary, a kind of English/financial-speak translation guide that will have you sounding like an expert in short order.

The Absence of a Clear Vision

As Yogi Berra once said, in his inimitable way, "If you don't know where you're going, you might not get there." It's true in business, and it's true in life. As a financial counsellor, I find that one of the biggest obstacles to achieving financial well-being is that we don't know what it is. We assume that more of everything must be better. Then we run into reality, which teaches us that we have to pay for everything we take from the world, and we conclude that the price is too high. We give up. We conclude that we must sacrifice time with our families to have a healthy investment portfolio, or sacrifice a great income in order to enjoy a high quality of life. There is a better way, and you'll find a path from here to there in this part of the book.

Overlooking the Basics

Too many people waste their time worrying about which mutual fund to buy and which new dot-com stock is going to the moon without ever having addressed the fundamentals. The truth is that we are in control of our financial well-being—external influences are important only after we've covered the basics of good money management. We'll take a look at all of the basics in the next few chapters. Then you can feel free to worry about the stuff we don't control if you so desire. Until then, conserve your energy—you're going to need some of it along the way.

In personal financial planning, as in life, there's the stuff we can control—and the stuff we can't. Human beings have an interesting tendency to spend lots of time and energy focusing on those things they can't control—the stock markets, for instance. For most of us, however, the ups and downs of the stock market, at least in the short term, have little or no impact on our lives whatsoever. Moreover, focusing on the stuff we can't control drains our energy and keeps us from taking care of the things that need taking care of— the things we'll look at in this part of the book.

Tip

Personal financial planning puts us in the driver's seat and helps us control the course of our well-being.

You're on Your Way!

You've taken a wonderful first step on the path to financial well-being by picking up this book, and by the end of it, you'll be able to consider yourself someone who knows your way around this personal financial planning stuff. Unfortunately, knowledge alone will not change your life. You also need to take action. Before you rush off headlong and open a day trading account or hire a tax specialist, however, you have to figure out where you are. Now. Today. It's time to face the music. Chances are you'll find you're better off than you thought, and you can breathe a sigh of relief. If that isn't true, and things are worse than imagined, the situation isn't going to improve without action. (Self-flagellation is not helpful—don't bother. Save your energy for something more creative.)

Who Knew?

Most North Americans are net spenders until the average age of 46.

In the first two chapters, you're going to measure your financial health. Think of it as a check-up—but, please, leave your clothes on! This is the kind of check-up that you do with a pen and paper—and a lot of self-honesty. Blame and shame won't help you here, and neither will excuses and rationalizations. The reality is that, perhaps with the exception of your creditors and parents, the world doesn't care about your financial health, and no matter how bad it seems, if they aren't in the same condition, they probably have been at some time. When I worked as a financial advisor, my clients tended to be people of some affluence—that is, they had money to invest. Even so, I can tell you, both from first-hand experience and through working with hundreds of other people, that this idea we have that everyone except us is making maximum RRSP contributions and paying off the mortgage early is an illusion. Most Canadians are net spenders (that is, they spend as much or more than they earn) until their late thirties. Until then, most of us are either just getting by, or we are investing in our education, in career development, in our first homes, and/or in the well-being of our children. Believe me, if you're breathing, there is still time to achieve financial success. The earlier you start, though, the easier it is.

The Real Road to Riches: The Element of Attitude

One only has to look around to realize that the greatest inheritance our parents can give us is not money at all, but an unshakeable belief in our own potential. Our neighbourhoods are full of examples of men and women who landed on our shores with only the clothes on their back and a head full of dreams, and who created financial miracles.

Who Knew?

Research has shown that our financial success is less dependent on inheriting money from our parents than inheriting good money skills from our parents. People whose parents invested money regularly tend to be better off than people who received an actual inheritance.

On the other hand, the opposite is equally true—if you believe that you'll never have enough money to live the life of your dreams, you'll undoubtedly prove yourself right.

If you find that you generally do the right thing when it comes to money, and you're just reading this book to sharpen up your skill set, you can probably skip this section. But if you find that you too often end up in more debt than you know is wise, or that you can't seem to save, no matter how often you decide you're going to, this section may be the key to your future financial success. Don't overlook it.

Since the time of Socrates, our wisest teachers have taught us that our beliefs determine our behaviour, and our behaviour then creates our reality. Yes, there are at least a thousand obstacles on any path, and yes, there are very significant factors over which we have absolutely no control whatsoever. That doesn't change the bottom line: *If we believe we can, we're right. If we believe we can't, we're right.* Business leaders know it, the great sports coaches know it, and when we know it, we will also have the power to succeed in ways we can only dream about today.

The challenge here lies in the illusion that our beliefs are beyond our control. Nothing could be further from the truth. In fact, it is simple to reframe our belief system, because the unconscious mind (where those beliefs are stored) has no ability to argue with us. It believes what it's told, and because many of the messages we send our unconscious are in conflict with each other, it decides what is true on the basis of quantity and quality of messages. Therefore, we must scientifically control the messages that our unconscious receives. Here's how.

Evaluate Your Beliefs

First, we need to determine what it is we believe at the present time. For the sake of this exercise, please just suspend any disbelief you might be harbouring and make the assumption that our beliefs really do create our reality. Assume that the pattern for our life right now lies in our belief system—what kind of pattern would create our financial situation now? How do we behave? What does our life look like? Where do the problems lie?

Make a list of the financial issues in your life right now. Here are a few examples to get you started:

> ➤ "I never have any money left at the end of the month, so I can't seem to get ahead. I'm always living paycheque to paycheque."

> ➤ "No matter how much money I make, I seem to spend more. I'm worried about my credit card bills."

> ➤ "I have no problem saving money, but I still worry, and I wish I could treat myself occasionally without feeling like I'm being a fool to spend unnecessarily."

> ➤ "Everything is going okay in my life financially, but I have this unshakeable anxiety about my future."

Now answer the following questions:

1. When you were a child, did your parents have any problems that involved money? If so, what were they?

2. Are there any similarities between the way you handle money today and the way either or both of your parents managed money?

3. Are there any ways in which your money management styles are different from those of your parents?

Who Knew?

Our spending and saving habits are usually developed by the age of 12, although we may not have the chance to practise them until years later.

4. When your parents discussed money with you, how did you generally feel afterward?

5. If you tend to spend money irresponsibly, do you feel this may be in reaction to feeling that your parents deprived you of the things you wanted and needed?

6. Are there any other ways in which your childhood experiences with money may be having an impact on your behaviour today? If so, are these primarily positive or primarily negative influences?

One Belief's Better than Another, Believe Me

Luckily, the truth will set us free. Whenever we become aware of a hindering belief, we almost inevitably have begun the process of being freed from its influence.

However, we can become active in the process, and take responsibility for reframing our beliefs in more creative ways.

Of each money belief you are able to identify, answer the following questions:

1. If my current beliefs are not achieving the results I want, what beliefs might work better?

2. What is the opposite of my belief?

3. If my belief were one side of a pendulum, and the "opposite" were the other side of the pendulum, what might be in the middle? (For example, if I believe that I will never have enough money, the opposite belief might be something like "I will always have more money than I need." In the middle might be something like "There is no difference between my ability to create wealth and that of other people. I can have as much money as I really want and need.")

4. If the "moderate" statement were true, how would it influence my behaviour? What things might I do differently?

5. What things that were true about money for my parents are no longer true today?

6. What do people I admire and whose lives I would like to live believe about money?

Behaviour Modification

Now that we've begun to think about ways in which our belief systems do not support our well-being, let's begin to think about ways in which our behaviour has the same effect.

Remember, our subconscious mind is "programmed" by the messages we allow into it. This programming then begins to influence our behaviour, which then creates our reality, which in turn sends further messages to the subconscious. It is similar to physical health—if we want to have healthy, vital bodies, we don't fill them with junk food. Once you've become aware of your hindering beliefs and thought of some more creative beliefs, practise affirmation. Each time you find yourself acting or thinking in a negative way, cancel that though or action with a positive one. In addition, try the following behaviour modification exercises:

1. Do your very best to come up with ten ways that you *don't currently* act in your own best financial best interest. (Some examples: *I'm always lending money to friends and family, and they never pay me back; I mean to pay off my credit cards monthly, but something always comes up, and the money just isn't there; I know that I should always "pay myself first" but there is never any money to pay myself with; Whenever I get depressed, I end up buying something on my credit cards.*)

2. Of each of the behaviours you listed, think of one thing you could do to change that behaviour.

Tip

A good habit takes 21 days to become established. If you have a difficult time saving, you can modify your behaviour by simply taking five dollars out of your wallet each day and depositing it into your savings account (via bank machine) or just into a "piggy bank" of some sort in your home. (Depending on the type of account you have, some banks charge up to $1 per transaction to use a banking machine. If that's the case, put your $5 into a piggy bank till the end of the week, then deposit $35 at once.)

3. Now, let's get rid of the excuse list—what's the pay-off for *not* changing your behaviour? For example, if you tend to lend money to friends and rarely get it back, the pay-off may be that you feel your friends will like you more, or that you feel good about being able to help them. If there's never any money to save at the end of the month, might it be simply that you enjoy spending more than saving?

4. In each instance, answer this about the pay-off for your self-sabotaging behaviour: Is it worth it? Or do you want to change?

Whatever we are doing to stand in our own way, we can stop. We can turn it around.

If you're reading this book, you are well on your way. The fact that you're interested enough to start reading is evidence enough that you have everything it takes to succeed.

Now that we've learned how to get out of our own way, let's move on, and create order, the structure that will support our growing abundance mentality.

Creating Order

Does this sound familiar? You leaf through your mail, only to find three bills, one for your credit card, one from the phone company, and another for a magazine subscription that is about to run out. You open them, examine them briefly, feel a little sick, and drop them on the table by the door with the other bills that have been collecting there for the last few weeks.

As you're about to fall asleep, you get a nagging feeling that the hydro bill might be due this week ... or did you pay it already? Oh, well, tomorrow. Now that you've started thinking about it though, you're a little worried about whether or not you might have forgotten to record that last cheque—do you have enough in the account? An hour later you're still tossing and turning, and when the alarm clock goes off six hours later, you're beat.

Well, my friend, those days are over. You are about to get organized.

Nothing thrives in chaos. Except, of course, chaos. Getting your financial records in order will make it possible to move on to the next steps, but keeping them in order is equally important. Again, if you already have a reliable record-keeping system in place, move on. (Picture me, briefly, bowing from the waist—with my hat off to you!) However, if you are dreading the next step because you have no idea how much you owe on your credit cards or where your last bank statement is, you're going to need to devote some time.

Create a Simple Filing System

I now have a filing cabinet, with real files, because I'm self-employed. When my record-keeping needs were simpler, however, I used large manila envelopes, and they worked fabulously. Every financial record, from statements to parking receipts, went into a large "current month" envelope, which I sorted each month after paying my bills. Each piece of paper went into the appropriate envelope—"financial statements," "paid bills," "tax receipts," and "general receipts." (Use a three-hole punch to make these envelopes binder-friendly.) At the end of the tax year, I put a rubber band around the annual set, marked the date on the outside, and moved them down into the box I keep in the storage room for that purpose.

Simple is always better. Remember the 1980s, when everyone *had* to have a closet organizer? Whatever you do, don't go out and buy the filing cabinet equivalent of a closet organizer until you find out if a simpler system will work for you.

Whatever you do, do it regularly. Don't let paper accumulate in your pockets and in piles on your kitchen counter. There is a kind of magic to order—something about it attracts prosperity. So even if you're kind of messy by nature, think about order as a money-magnet, and chaos as a money-repellent.

Bill Paying 101

Right now ... yes, right now, stop reading and dig up a basket, shoebox, file folder, or any other receptacle that will hold your bills and receipts. Find a place to put it near the front door, or wherever you come in with your mail. From now on, every bill and receipt you receive *must* go in your bill and receipt receptacle. Now, take out your calendar, or put a note on your refrigerator. Designate a day each month, on which you are going to pay your bills. (If you don't have enough money to pay your bills, proceed to Chapter 6, "Managing Credit and Crisis.")

Okay. Collect all your bills for the last month. (You may have to do this next step on your lunch hour at the office, because it will have to be done during business hours. It will be worth it, I guarantee.) For each of your monthly bills (car payments, rent or mortgage, hydro, telephone, Internet service, and so on) call your service provider (there will be a service number somewhere on the bill) and ask if they have a monthly automatic payment option. If so, do whatever is necessary to have the payment automatically debited from your chequing account. Create a record of each payment that will come out on each day, and the approximate amount. For future reference, try to set up any annual costs on a monthly basis, too. For example, my auto and home insurance are now debited monthly, and most of my charitable donations are also debited directly from my account on the same day each month.

Once you have set up the automatic payment, when the bill comes in the mail, you can put it directly in your "paid" file. (We'll set that up in a bit, don't worry.)

There will be some bills that can't be paid automatically—credit card bills, for instance. From now on, put them in your incoming bill receptacle, and sit down on your designated day each month to pay them. Think about how you feel writing those cheques—if your financial affairs are in order, bill paying can be a very satisfying experience. If your financial affairs are not in order, it can be very unpleasant. Therefore, when something doesn't feel good, the discomfort is worth examining. Do you regret spending your money the way you do? Are you anxious about not having enough?

Get Rid of the Paper Overload

Think about how you handle your mail. If you aren't already in the habit of doing so, it's a good idea to start with a handy recycling bin for junk mail. Keep only what's necessary. (No, you will not read it later.)

Beware

Pay your bills on time. Late bill payments are energy-draining and anxiety-provoking. If for some reason you *can't* pay your bills on time (because you've lost your job, for instance), call your creditors and let them know what's going on. Taking the bull by the proverbial horns will make you feel a lot better and will make your creditors a lot more understanding. It can also save your credit rating!

Tip

Think of order as a money-magnet, and mess and chaos as a money-repellent. It will make it a lot easier to remember to put those unpaid bills in the designated spot!

Who Knew?

There's more than one bank savings account open for every person in Canada. A few of us don't have any at all, but a lot of us have two or more.

Now that the junk mail is in the recycling bin, you'll have two kinds of mail in your hands—good mail, like postcards from your world-faring friends, and bills. Do whatever you'd like with your good mail, and put your bills in the bill container.

Limit Your Accounts for Ease of Handling

If you have multiple chequing accounts, do give some thought to closing all but one. Who needs unnecessary complexity? Ditto for your credit cards. There are few good reasons for having more than one.

Account for Your Money

Most Canadians keep their money in bank savings accounts. This is a big financial mistake. The bank may love you, but you're cheating yourself.

Savings accounts will never pay you enough money in interest to stay ahead of inflation. So you should use them only as a temporary storage place, while you decide what to do with your money.

Conventional or Daily Interest: Which Is Best?

Do you have a conventional savings account or a daily interest account? Many of us aren't even sure.

➤ For a conventional savings account, the interest is tabulated monthly. Money deposited in a conventional account after the first day of the month doesn't earn interest for the entire month.

➤ For a daily interest account, the money earns interest on the first day that you deposit it and every day after that, until you remove it. Even if you leave it there for only one day, it will still earn interest, at a slightly lower rate than it would earn in a conventional savings account.

Beware

At an interest rate of half of one percent a year—the rate paid on some savings accounts—it'll take 144 years for your money to double.

Most of us get paid every two weeks. And we usually deposit our paycheque in the bank after the first day of the month. Then, we're so busy paying bills that our money comes out of the account just about as fast as it goes in. So it makes a lot more sense to calculate interest on a daily basis than to do it once a month, even if the monthly interest is calculated at a rate half a percent higher.

Tip

Say you get paid every two weeks, and your take-home pay is around $900. If your paycheque is deposited into a daily interest account earning $2\frac{1}{2}$% annually, and if you can leave your cheque in the account for only eight days, you'll earn about 70¢, 26 times each year. That comes to an extra $18 to $20 each year. You get this money for doing nothing more than opening a daily interest savings account rather than a conventional savings account. That's a no-brainer.

Strategy 1

Have your paycheque deposited directly into a daily interest savings account. Then withdraw the money as you need it to pay your bills and buy investments.

Strategy 2

Check which bank, trust company, or credit union offers the highest yield on its daily interest savings account and then, providing it's convenient for you, have your money deposited there.

Is Your Money Safe in the Bank?

Keeping your money in Canadian banks, trust companies, or credit unions is very safe. Any institution that displays the Canadian Deposit Insurance Corporation (CDIC) sticker provides guaranteed protection of all funds deposited up to $60 000. If you don't see any sticker displayed, make sure to request proof of CDIC coverage.

How Does CDIC Insurance Work?

Any money that you have in a savings account, chequing account, guaranteed investment certificate (GIC), or term deposit is guaranteed up to $60 000 per institution, not per branch. If you have over $60 000 sitting in a bank, you can get around the guaranteed limit by keeping up to $60 000 in your name, up to $60 000 in your spouse's name, up to $60 000 in a joint account, and up to $60 000 in an RRSP, all within the same institution and all guaranteed.

Tracking Your Expenses

If you aren't using an expense-tracking program like Quicken or Microsoft Money, and you have a home computer, do give some thought to getting such a program. (I've found that people tend to love whichever they try first, and you can generally download a trial copy from their Web sites.) Particularly if you can't seem to figure out where the money goes, these programs can be wonderfully helpful. They can also make tax time a breeze—you can just print a report, add up your receipts, and insert the numbers on your return. It doesn't get any easier than that.

I do my very best to put all personal expenses on my debit card, and all business expenses on my credit card. That way, my record keeping is essentially done when I get my statements in the mail. By the way, after five years of carefully examining my bank statements, I found that they never made one mistake. (I made a couple, however.) I don't balance my chequebook anymore, because I very rarely use my chequebook anymore. By using my debit card, credit card, and setting up automatic bill payments,

Tip

When setting up your Quicken or Microsoft Money programs, be sure to use detailed categories. We all know that "dining out" is not the same as "groceries," but I've interviewed people whose "grocery bill" was outrageous until we subtracted the daily Starbucks latte and the regular lunches out. The more detailed your categories, the more revealing your record keeping.

the only cheques I generally write are to my daughter's school. Since I download my chequing account records online into my Microsoft Money program, I can quickly enter the cheque I've written, and I don't have to worry about forgetting them and spending more than I have in the account.

I do, however, check my credit card statements every month, as should you. Research has shown that 14 percent of all retail transactions result in at least one error—check your receipt before leaving the store or restaurant, and check the receipt against the credit card bill when it comes in.

The Least You Need to Know

➤ Our beliefs create our behaviour, and our behaviour creates our reality—the obstacles between us and financial well-being always begin with us!

➤ Nothing thrives in chaos—we need to create order in our money management before we can move on to things like investment planning.

➤ Multiple chequing accounts and credit cards add up to unnecessary complexity.

➤ Think about using a software program like Quicken or Microsoft Money.

Chapter 2

Money Diagnostics

In This Chapter

➤ Figure out where your money is coming from

➤ Where it's going

➤ Create a net worth statement and start measuring your progress from year to year

Money In: Where's It Coming From?

Believe it or not, most of us don't have a clue how much money we earn. Okay, we have a clue. We know we make X dollars in salary, and we probably know what our net pay is each payday. Unfortunately, we usually don't know the useful stuff—like how much we pay in taxes, how much we spend to earn our income (in transportation costs, clothes for work, etc.), and what we're actually netting at the end of the day.

Now, dig up last year's T4. Let's begin by looking at our income as if we were a business. A business doesn't view its earning as its revenues, or the money coming in the door. From a business perspective, income is whatever is left after we pay all the costs related to earning it. Also, remember to add in your benefits. If you belong to a decent company benefit plan, your benefits may be worth anywhere from 15 to 25 percent of your salary. (If you have a benefit plan that pays for disability insurance and life, you may wish to approximate and add 15 percent of your salary; if you have a benefit plan that provides pension benefits, add in the "pension adjustment" figure that appears on your T4.) Table 2-1 provides an outline to use to figure out your true income.

Table 2-1
Calculating Your True Income

	Income	Expense
Gross annual income	_____	
Value of company medical and dental benefits	_____	
Value of company pension benefits	_____	
CPP and Employment Insurance deductions		_____
Any other deductions from gross pay		_____
Annual taxes paid (Add whatever was withheld to the value of your tax refund or payment)		_____
Net investment income (Now we're talking!)	_____	
Net rental income	_____	
Gifts, inheritances, lottery winnings	_____	
Bonuses, commissions, or royalties	_____	
Cost of business wardrobe		_____
Dry cleaning of business clothes		_____
Transportation to and from work (auto costs plus parking or public transportation)		_____
Additional food costs (lunches out, fast food dinners, etc.)		_____
Health costs relating to work		_____
Additional income	_____	
Additional expenses		_____
Total Income	_____	
Total Expenses		_____

Subtract total expenses from total income to get your net income: _____ (a)

No. of weeks worked per year: _____ (b)

No. of days worked per week: _____ (c)

No. of hours worked per day: _____ (d) (Include travel time)

Multiply (b) times (c) times (d) to calculate the number of hours you use to create your income: _____ (e)

Now calculate how much you actually earn per hour of labour:

Divide (a) by (e) = _____ (f)

Tip

A dollar saved is at least two dollars earned. Yes, by the time we add up all of our taxes, we generally have to make at least $2, and often $3, in order to have an extra $1 to spend.

Before you purchase anything, do the life exchange calculation. Simply divide the cost of the purchase (including tax and any interest charges you'll pay over the life of the loan if you're thinking about buying on credit) by the amount you really earn per hour to calculate the number of hours you'll have to sacrifice for that purchase. Is it worth it?

Cash Flow Statement

It's as simple as this. Enjoying life depends on spending less money than we earn. No exceptions. Unfortunately, in this age of advertising dreams and pre-approved credit cards, this is more challenging than it should be. Taking on debt to finance things that depreciate in value, like cars, vacations, and big-screen TVs, is a sure way to financial ill-health. As much as you might like to think so, your credit card limit is not an extension of your paycheque.

If you aren't sure of your expenditures, don't guess. Try using a chart like the one in Table 2-2. Check your bank statements and credit card statements. Beware of the mystery amounts. You should be able to account for at least 95 percent of your income. If more than 5 percent of your income is

Beware

A $4 latte, five days a week, adds up to $1040 over the course of a year. If your net hourly income, after taxes and work-related expenses, is $15 an hour, you're working almost nine days a year for that afternoon coffee. Is it worth it?

"disappearing," you're going to have to track all of your expenses for a while, including your "walking around" money. You can do this two ways—either carry a little notebook around and make a note of every cent you spend, when you spend it, or start paying for everything on your debit card. Carry perhaps $20 in cash per week, and write that amount in the miscellaneous spending column.

Table 2–2
Cash Flow Statement

	Annual Expense	Approximate Amount	Amount Divided by 12
Car insurance	_____	_____	_____
Home insurance	_____	_____	_____
Vacations	_____	_____	_____
Car tune-ups	_____	_____	_____
Furnace tune-up	_____	_____	_____
Contact lenses	_____	_____	_____
Lump sum RRSP contribution	_____	_____	_____
	_____	_____	_____
	_____	_____	_____

	Annual Income	Approximate Amount	Amount Divided by 12
	_____	_____	_____
	_____	_____	_____
	_____	_____	_____
	_____	_____	_____

Monthly Income and Expenses

Description	Income	Expense
Income from salary	$_____	
Income from bonus or commissions	$_____	
Rental income	$_____	
Self-employment or professional income	$_____	
Income from investments	$_____	
Child support or maintenance	$_____	
Pensions	$_____	
Other	$_____	
RRSP contributions		$_____
Savings or investment programs		$_____
Loan or credit card payments		$_____
Mortgage/rent		$_____
Home or contents insurance		$_____
Property taxes		$_____
Home repairs and maintenance		$_____
Utilities (gas, electricity, water)		$_____

Telephone	$_____
Cable	$_____
Domestic help	$_____
Groceries	$_____
Take out and fast food	$_____
Dining out	$_____
Household maintenance items (cleansers, supplies, etc.)	$_____
Car payments	$_____
Car maintenance and repair	$_____
Gas and oil	$_____
Parking	$_____
Public transportation	$_____
Car insurance	$_____
Pets—food, veterinarian services, licensing, etc.	$_____
Clothing	$_____
Education and school fees	$_____
Personal care (cosmetics, vitamins, fitness centre fees, hair care)	$_____
Baby sitting	$_____
Day care	$_____
Entertainment	$_____
Crafts and hobbies	$_____
Vacations	$_____
Medical insurance	$_____
Prescriptions	$_____
Dental	$_____
Disability insurance	$_____
Life insurance	$_____
Bank charges	$_____
Professional fees (lawyers, accountants, etc.)	$_____
Optical expenses	$_____
Gifts	$_____
Memberships	$_____
Charitable donations	$_____
Other	$_____

Total Income	$_____	
Total Expenses		$_____
Net Cash Flow	$_____	$_____

Net Worth Statement

Now that you know what you're actually earning, let's figure out how you've done so far. A net worth statement (see Table 2-3) can also provide a benchmark against which you can measure your progress. It's important to do one of these annually—it feels great to measure your progress and start to see the impact of good planning.

Table 2-3
Financial Net Worth Statement

Assets Description	Approximate Value
Personal Assets	
Residence (as of last tax assessment)	$_____
Jewellery, rare coins, art	$_____
Collectibles	$_____
Furnishings (resale value)	$_____
Automobile (approx. resale value)	$_____
Other	$_____
Total Personal Assets:	**$_____**
Liquid Assets	
Non-RRSP savings accounts	$_____
Chequing accounts	$_____
Money market funds	$_____
Canada Savings Bonds	$_____
T-bills	$_____
Term deposits and GICs under one year	$_____
Total Liquid Assets:	**$_____**
Investment Assets	
RRSP investment accounts	$_____
Non-RRSP investment accounts	$_____
Commercial or non-residential real estate	$_____
Cash value of insurance policies	$_____
Small business assets; or outstanding loans to individuals or small businesses	$_____
Total Investment Assets:	**$_____**
Total Assets:	**$_____**

Liabilities Description	Approximate Balance Owing
Credit Cards and Personal Debt (short-term loans, car loans, lines of credit, loans to family members). Include interest rates and payment terms in description.	$_____ $_____ $_____ $_____
Total Short-Term, Non-Deductible Personal Debt:	
RRSP Loans	$_____ $_____ $_____ $_____
Total RRSP Loans:	$_____
Mortgage(s) on Primary Residence	$_____ $_____
Total Mortgages on Primary Residence:	$_____
Deductible Investment Loans or Mortgages	$_____ $_____
Total Deductible Investment Loans or Mortgages:	$_____
Total Liabilities:	$_____
Total Assets – Total Liabilities = Net Worth	$_____

How Are You Doing So Far?

How do we know we're on the right track? I prefer to think in terms of progress rather than amount. One calculation you might apply is this:

1. Calculate your *net* average annual income for the years you've worked. It doesn't have to be precise. If you've worked for ten years, started at a net income of $25 000 a year, received regular raises and now make $42 000 in take-home pay (another term for net income), it's generally safe to choose the midpoint of $33 500.

2. Multiply 10 percent of that (just add a decimal place—$3350.00, in the above example) by the number of years you've been working.

3. If you've paid off a student loan, or put two kids through university, subtract that amount from the total.

4. Now, subtract any depreciable personal items (like your car and furniture) from your net worth.

5. Compare the two totals. If you are anywhere within range, you are a superstar. If your net worth is negative, you need to take some serious remedial action, which you are obviously in the process of doing.

It should look like this:

10 (no. of years worked) times 10 percent of $33 500 (net income) = $33 500

$33 500 minus $6500 (paid off student loan) = $27 000
(compare to net worth minus "personal assets")

In this case, a net worth of $27 500 or above would be absolutely stellar, and anything in the range of 75 percent of that would be considered very good.

Definition

Gross income is your total salary, before deductions and tax. **Net income** is what you actually take home, or the amount that is deposited in your bank account on payday. **Real net income** is the amount left after deductions and the money you spend earning that money.

Another rule of thumb that can be applied is a simple calculation based on net income. If you are in your 20s, and your net worth is positive, consider yourself on track. If you're somewhere in your 30s, you should aim for a net worth of at least 50 percent of your annual net income. In your 40s, if your net worth is more than the equivalent of two years of net income, congratulations!

Wow. You've made so much progress. Take some time now to celebrate your accomplishments. How does it feel? Are you proud and pleased? Or glad to have done it, but feeling a little worried and dejected?

Either way, remember that this is only one snapshot of your financial situation. It is important to know where you are today, but it is more important that you are on the path to creating the life of your dreams.

This is just the launching pad, and your assets are the foundation of your future. That's true whether those assets are in the form of stocks and bonds, a good education, the experience of world travel, or just a lot of lessons about what *not* to do. Whatever you do, don't waste energy on regret. Now that you know where you're starting from, you can begin to plan the journey.

The Least You Need to Know

➤ Financial well-being is something you are responsible for creating—it won't happen by accident.

➤ Knowing how much we really earn, per hour of precious life, allows us to make sound spending decisions.

Creative Saving, Creative Spending

Don't you hate investment and personal planning books that tell us we must save money and don't give us a clue how to do it? From an author's perspective, however, there is a certain wisdom in the oversight. First of all, everybody (and I mean everybody) hates to be told what to do; and, second, what may be important to you may not be important to me, and vice versa.

The Real Value of Saving

Saving money is much more important than most of us recognize—in part because we were raised with that old saying, "a penny saved is a penny earned." Whoever first said that lived before the days of taxation, because a penny saved today can be worth anywhere from one-and-a-half to two pennies! Add in the costs of work-related expenses and interest (if you're buying on credit) and a penny saved can be three pennies earned. Doesn't sound like something significant enough to waste your precious time contemplating? Let me rephrase it—an extra $1000 on a new car can cost as much as

$3000 in before-tax, before-expense, before-interest income. So, which would you rather do: shop around to shave $1000 off the purchase price or work to earn an additional $3000?

Beware

A penny saved *is not* a penny earned—if you factor in all taxes and employment-related expenses, a penny saved is more like *three pennies* earned—and don't forget, we aren't really talking about pennies, but about thousands of dollars. Cutting $5000 in spending out of your annual budget really saves in the range of $10 000 to $15 000 in income. That's like having a good part-time job—without the job!

The Way to Save Money Is Simple

Saving money can be simple if you make an effort to do the following:

➤ Have a clear vision for your future.

➤ Earn enough to pay for life's necessities and have a bit left over.

➤ Set up your savings plan so that it comes out of your account every month when your paycheque goes in.

➤ When your income increases, through whatever means, put the difference into your investment plan.

Tip

Choosing *not* to carry a balance of just $1000 on your department store credit card will save you almost $300 in one year!

It's Simple to Spend Less

The way to spend less money is also simple. Figure out how much of your life you spend earning your income, calculate the hourly rate (from Chapter 2), and then stand before those pair of designer shoes and say "Shoes—yeah, you, snappy little black leather numbers there—are you really worth seven hours of my precious time? Will you give me seven laborious hours worth of pleasure and satisfaction?" If so, and you've got the money, get them.

If you're thinking of buying them on credit—don't. You may be able to calculate the amount of interest you'd pay on a $100 purchase, but how can you calculate the emotional price of selling yourself into indentured servitude to a credit card company?

Dozens of Ways to Enjoy Money More

The objective of good money management is *never* deprivation—it's getting the absolute Biggest Bang per Buck. Now that you've established how much you're really earning per hour of labour, you are probably also finding that you are much more discerning about how you spend your money. Here are some tips I wish I'd known in my 20s, when money was really tight, but which continue to add real richness to my life on a not-at-all-extravagant budget. I don't think I invented any of these—some are just common sense tips you may not have thought of yet, some I've read in other books, and some I learned from my mom or by following my sisters around thrift stores. I hope you find at least a few of them to be of help.

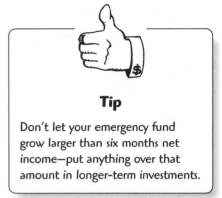

Tip

Don't let your emergency fund grow larger than six months net income—put anything over that amount in longer-term investments.

Tips from 1 to 10: Keeping More of the Money You Earn

1. Never use department store or gas credit cards if you don't pay them off monthly. (The annual interest rates can be as high as 30 percent, with interest calculated from the date of purchase).

2. Get over the thrill of New. Think instead about the shadow side of retail—mark-up. When buying household and sporting goods, at least take a look at the second-hand shops. You may be amazed—and you will certainly be richer.

3. Buy the highest quality you can afford, but never pay full price.

4. Take your lunch. Buying lunch at the office cafeteria is one major expense that gives most Canadians little or no pleasure whatsoever. (Unconvinced? Do the math: soup made from powdered mix and a dreary tuna sandwich = $7; $7 × 235 working days = $1645). If having lunch out is a real treat for you, try bringing your lunch nine days and splurging on the tenth—but have something you enjoy, not a sandwich you could make at home for one-quarter of the price. If you have a fridge at work, stock it with cream cheese and bagels, cheddar cheese and English muffins, raw fruit and vegetables, hummus and pita, bean salad, and anything that tickles your fancy. Keep canned soup and dry oatmeal in your desk.

5. Never buy anything without comparing prices. Not one thing.

Beware

Just one coffee-shop latte per working day can easily add $1000 a year to your expenses. Remember, when you factor in all taxes and work-related expenses, that can easily be the equivalent of $3000 in income.

6. Call your bank, telephone company, cable company, cell phone, and Internet service provider to ask if you have the best service package for your style of usage. They won't tell you if you don't ask, and you may be missing out on big savings.

7. If you smoke, please stop. I know how hard it is, but I promise you, it's worth it just for the money you'll save, let alone the years you'll add to your life (which you'll have to pay for, but that's another story).

8. Too much of the spending we do is an unsuccessful attempt to ease longings that have nothing, really, to do with stuff. The price is high, the pleasure fleeting. Eat well, go outside and exercise regularly, and get eight hours sleep each night. Everything else will be more satisfying.

9. Pay your neighbourhood teenagers to wash and wax your car. Never pay until the work is done, and be specific about your expectations. You may only save a couple of dollars a wash, but you'll get to know your neighbours and remember what it is to be young.

10. Unless you will need it forever, buy term insurance rather than universal or whole life.

Another 9 Tips on Keeping More of the Money You Earn

The tips just keep on coming. Here are another nine hot pieces of advice that might save you some money. (And, hey, they're fun to read, even if you never put them into action.)

1. Whenever possible, barter for services. For example, you might baby-sit for your gardener.

2. Be nice. Or in more modern phraseology, network. If you lose your job, the length of time it will take you to get a new one will depend entirely on how many people you know and how they feel about you. Your health will improve, you'll have more energy, and you can save thousands of dollars in income that might otherwise be lost between jobs—just by smiling, saying hello, and showing sincere interest in the well-being of the people you meet.

3. Remember that gifts are tokens of love. An expensive gift does not indicate greater love than an inexpensive gift. A considerate gift, one that shows you understand the nature of the receiver, will be even more welcome.

4. Collect inexpensive, thoughtful gifts throughout the year. Once you get in the swing of it, you may even begin to enjoy Christmas again.

5. When buying property or car insurance, always get the policy with the highest deductible you can afford to pay if something happens.

6. Don't buy the little insurance packages—you know, the extended warranty on the computer that comes with a decent warranty or the insurance on your RRSP loan. In particular, skip the unemployment insurance on your credit-card balance. Insure against catastrophe, not inconvenience.

7. Believe it or not, you can still drink Canadian tap water. I know it seems weird, but it's true. You can even filter it, and take it with you in bottles.

8. If you're of a radical nature and can resist the lure of owning your own home, you may be better off renting. See Part 3, "Home Sweet Home," for details.

9. Unless you're living on a sailboat or on your way to Europe, don't ever rent storage space. If you need it, you probably have too much stuff. Think about downsizing first. How about a garage sale?

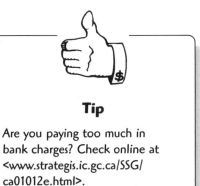

Tip

Are you paying too much in bank charges? Check online at <www.strategis.ic.gc.ca/SSG/ ca01012e.html>.

Reconnect to Your Community and Save Big at the Same Time

Here are four ways to get in touch with the people around you, while saving money at the same time. At the very least, if you follow some or all of these tips, you'll have more people to call on a rainy Sunday afternoon.

➤ Think about starting a lending library in your community for things like tools, toys—even extra chairs or glassware that can be borrowed for parties—staffed by volunteers.

➤ Consider setting up a "community hours" bank. Members earn credits by providing hours of service and can then exchange them for other services. For instance, someone with computer savvy can earn community hour credits for pulling the local YMCA through a systems crash, and spend their hours taking yoga classes at the community centre. Not only does it save money, but it creates an amazing sense of community and belonging, something that is in too short supply. (This idea was created by Paul Glover in Ithaca, New York, which now has hundreds of thousands of "Ithaca dollars" in use. The idea has spread to Toronto, where you can pick up "Toronto dollars" at certain locations around the city, like the St. Lawrence Market.)

Who Knew?

The "Toronto dollar" is a community currency for the community minded. You can exchange Canadian dollars for Toronto dollars at several locations. You can spend your Toronto dollars at par with the over 100 participating businesses including 40 St. Lawrence Market merchants and more than 20 restaurants. As soon as you make an exchange to Toronto dollars, 10 percent of that exchange goes directly into a trust fund that is used to help community organizations. You can get more information from Toronto Dollar Community Projects Inc., 49 Wellington St. E., Fifth Floor, Toronto, Ontario, M5E IC9, Phone: (416) 361-0466, Fax: (416) 361-1123, or check their Web site at <www.web.net/~tordoll>.

Who Knew?

Local employment trading systems (LETS) were started in British Columbia by Michael Linton in 1983. With over 1000 independent LETS organizations now operating throughout the world, LETS also form an important network of communities. Get more information at <www.web.net/~lets>.

➤ Set up a food co-op, where members can save money by buying in bulk and dividing up their purchases.

➤ Take the food co-op a step further and create a co-op kitchen in a community centre, where members can meet and cook up batches of frozen casseroles and baked goods.

Reducing Food Expenses

Here are some tips that will save you money and perhaps even improve your diet. At the very least, you'll have fun trying.

➤ Have you ever noticed that every trip to the grocery store costs a minimum of $35, even if you only go for milk? Keep a well-stocked pantry, with lots of canned and dry goods that can be put together to create a palatable meal, and eat the food you have at home.

➤ Eat five small meals a day. It's better for your health and, because it curbs impulse junk-food buying, better for your wallet.

➤ Eat simply, nutritious dinners like salmon filets basted in teriyaki sauce with steamed rice and carrots; pita bread spread with prepared spaghetti sauce, sprinkled with grated cheese, topped with bean sprouts and broiled for five minutes. I'm sure you can think of others.

➤ Buy fruit and vegetables in season from fruit and vegetable stands.

➤ Buy no-name brand stuff if it doesn't matter.

➤ If it does matter, buy house products, like President's Choice, for great quality and good value.

Here are some tips on eating a better diet, which can usually translate into lower food costs.

➤ Eat five half-cup servings of fruit and an equal amount of vegetables every day. It will improve your health, and you'll spend less money on prepared snack foods.

➤ Bring nutritious snacks to work: Roasted almonds, yogurt, cheese, vegetable sticks, popcorn, oatmeal, grain bread, crackers, fruit, cold cereal with or without milk, fresh bread and peanut butter, bagels and cream cheese ...

➤ Eat less meat. Start by having one vegetarian meal a week.

➤ If you have time to cook, plan your menus around what's on sale. Check the flyers.

➤ Eat before you go grocery shopping—never shop for food when you're hungry. (This strategy does not work at the liquor store.)

➤ Learn to cook at least one delicious seafood or fish dish. The secret is always in the sauces.

➤ Don't buy processed food. Before there were frozen dinners, there was pancake night, omelet night, hamburger night, and soup and grilled-cheese sandwich night.

➤ Unless you love it, don't bake.

Beware

Use coupons, but don't get attached to them. The store brand may be less expensive than the name brand even after the coupon discount.

Reducing Clothing Expenses: Look Like a Million Bucks for Significantly Less

You can dress for less and still find success. (Okay, there's a bad poem in there somewhere.) Here's how to do it:

➤ Face it—there are days when we just need to *buy*. Find a favourite thrift store and stop by when the mall therapy urge hits. If you go looking for one especially-for-you treasure rather than with preconceived ideas about what you'd like to find, you'll almost never be disappointed.

➤ If fashion is your passion, don't buy designer goods from designer stores. Look for wholesale outlets and clearance and consignment stores.

Beware

Have a shoe fetish? If you spend an average of $100 per pair ($85 plus tax) and own just 30 pairs, you have a $3000 footwear investment—$9000 in pre-tax, pre-employment cost dollars!

➤ However, if you find great clothing at a great price, buy two. I rue the day I only bought one pair of those perfect black pumps.

➤ Have your clothes tailored to fit perfectly—you'll wear them more and feel better about it. Find a good neighbourhood tailor and make friends.

➤ Have rubber soles put on your shoes—they will last forever.

➤ Clean and polish your shoes regularly.

➤ Buy neutral basics (black, gray, white, tan, ivory, navy, red, taupe, browns) and use colour to accessorize.

➤ Pick a couple of sock styles and colours and stick with them. You'll have an endless supply of extras.

➤ Don't collect lingerie. Find a style and price that suits you, buy enough to get through the week, and then replace the pieces as they get worn.

➤ Limit the clothes that you dry clean, and limit the amount of dry cleaning you do. Take off small spots yourself, and do your own pressing. Overuse of your dry cleaner can easily add up to $500 a year. (I know—that was my bill.)

Reduce Personal Care Expenses

There are ways to look good without feeling poor. Just follow these tips. (Most of them are directed at women, but men will find a few useful ones, too.)

➤ Don't buy designer cosmetics, but buy a great compact, and a great-looking lipstick. If you aren't going to take it out of your purse and put it on in a restaurant, don't spend money on packaging.

➤ Experiment until you find an inexpensive cleanser, antiperspirant, moisturizer, shampoo, conditioner, hair spray, soap, and body lotion. (The best moisturizer in the world is Keri Lotion at $12 a litre.) Once you find them, stick with them. Not everything can be improved.

➤ Wrinkle creams, dark circle remover creams for your eyes, cellulite creams, thigh-toning creams—if they worked, don't you think we'd all have them? Come on.

➤ Get a good haircut from a skilled technician, but don't assume that someone who charges outrageous prices is skilled. I used to know a fellow who was the priciest hair-stylist in the city. He knew only one haircut—in short, medium, and long.

➤ If you're going home anyway, dry your own hair when you get there. A blow dry can cost up to an extra $20. (Don't do this with a new style—you'll never know how it's supposed to look.)

➤ If you colour your hair, retouch your own roots at home. Get a professional colour every three months.

➤ Don't sign that fitness membership agreement, I beg you. Walk. Play. Skip. Run up stairs. Have you ever thought about the real place of a stair master—in a world full of stairs?

Entertainment: Have More Fun for Less Money

When you were three years old, you could spend a whole day playing with a cardboard refrigerator carton and never get tired. You still can, although now you can forget about the cardboard. Here are several ways to have fun without spending a fortune:

➤ Get a library card. You can rent movies, CDs, books, and magazines—for FREE.

➤ Take advantage of community events, community fitness facilities, and community learning.

➤ Rent movies with friends. Make some popcorn, break open a six-pack of something. Instant party.

➤ Trade Halloween costumes. Save them all—never throw a costume away.

➤ Don't buy new novels in hardcover (unless you feel, as some people do, that good authors deserve to make a living, too). Don't tell me you've read all the great old ones yet.

➤ Subscribe to a newspaper rather than buying it at the newsstand every day. You'll save about three dollars a week.

➤ Find the cut-rate movie theatres in your city.

➤ If you really want to own a video, buy your favourite, previously viewed, from the big video rental places. I bought *Enchanted April* for $8.99—and I've watched it at least twenty times. That's less than fifty cents a viewing, and it's still precious to me.

➤ What would you do if you didn't have cable TV? As a matter of fact, who would you be? Are you courageous enough to try it for six months?

➤ If you drink wine regularly, bottle your own. The savings are huge.

Tip

Take a dream vacation in your home town by visiting the places where you'd take guests from out of town but seldom visit otherwise. Or invite your friends to your home for a spa weekend. Swap manicures, go for a hike, and give each other facials.

The Dining Dilemma: Can I Ever Eat Out Again?

You can spend a lot of money going out for dinner when you can have more fun, and spend less, by staying home. But on those occasions when you just have to go out for dinner, here are some ways to keep the bill down:

➤ When you eat out with a significant other, choose an appetizer each and split an entrée. Unless you're a sumo wrestler, you'll have more than enough food, and you'll save from $9 to $30 every time.

➤ Don't have dessert when you go out for dinner or lunch. Instead, make dessert a separate occasion. You'll enjoy it far more than after a big meal.

➤ When you dine out, limit your alcohol. It can quadruple your bill. Have liqueurs at home later, in front of a roaring fire. Very romantic. (Don't try this if you don't have a fireplace!)

➤ Drink water rather than soft drinks when you have fast food. It's WAY better for you, and can significantly cut the cost of the bill. Even better—carry your own water from home.

➤ If friends suggest meeting at a pricey restaurant for dinner, offer to host a potluck dinner instead. Then you can afford a better bottle of wine and enjoy each other's company in the comfort of your own home. If you're not up to cooking, take-out potlucks work too.

Hanging on to a Few Dollars Even After You Have Kids

When the kids arrive, the bills do, too. Or so it seems. Yet there are ways to do everything you can for your kids, without driving yourself into the poorhouse in the process. Here are some tips:

➤ Join a toy library, or shop at consignment and thrift stores for next-to-new educational toys at half the price of new. (Sterilize them in the dishwasher when you get them home. Not the teddy bears, silly.)

➤ If you have younger kids, set up a baby-sitting co-op service in your community with other parents you trust. Trade hours rather than after-tax dollars.

➤ Teach your kids to be fashion originals. Following trends is incredibly expensive.

➤ A peanut butter and jelly sandwich is still more nutritious, less expensive, and just as fast as one of those $4 snack/lunches that are so popular with kids these days. Remember, the appeal is really the 25-cent candy bar inside—if you're willing to put one of those in your kids' lunches, you'll find they couldn't care less about the packaging. (Nowadays, you may have to replace the peanut butter with something else, since many schools no longer allow allergy-causing peanuts on the premises.)

➤ Don't buy your kids video games. You can always rent the machines and games from the video store on special occasions, like when you're about to lose your mind. Then, when your children are about to lose their minds, you can return them.

➤ Don't buy your pre-school kids designer clothes. Shop for used jeans and overalls. You can get tremendous quality for low prices at thrift and consignment stores.

➤ Limit your kids' after-school activities to one or two per season. If they're playing little league and taking karate, they don't need piano, voice, and Japanese lessons too. Whenever possible, enroll your kids in community activities rather than private ones, and take advantage of free programs offered by the school or your municipality.

Rolling, Rolling, Rolling: Take the Bite out of Transportation Costs

If you have time to use it, your imagination can keep you entertained for hours, even as you go from A to B and back again without your car. If you really have to drive, do it as cheaply as possible. Consider the following suggestions:

➤ Leave your car at home. Walk as much as you can. You'll learn to love it, and it will create a light inside you.

➤ Oh, I know how you hate to hear this. Don't buy a new car unless you can walk in and lay down the cash. It's a myth that a new car will cost less to operate—as a matter of fact, you may find yourself paying more for maintenance to keep the warranty valid than your older car cost to fix. (Remember, when you drive by in that sporty new automobile, the woman or man of your dreams is just as likely to think "what a foolish waste of money!" as they are to think "hot car!" Depending on your dreams, of course.)

➤ Think about taking a cab, joining a car ownership co-op, or even renting a car when required rather than buying a vehicle that you'll rarely use.

➤ Shop around for the lowest parking rates. You may save hundreds of dollars a year by parking five blocks from work and walking—and you can save on the gym membership you'll no longer need, too.

The Least You Need to Know

➤ Saving $1000 can easily be the equivalent of earning an additional $3000 after taxes and income-related expenses are factored in.

➤ Getting past our infatuation with the Hottest, Newest, and Trendiest can help provide us with financial well-being and the Rich, Sweet, and Satisfying life of our dreams.

➤ There are dozens of ways of trimming your spending, and probably hundreds more that we haven't thought of. They all require a bit of planning, creativity, and effort, but it's worth it!

Part 2

Hitching Your Wagon
to a Star

As with any long journey, we have to know where we want to go before we can pursue our financial goals.

The next five chapters will help you identify what you want in the future, financially speaking. Then I'll help you figure out how to get what you want.

We'll also look at some of the pitfalls and dead-ends of credit abuse that might impede your successful journey. And we'll examine some of the sources where you might find some help along the way.

Chapter 4

The Destination: Our Personalized Vision of Financial Freedom

> ## In This Chapter
> ➤ Explore the difference between deprivation and motivation
> ➤ Develop a vision of your future that will inspire you to make the right decisions today
> ➤ Calculate the cost of retirement

Let me give you the bottom line on this personal financial planning stuff. First, it's up to you. Second, the first key to success is spending less than you earn. Ouch! Oh, I know, it hurts to hear—but it really doesn't have to be painful at all. As a matter of fact, let's begin by rejecting the whole concept of budgeting. Budgets are a lot like diets— they consume our attention and energy, make us feel deprived, and work only as long as the deprivation continues. The moment we let down our guard and start enjoying ourselves again, trouble looms.

Therefore, you won't find me using the word *budget* again. Instead, let's focus on our dreams.

Vision: The Master Motivator

Imagine, if you will, a 14-year-old girl being forced by her well-meaning parents to get out of bed at 4 a.m. every morning. She must then go to a cold ice rink and skate, half asleep, for two hours, until her feet ache in her skates. She has a quick shower, and then eats breakfast in the car on the way to school. After, she has to rush straight home to do her homework, while her friends are hanging out and doing teenage sorts of things. Then, while the rest of her family relaxes and watches a bit of TV, she goes back to the rink for another two-hour session comprised of doing things she thought she could not do and being barked at by a tough coach.

Absolute torture.

Now imagine this conversation between a coach and the same teenager:

> I believe you've got it in you to make the Canadian Olympic team. It's going to take a lot of practice—I need to see you here for two hours every morning before school and two hours after. You're going to have to work harder than you've ever dreamed of working, but if you do, I believe you're going to make the team, and there is no reason you won't be on the podium in the next eight years.

The difference is clear—this coach knows how to move from "process" to "vision." We need to do the same with our financial plans. Believe me, namby-pamby objectives like "I want to have a comfortable retirement" don't have any power whatsoever when they are up against a Hawaiian vacation or even a designer suit. If we want to change our spending habits, we have to have a clear vision of the destination.

Tip

The most successful savers have a clear objective in mind. Knowing exactly how much you need to reach your dreams can turn delayed gratification into a joyous sense of accomplishment as you watch those numbers move closer to the target.

The Canadian Dream—Ahh, What Was That Again?

For most Canadians, our general objectives include:

➤ Owning our own home (the mortgage burning ceremony!)

➤ Providing our kids with a good education

➤ Saving for our retirement

➤ Freedom from indentured slavery—having enough to quit our job and try our wings in the world of self-employment or small business

For most of us, however, the reason we worry about money, the reason we're reading this book right now, and the reason we are willing to defer spending is—*fear*. We're afraid of not having enough. It's motivating, to be sure, but the problem is that we have to *stay* fearful in order to stay motivated. In addition, fear becomes a painful habit.

Who Knew?

According to Malcolm Hamilton, an actuary with William M. Mercer Ltd., a retired couple living solely on Canada Pension, Old Age Supplement, the Guaranteed Income Supplement, and tax credits will have equivalent "consumable income" to a middle-income family earning $63 400 after tax, retirement savings, and mortgage payments are factored in.

When I first began working in financial services, it quickly became clear to me that this thing we refer to as "financial security" is not the result of accumulating a pile of assets. People with a high net worth are often as anxious and fearful as those who are struggling to make it from paycheque to paycheque.

Are You Motivated by Vision or Fear?

If we are to achieve authentic financial success, we have to reach financial freedom— that is, freedom from fear and anxiety about money. Doing so often involves reframing some of the beliefs we talked about in Chapter 1, but it also involves knowing our destination. Try on some of the following statements for size. Read them aloud, and be aware of how you feel. Does it have the ring of truth for you?

	So True	True	Not True
I need to know that I'll be okay even if I get sick or have an accident.	☐	☐	☐
I want to know that I won't be poor when I'm old and can't work anymore.	☐	☐	☐
I'm worried about getting my children through university.	☐	☐	☐
Owning my own home would make me feel a lot more secure about the future.	☐	☐	☐

	So True	True	Not True
I want to know that my family will be comfortable even if something happens to me.	☐	☐	☐
I want to be able to enjoy my retirement, to have money to travel or take up golf or visit my grandkids.	☐	☐	☐

Now, let's reframe these statements:

	So True	True	Not True
I have enough disability insurance to know that I'll be okay no matter what happens.	☐	☐	☐
I know exactly how much I'll need to retire comfortably, and I have a plan in place to get there.	☐	☐	☐
I'm not worried about getting my children through university—I feel really good about making regular RESP contributions. It's going to be okay.	☐	☐	☐
I'm looking forward to paying off my mortgage on _____ [date]. Yahoo!	☐	☐	☐
If I were to die tomorrow, my life insurance would give my family the same kind of lifestyle I can provide for them today.	☐	☐	☐
I'm saving _____ dollars per month so that I can really enjoy my retirement.	☐	☐	☐

See the difference here? Vague worries are destructive. They reduce our quality of life. Clear visions, accompanied by plans to achieve those visions, vastly enhance our quality of life and make it far more likely we'll achieve everything we're dreaming of.

Now it's your turn. Think about what you really want. Make yourself a cup of tea, or pour a glass of wine, and dream. What does your future look like? Don't allow yourself to stumble over the roadblocks—for the sake of this exercise, imagine everything is possible. (It is!) When something occurs to you, write it down on your list.

Next, let's take this a level deeper. For every statement you made about your future vision, answer these four questions:

    1. How would achieving this objective add to my happiness?

2. Is this something I want for myself, or is it something that would make my
   _____ [spouse, partner, family, parents] proud of me?

3. Is this something I really want and need to accomplish in my life, or have I
   just unconsciously accepted the social message that this is a good thing?

4. Is this something I really want, or am I just afraid of what might happen if
   I don't?

Defining a "Comfortable Retirement"

A "comfortable retirement" is a good example of something that needs to be clearly
defined from a completely individual perspective. For instance, I'm self-employed, and
absolutely love my work. As a counsellor, educator, and advocate, there is nothing that
fulfills me more than working. I'll work until my physical health no longer permits it,
and I take very good care of myself to ensure that is a long time from now. However, I
plan to travel at least three months of each year beginning 10 years from now, so my
"retirement planning" consists of figuring out how much that will cost—and ensuring
my dreams aren't hindered by my bank account. I also have to plan for the possibility
of catastrophic illness or accident. Although my best "insurance" is my own behaviour
—eating right, exercising regularly, maintaining serenity, driving carefully, and avoiding
tobacco and excessive alcohol consumption—I can also purchase insurance that will pay
me a lump sum if I become severely ill. (This is a good choice for people who find it
hard to qualify for disability insurance—see Chapter 25 for more details.)

The happiest couple I've ever met had exactly $25 000 in assets. They were both 69—
she still managed their apartment building, they were in sparkling good health, and
they were receiving as much from CPP, OAS, and GIS as they had ever earned together
in a lifetime of what many would see as brutally hard work. When they spoke of their
children and grandchildren, about their beginnings as peasant farmers in the Ukraine,
they absolutely beamed. They had a wonderful life. Their needs were simple, their
relationships rich. When I asked if they had any plans to travel, they both looked
horrified. "How could we leave our grandchildren?"

Conversely, a colleague of mine told me recently about a couple he works with who are
now on a year-long safari in Africa. They managed to accumulate a very impressive
portfolio, and they plan to spend it seeing and enjoying the world.

Do you see what I mean? It is integrally important to get a clear picture of your real
objective. It's amazing how many people are working long hours in jobs they hate to
prepare for a "comfortable retirement." In the meantime, they drink too much, eat too
much, and veg out in front of the TV in an attempt to get some relief from their misery.
Not only are they not enjoying life to its fullest now—but they are almost guaranteeing
painful (and expensive) health problems in their future.

Don't fall victim to this trap. Think about what you *really* want.

If You Want to Maintain Your "Current Lifestyle"

If what you want is to be able to maintain your current lifestyle in retirement, it is easiest to get on the Internet and use one of the many available retirement planning programs. My favourite is at <majestic5.vanguard.com/GUIDE/DA>, but you can find retirement planners at almost any personal financial planning site. (Check out Appendix A at the back of the book.) However, don't lose sight of the fact that your "current lifestyle" probably includes major expenses you won't have in retirement. Your mortgage will hopefully be paid off, your employment-related expenses will end, you won't be saving for retirement, and, God willing, your children will be self-supporting.

If you don't have access to the Internet but do have a computer, Quicken and Microsoft Money both have retirement income calculators. If there is no computer in sight, your bank may be able to provide you with a retirement planning booklet that will take you through the calculations.

To give yourself an idea about what you should probably be saving, you might try the calculations using Tables 4-1 and 4-2.

Table 4–1
Saving for Retirement

		Example (at Age 41)	Your Figure
A	Your family income today.	$ 40 000	$_____
B	CPP and OAS benefits (call the CPP hotline to find out what you can expect)	$ 9 400	$_____
C	Any pension benefits already ensured (if you belong to a pension plan, call your HR department to get this information). If your pension isn't indexed for inflation, multiply benefits by 0.6.	$ 8 400	$_____
D	Subtract those costs or payments you'll no longer have during retirement-the amount you are currently saving, investing, paying for life insurance, and/or spending on income-related expenses	$ 6 000	$_____
E	Investment income required in retirement [A – (B + C + D) = _____(E)]	$ 16 200	$_____
F	Savings needed to retire at 65 (E × 18)	$291 600	$_____
G	Amount of current savings/investments	$ 45 000	$_____

H	Value of current savings at time of retirement* (E × "investment growth factor" in Table 4-2)	$148 500	$_____
I	Savings required in today's dollars	$143 100	$_____
J	Monthly savings required (I × "monthly savings factor" in Table 4-2)	$257.58	$_____

*Assumes growth of 8%, inflation of 3%, and investment in an RRSP or RPP.
Source: Adapted with permission from *The Coffeehouse Investor* by Bill Schultheis.

Table 4-2
Retirement Worksheet Factors

Your Current Age	Investment Growth Factor	Monthly Savings Factor
19	9.9	.0005
21	9.0	.0005
23	8.1	.0006
25	7.4	.0007
27	6.7	.0007
29	6.0	.0008
31	5.5	.0009
33	4.9	.0011
35	4.5	.0012
37	4.0	.0014
39	3.7	.0016
41	3.3	.0018
43	3.0	.0021
45	2.7	.0024
47	2.5	.0029
49	2.2	.0034
51	2.0	.0041
53	1.8	.0051
55	1.6	.0064
57	1.5	.0085
59	1.3	.0119
61	1.2	.0188
63	1.1	.0395

That's enough about retirement for now. Let's talk about life.

Living Deep

Although it can create quite an effective distraction from unhappiness, at least for short periods of time, money doesn't buy happiness.

Money buys freedom, and freedom allows us to do what we are here to—become ever more fully ourselves. In recognizing and following our heart's desire, we learn to finally reach that place in which our passions and abilities intersect with the needs of the world. It is then that we come to understand that happiness is a by-product of doing what we love to do. If we wait until retirement to find out what that is, we are wasting so much precious time—and for some, it's too late altogether.

Definition

Umbrella liability coverage *is* an economical alternative to high-cost liability coverage on your home and auto insurance policies. It insures you against a situation in which you are sued for damages caused in or by your car, home, and/or watercraft (*if applicable*).

Tip

Saving for retirement should be more of a concern for high-income Canadians than for those in lower income brackets if they want to continue in their current lifestyle—reducing expenses can add as much to our comfort level as increasing income.

Whatever the advertisers would have us believe, however, more is not necessarily better. "More" can trap us in a situation where we have to devote ever larger portions of our time and energy—our life essence—to debt repayment and the quest for stuff. Financial freedom is achieved through a two-part endeavour—increasing your income to that place at which your needs are amply met, and reducing the cost of whatever it is you need in order to be comfortable and fulfilled. Many people, perhaps the majority of people, will go through life without ever having a clear understanding of what it is that makes them happy, and how much it costs—sort of like setting out on a trip without any idea of the destination.

I recently did some counselling for an amazing couple—these two could be poster children for personal financial planning. Still in their early 40s, they give generously to charity, have a beautiful home, and are just months away from being mortgage-free. They make their maximum RRSP contributions each year, are educating themselves on investing, have ample life and disability insurance in place, and minimize their property insurance costs by using umbrella liability coverage.

We were discussing the impact of saving an additional monthly amount outside of their RRSP. She wasn't convinced.

"I could spend that money enjoying life now!"

I was a little surprised. From a material perspective, this couple really seemed to have it all.

"Aren't you enjoying life now?" I asked.

There was a moment of silence, followed by laughter, but it struck me that something really important had just happened. Without a vision, saving is a struggle and spending is less than satisfying. Decisions *must* be made in the context of a larger plan, or we risk feeling unfulfilled whatever we choose to do.

The reason that personal financial planning is important is that it enables us to enjoy life as much as possible, now and later. Whatever you do, don't sacrifice the present in an attempt to control anxiety about the future. You may not be able to have it all, but you can, if you plan well, have most of it.

On the other hand, don't squander money today. It's your life you're frittering away, your precious hours, your energy.

The key is to stop spending money on stuff that gives you little or no pleasure at all. Think about it—do you really need two cars in your family, or would it be enough to have one? Worried about negotiating use? What if you could? What would that look like? How long did that new car really turn your crank? The stereo you absolutely had to have—when was the last time you sat and listened to it, thinking about how happy you were you bought it? The Club Med vacation you put on your credit card last year and are still paying for—would you need it, even want it, if you had work that you loved?

The Least You Need to Know

➤ Spending and saving are both more fulfilling if they occur in the context of a larger plan.

➤ Fear and anxiety are far less effective motivators than a compelling vision.

➤ At the very least, calculate the cost of your retirement, and know what it is you need to save monthly in order to get there.

➤ It is up to you to define the meaning of a "comfortable retirement."

Chapter 5

Increasing Your Income

In This Chapter

➤ What to do if your income simply won't meet your needs or dreams

➤ Everything you need to know (and, more importantly, do) to expand your employment income

➤ Prosperity Law #1: Stop working for money and put your money to work for you

If you see the future you want to create, determine what it will cost to get there, and realize that you simply have to increase your income, you may want to try some of these ideas. These are tried and tested, fool-proof methods. I have applied them successfully in my own life, and I have watched them work for others.

Work More

This may not be an attractive option, or even a realistic option right now, but it is worth thinking about. Get a part-time job, in addition to your full-time job, or simply put in more hours at the job you have now. Ironically, this doesn't necessarily mean that you have to spend more time at work. There have been a number of times in my own career when I stopped taking my heart to work with me. During these periods, I often spent eight, ten, even twelve hours a day at the office. Fifty percent of those hours may have been productive. As a manager, I've seen this syndrome hundreds of times. We feel like we're working, because the very effort required to be present is so excruciatingly hard, but our productivity is dangerously low.

As long as you really are working more, and not just spending more time at work, you will eventually be promoted and you will get a raise. If you work for cretins who don't notice, rest assured that someone will—some co-worker, client, or customer will notice. And when they need someone at their new firm, they'll think of you.

Remember, if you can't make yourself be productive at work (as opposed to just *there*) there's a message trying to break through—it's time to move on. Start thinking about what you want the future to look like and how you can begin to move in that direction. In the meantime, see if you can invite some energy into your current job performance by thinking of it as a temporary launching pad as opposed to a permanent indentured servitude contract.

Educate Yourself

If you think your education ended when you got your degree or diploma, you are robbing yourself. If you read nonfiction material for one hour a day for the next year, you will make more money. If you can, take adult education courses. Attend seminars. Take correspondence courses. Many of North America's most successful business people never received a formal education, but they never stopped educating themselves through the means available to them.

Market Yourself

Think of every professional interaction as a possible career contact. How would you handle this client if you thought he or she might make you a job offer next week? You know what? That person just might. When you do get offers, even little wisps of semi-offers, like "I wish you worked for me," let your employers know. Sound like bragging? How do you think Sarah McLachlan would have done without marketing? Estée Lauder? Mary Kay?

Unlike Sarah and Estée, no one is going to do it for you. And hey! Who is more excited about the product?

Work Less—But Do What You Love

Leaving a job that you hate, a career that drains you, can prove to be the most fruitful move you could ever make. If you are stagnating in your career, ask yourself why. Is it because of the industry? Or the economy? Or is it because your heart is no longer in it?

Increase Your Value to Your Employer

Even if that employer is you. (Ultimately, the employer is always you.) Education is one way; greater time commitment is another. But they aren't the only ways. As my nine-year-old daughter once asked, "What do you do that makes money for that company?" Once you have the answer to that question, do more of it!

Take a course to hone your skills in that area. If social skills are holding you back, get some counselling to put those old issues to bed once and for all. At the time my daughter asked the question, I was doing consulting for an investment services firm. In an effort to answer her question, I became aware that I was missing the mark. I had been hired to improve operational processes and strategies, and although I worked very hard to do that, the greatest obstacle was the managerial style of the principal. I had attempted to work around this handicap to avoid offending anyone. My daughter reminded me that the way I made money for that company was in eliminating obstacles, not enabling them. I overcome my fear of giving offence, and finally did what I had been hired to do.

Show up at work healthy, well-balanced, rested, serene—you wouldn't believe what you can accomplish. Abe Lincoln once said that if he had eight hours to chop down a tree, he'd spend six hours sharpening the axe. Very wise. We forget that we are the "axe"—in order to bring as much as possible to our work, we must also constantly replenish and nurture our body, mind, and spirit. Allowing ourselves to become one-dimensional drains our creativity, compassion, and energy. Ultimately, our work suffers too.

Ask for a Raise

Employers in general are unlikely to offer a raise out of the goodness of their hearts, so it's up to you to establish what you're worth and ask for it. Do a bit of research on salary ranges for people in your field. The employment ads are a good place to begin. Do some research on the Internet. If you are having a difficult time, you can try my method: call two or three of your employer's competitors, and ask to speak to the person working in your position. Tell him or her that you are trying to establish a reasonable salary range for your job because you are going to request an increase. You may be surprised at how forthright people are willing to be in order to help.

Once you've established an industry range, prepare a presentation demonstrating where you should be in that range, using your experience, education, and your accomplishments to your best advantage. Spend some time thinking about how you've improved your employer's business over the past two years, and highlight those contributions while making your presentation. While you're at it, it doesn't hurt to say something like, "I'd like to increase my income as much as possible. Is there anything that you would suggest, like courses I could take or extra projects I could take on, that would make that possible?"

Pay Less in Tax

Check out Chapter 7 for ways to reduce the taxes you must pay. Remember, a dollar saved is two to three dollars earned.

Become Self-Employed

Leverage your assets into the market at the highest possible price—market yourself as a consultant or contractor. The benefits are endless:

➤ more tax breaks

➤ more independence

➤ more variety

➤ more respect in the workplace

➤ more flexibility

➤ more opportunity to do what you do best

➤ more freedom to leave situations that aren't comfortable

➤ more ability to increase your income as your skills increase.

And those are just the benefits I know about!

Be Assertive in Expanding Your Range of Contribution

Let go of the illusion that being nice will get you want you want. The most underpaid people I've worked with are paralyzingly nice. Ask for what you're worth. Find out what other companies are paying. Every year, if you are educating yourself and working hard for your employer, your value to that employer is increasing. If they won't acknowledge it, someone else will. Two of my promotions came as counteroffers after I had accepted employment from other firms.

The man that first promoted me to a managerial position once told me that, as a manager, you have to be very careful about what you ask people to do. If you ask or allow staff to take on projects outside of their job description, you are providing them with training. Once you have trained them, you may have to pay them more money.

Now you have the secret to advancement. Use it to your advantage.

Negotiate Better Benefits Within Your Relationship

If you are in a life partnership where the deal is that one of you will take time off to stay home with the kids (or do the majority of the home caring so the other partner can concentrate on his or her business), negotiate a raise.

If you are in a traditional marriage, request that your partner make spousal RRSP contributions. Increase your household expenditure budget to include a monthly savings plan, so that you can create an emergency reserve account—for you! Remember, please—I beg you—every calorie of energy you put into doing more than your share domestically is a calorie of energy that is lost to your career, whatever that may be. Your time and energy are not free, nor are they limitless!

If you generally make $30 000 a year, it's costing you at least $30 000 a year to stay home! Just as importantly, you are losing Canada Pension Plan room, access to RRSP contribution room and/or a pension plan, cost of living wage increases, and the opportunity to move up the corporate ladder.

And the #1 way to increase your income ...

Send Your Money Out to Work for You

This is the second level of magic—the magic of compound returns.

First, a very simple illustration. I save 10% of my net income in an RRSP. Let's say my net income is $36 000, so I save $300 per month. I invest it at 9%, and I keep contributing for 25 years, until I'm in my sixties. In all, I will have contributed $90 000. But in my account, I'll have ... $317 306. That's the power of compound return.

Joanne Thomas Yaccato, in her book *Balancing Act*, gives us an even more powerful example:

> Twin sisters, Krystal and Vanessa, are discussing their impending retirement. Vanessa, who had been saving diligently since the age of thirty, was very concerned about her sister. Krystal was a homemaker, who stopped working at age 30, didn't qualify for CPP, and couldn't contribute to RSPs, even if she had the money, which she didn't. Her husband had just died, "leaving nothing behind but funeral expenses."
>
> But Krystal had the last laugh. In the ten years she had worked (between age twenty and age thirty), she saved $2500 per year, and invested it at 10%.
>
> Vanessa had started saving ten years later, when she was thirty, and had invested $2500 a year at 10%—for thirty-five years.
>
> The total of Vanessa's nest egg, after thirty-five years of saving, was $745 317. By starting ten years earlier, Krystal accumulated $1 231 671!

If you are more like Vanessa than Krystal, or are in your later thirties, forties, or fifties, this example can be depressing. However, the underlying principle, the power of compound return, is a powerful force at any age, within any period.

As they say, the best time to invest was 20 years ago. The second best time is now.

The Least You Need to Know

➤ Your income will keep growing as long as you do—and we aren't talking about your waistline.

➤ Be assertive in making your worth clear to both employers and partners.

➤ Our time and energy are limited—our money is not. Only investors achieve great wealth.

Chapter 6

Managing Credit and Crisis

In This Chapter

➤ Indentured servitude—the real toll of being a member of a consumer society

➤ Best practices for managing credit

➤ Considering bankruptcy, and if need be—recovering afterward

➤ Crisis management for times of trouble

"Working for a Dying"

As Vicki Robin and Joe Dominguez so sagely stated in their revolutionary book, *Your Money or Your Life*, most people are not working for a living—they are "working for a dying."

Despite the fact that present-day North America is the richest society in the history of humankind, we suffer from collective money anxiety, and have enslaved ourselves to creditors. "Pay day" has become "payment day," and we work at jobs we hate to pay off cars, houses, and do-dads that we have long since fallen out of love with. Credit can be a convenience, and it certainly seems necessary to make us "legitimate" citizens in this day and age—but as a society, our inability to handle credit well is profoundly destructive to our quality of life.

Consider this fact from the *Complete Idiot's Guide® to Personal Finance in Your 20s, 30s, and 40s*: "In 1996, the average total debt for people in their 20s, excluding mortgage debt, was nearly $17 000."

Tip

Credit card rates range from 8.9% to 18.9%. Particularly if your credit is good, shop around. Begin by asking your bank for their best rate.

Unless you're in the same boat, you might be tempted to ask how that is possible. When you look at the spanking new cars clogging our roadways, flip through the "no money down, no interest" furniture and electronics advertisements in the weekend paper, and then add student loans into the picture, it becomes a lot easier to understand.

There are billions of advertising dollars spent every year to program us into the kind of buy-happy consumers we have become. Somehow, an invisible credit card debt of $17 000 (and that's the *average*) is not damaging to our self-esteem but driving a 10-year-old car is. I think not. Say it with me, people—break free!

Tip

If you're carrying a balance, you don't need to pay it off before moving to another credit-card company—most credit companies are happy to do what's called a "balance" transfer, and you may get low interest (or even no interest) for the first six months. But don't be so dazzled that you forget to ask what the usual rate is.

The First Law of Financial Well-Being

The First Law of Financial Well-Being is this: "Never borrow money for anything that is not going to increase in value."

That immediately cuts out cars, furniture, computers (except for business), vacations, restaurant meals, clothing, alcohol, entertaining, sports, and electronic equipment—you're getting my drift, I'm sure. If you tend to put stuff like this on your credit card believing that you will pay it off when the bill comes, only to find yourself carrying the balance for three months—wake up, dude.

No Credit Problems? Here's How to Ensure It Stays That Way ...

First of all, let's assume that you don't currently have a credit problem. You haven't had any problems paying your bills, you haven't bounced a cheque in the last year, and things generally seem to be going okay. Here a few helpful hints to keep you striding in the right direction.

Reduce Your Number of Credit Cards to One, or at the Most, Two

The Strategis Canada site provides a fabulous calculator to help you determine which credit card is best for you based on your spending (and paying) habits. If you have Internet access, check it out at <strategis.ic.gc.ca/SSG/ca00458e.html>. If your credit rating is good, financial institutions love to grant you credit, so take advantage of the goodwill to get the best deal possible. If you pay off your balance each month, for instance, look for a card with no annual fee. If you tend to carry a balance from month to month, the interest rate also becomes important, and you may save money by paying a small fee for lower interest. The rates shown in the Strategis Web site on May 8, 2000, ranged from 8.9% for a LowRate MasterCard to 18.9% for a Canadian Tire MasterCard.

Are You at Risk?

Answer these four questions:

1. When you get approved for a credit card, do you feel as if you've just received a gift?
2. When you are deciding if you "can afford something," do you tend to think about how much room you have left on your credit card rather than if you earn enough discretionary spending money?
3. Do you make only your minimum payments more than three months out of the year?
4. When considering a major purchase, like a car, a boat, or a new stereo system, do you simply figure out if you could manage the minimum monthly payments?

A "yes" response to any *one* of these questions means that you are at risk.

Your Credit Card Is Not a Paycheque Extension

The most common beginning of credit card problems is viewing them as income—sort of a paycheque extension. If you are someone who tends to see it that way, you'll want to keep one credit card with a very low minimum, or none at all.

If you carry a debt balance of just $3000 ($14 000 less than the Canadian average) at 18 percent, you will pay over $550 in interest in one year. Imagine all the perfectly nice things you could spend that $550 on! And if you need further encouragement, remember that if you are in a 50 percent tax bracket, you had to earn more than $1100 before tax to get that $550. For most of us, that is a week's work or more—for Mr. Visa or Ms. MasterCard, and the privilege of buying stuff sooner so we can tire of it faster.

Avoiding the Emergency Spending Trap

Another source of credit card problems is emergency spending. Have you ever noticed that your washing machine will inevitably break down as soon as you pay off your line of credit? Or that your car will need new brakes as soon as you get a raise?

Get in the habit of putting $50 or $100 into a mutual fund money market account each month. I don't know about you, but savings accounts *never* worked for me—it was just one more place to transfer money from when I ran out. A money market fund is kind of magic—you can set up a pre-authorized plan that comes out of your account every payday. Unless you are already struggling to get by, you won't even notice the missing money, I promise. Your savings will earn in the range of 4 percent, and you can generally access the money by calling for a redemption within two or three days of the time you need it. Not only are you going to feel like a paragon of virtue watching that balance go up every month, but you will have a supply of emergency money when your car breaks down. No more rainy day blues for you!

Save for Annual Purchases, Don't Charge Them

It is so easy to put your car insurance, house insurance, and property tax on your credit card when they come due, isn't it? Of course, once your credit card bill is that high, any income not used for necessities goes to make your minimum credit card balance and pay the interest. Use the money market solution mentioned above instead. Many insurance companies now provide the option of monthly payment, too, and the interest charged can be as low as 2 or 3 percent, rather than 18 percent. Check it out.

No Interest, No Down Payment? Clutch Your Wallet!

Never fall for those "no interest for six months" advertisements. Things rarely change for us over a six-month period, and if you read the fine print, you'll probably find that if you don't pay your purchase off within the six-month period (or whatever the time frame) the interest clock started ticking the moment you made the purchase. When that happens, as it too often does, the interest rate is usually the department store rate of 28.8 percent.

I Work So I Can Drive: The Car Trap

Buying a new car? Oh, please don't buy a new car. Okay, if you must buy a new car, at least do not fall for the 1 percent financing deal. Remember that other rule of personal financial planning—nothing is free, and consumer credit does not come in a 1 percent interest version. Instead, the car dealer "buys down" the true interest rate, and adds it to the purchase price of the car. If you can afford to buy a new car, you can afford to pay cash. And while you're at it, ask the dealership to discount the car's price by the amount that you would save between the car loan rate and 1 percent if you had financed it.

If you can't afford to pay cash, give some thought to getting a good second-hand car. Anything you've heard about a new car saving you money is *myth*—just be sure to have any used car thoroughly inspected and buy from a reputable dealer. (Call the Better Business Bureau for a record of complaints against any dealership you're considering.)

Financial Crisis Management—Is Bankruptcy in Your Future?

You're in trouble. You've flipped through some of the other sections and you feel more discouraged after each page. None of this stuff applies to you. You can't "pay yourself first." You can't even pay your creditors.

I've been there, and I'm going to let you in on a few little-known facts about the dark side of the consumer society.

Credit cards are a huge source of profit for financial institutions. That's why it's so easy to get credit. Most Canadians do not pay off their monthly balances—we have become a nation of debtors— We have sold ourselves into a life of indentured servitude. The majority of us still manage to get by. We may end up spending any discretionary income on interest payments, but we at least make all of our minimum payments and we've learned our lesson—we're not still buying on credit. We're among the lucky ones, and with discipline and hard work, we'll get back in the black and start moving in the other direction as our income increases.

Definition

Discretionary income is money not required to pay for the necessities of life—basic food, shelter, and costs relating to employment.

Some of us will not be so lucky. The worst thing that can happen to us is to have lots of credit when trouble strikes. So many really sad stories begin with "We were doing okay until I lost my job," or "I was just trying to get by until the child support started coming in."

By the time the new job starts or the child support finally arrives, we realize it is too little, too late. We're barely making enough money to live on—and now our creditors would like to get paid too.

Do You Need Help?

How do you know when you're in trouble? Well, if you think you are, you are. Like they say in Alcoholics Anonymous, "Social drinkers don't sit around wondering if they have a drinking problem."

How many of the following statements apply to you?

1. I make only my minimum payments the majority of the time.
2. When I've run out of money in the past, I coped by having my credit card limits increased.
3. I'm behind on my minimum payments.
4. I use my credit cards to pay for things like the phone bill, groceries, or the hydro bill that I wouldn't otherwise be able to pay.
5. My credit cards are all at their limits. I make the minimum payments and then use that room for spending.
6. My credit card and car loan debt is more than 25 percent of my annual income.
7. I'm receiving calls from creditors. They want their money and I don't have it.
8. I applied for a consolidation loan and was turned down.
9. I've used a cash advance on one credit card to make my minimum payment on another.
10. My debt is at least 25 percent high interest—I'm paying more than 25 percent interest on at least a quarter of what I owe.

If any of statements 1, 2, 4, 5, 9, or 10 apply to you, you need to rethink the way you use credit and get back on track. You're walking on a tightrope. Think about getting credit counselling now. You can find help in the blue pages. You need a disciplined spending plan, and you may need to consider moving to a less expensive home, trading down to a less expensive car, changing your lifestyle, or taking a part-time job to increase your income. I'm sorry—but you also need to cut up your credit cards. Now.

If any of statements 3, 6, 7, or 8 apply to you, it may be time to consider bankruptcy. See a credit counsellor, and if necessary, the counsellor will refer you to a bankruptcy trustee. Be aware of two conflicts of interest you may run into—the credit counselling agency may be partially funded by the financial institutions who are offering the credit cards, and the bankruptcy trustee will make anywhere from hundreds to thousands of dollars in fees if you decide to go ahead. You must ultimately decide what is right for you. In your heart, you know what you must do.

Before you decide, consider the following bankruptcy facts:

➤ One in 200 Canadian families will declare bankruptcy this year.

➤ Credit cards and consumer debt are a source of rather obscene profitability for financial institutions, and bankruptcies are very carefully factored into the business plan.

➤ Credit card companies encourage us to take on as much high-interest debt as we can possibly handle, knowing that some of us won't make it.

➤ Your creditors may very well prefer that you declare bankruptcy. They can then write off the loss against profits, and they don't have to take further expensive collection measures.

➤ Many people avoid bankruptcy because of the impact it will have on their credit rating. If you are in the kind of trouble that would cause you to consider bankruptcy, your credit rating is already in very bad shape.

➤ Once you break out of the downward spiral you're in, you'll find that life without credit is *preferable* to the life you're living now.

➤ "I spent the money. I'm going to pay it back." You spent the money, but what about the interest?

Bankruptcy, Consumer Proposal, or Debt Consolidation?

In some provinces, when you see a debt counsellor, you'll hear about two options—bankruptcy and debt consolidation. In addition, there is an option called a "consumer proposal." Debt consolidation and consumer proposals are similar in nature.

With debt consolidation, your credit counsellor will create a spending plan (budget) for your basic needs, and calculate the amount you'll have left over for debt repayment. There will be no fat in this budget—no movies, no eating out, no luxuries of any kind. Then a debt consolidation order will be served to each of your creditors on your behalf, and you'll begin the long, slow process of repayment.

There are three things you need to know about debt consolidation orders and consumer proposals. The first is that you're in for a very tight time of it. It's one thing to commit to living without luxury—it's another thing to tell your children, one more time, that they can't join that team, attend that class, or go to that birthday party because you can't afford it.

Second, your creditors will not thank you. They will not be one iota grateful for your sacrifice. They truly don't care.

Third, bankruptcy appears on your credit report for seven years following your discharge from bankruptcy. A debt consolidation order will appear on your credit rating for three years following the completion of repayments. That means that you won't be able to begin rebuilding your credit rating for 10 years. That's a long time.

Oh, and one other thing. If a crisis occurs and you fall behind in your consolidation payments, the deal's off, and you're back where you started.

The good news with either a debt consolidation order or a consumer proposal is that you get to keep your assets. This can be important if you're self-employed, or if home prices are depressed in your area and your equity would be wiped out by a forced sale.

The Dark Side of Bankruptcy

Bankruptcy should hurt. We all make mistakes, and we are incredibly blessed to live in a country like Canada where we are free to make them. Making the same mistakes twice or three times, however, is tragic. If you feel the need to declare bankruptcy, learn the lessons that this experience offers, pay the toll, and then move on. These are some of the challenges you may expect.

Double Trouble: Do You Have Any Co-Signers?

Perhaps the worst place to be as a debtor is facing bankruptcy with a co-signer on one or more of your loans. There is a saying "neither a lender nor a borrower be"—and I'd have to add co-signer to the list. If you have a co-signer, the loan on which you default will immediately become their loan, and they will be pursued for payment. If they don't have it, you are passing the collection phone calls on to them.

If you get in this kind of situation, approach the co-signer first, and tell them the situation. They won't be happy, obviously, but at least they'll be part of the process. It may be that they can cover the payments on that loan until you get back on your feet. Ask for advice from your credit counsellor—your co-signer may even want to go along.

Giving Up Your Assets

The more you have to lose, the harder bankruptcy will be on you. You'll be allowed to keep about $2000 worth of furnishings and $1000 worth of personal effects. If you can prove that your car is necessary for your work, you may be able to keep it, as well as a limited amount of "tools" needed for your trade.

The Emotional Toll

It can take a long time to get over the feelings of failure and humiliation. You'll be reminded of the experience for years to come—each time you think about paying by cheque in a store or at the dry cleaner, when you want to reserve a hotel room or a rental car. It's going to be a long time before you have a credit card again—but that might be the best thing that's ever happened to you.

For the period of your bankruptcy, from the time that you file until the time you are discharged, you have given up your right to financial privacy. You are required to be completely forthright with your trustee, including disclosing any assets (the ones you own now and the ones you've owned in the previous five years), statements, and financial records. Every month, you'll have to provide a spending and income report, including receipts. For the period of bankruptcy, the court may order you to pay whatever income you have above that required for basic necessities. They'll then distribute these payments to your creditors on your behalf.

Two tax returns will be filed—one for you and one for your bankrupt estate. Any refund will be used to pay off your creditors.

If you're thinking about withholding information, or not mentioning that $100 a month you get from baby-sitting, think again—you can be fined up to $10 000 or sentenced to three years in jail.

Starting Over

Whatever you decide to do, do your very best to let go of any shame you feel. It isn't helpful. Remember that you did the very best you could. Put your energy and efforts into making sure you never have to go there again.

Here are some things that will make the post-bankruptcy period less painful. You are now a cash consumer, and this can be an exciting period of your life. You are free from those awful calls, from the chronic gnawing anxiety.

➤ The worst thing about not having credit is not having money and vice versa. Start saving something, even if it is just $50 a month, so you'll have a stash for emergencies.

➤ If you haven't learned to be a creative shopper yet, now is the time. Refer to the savings tips in Chapter 3, and start applying them.

➤ If you have children and are living in poverty, contact Family Services in your area to see if you qualify for any assistance. You may find that there are income assistance, day care, low-cost housing, and other services available to you.

Avoiding Bankruptcy—When Crisis Hits

If it isn't time to think about bankruptcy—it's time to think about preventing it. What do you do when crisis hits? You've just received your lay-off notice, or your condo association has billed you for $10 000 worth of structural repairs. How do you cope?

➤ Revisit your spending plan. Hopefully, you've already done one, and you know where every cent goes—then you'll also know where to trim.

➤ Cancel any unnecessary services now. The cable, the extra phone features, magazine subscriptions—anything that isn't necessary must go.

➤ If your credit is otherwise good, you may want to call your creditors and ask to make interest-only payments for up to three months. Tread carefully here—one couple with a spotty payment history did this only to have all of their accounts turned over to a collection agency.

➤ Don't delay making the difficult decisions. Are you going to need to move? Sell your current car? If so, the sooner you make the decision, the better off you'll be—emotionally and materially.

➤ Try not to use your credit cards or line of credit unless absolutely necessary. Whatever you do, don't comfort yourself by overspending. What you don't need right now is expensive dinners out, a credit-card-sponsored vacation, or a new car to make you feel more prosperous. Things will get better, but it may take a while, and you don't want to start over with a debt load you can't bear.

➤ Be creative about increasing your income. If you're one of a partnership, could your spouse take on some overtime? Are there any services that you provided for your employer that you could now provide to them or other companies on a contract basis while you're looking for another job? What about registering with a temporary agency?

➤ Before taking on more consumer debt than you can handle, swallow your pride and think about a family loan. If Mom or Dad can help you through this rough patch, it sure beats credit card bills at 18 percent. (If ever you borrow or loan to family members, draw up a loan agreement and stick to it.)

➤ If you don't have enough money for necessities, don't try to continue monthly investment or savings plans. As a matter of fact, if you are unemployed for an extended period of time, and things are truly desperate, consider an RRSP withdrawal. You will lose that RRSP room forever, and it will be taxed as income, but if your income has dropped significantly, that may not be a problem.

➤ If you have non-registered savings or investments, consider cashing them in (if it won't create a loss) prior to taking on debt.

➤ Eat well, get eight hours of sleep a night, and exercise as much as possible. Taking care of your physical and emotional health in difficult periods like these will prevent the snowball effect from occurring. Just because things are bad doesn't mean they have to get worse.

Good luck to you—if you are brave and resourceful enough to be reading this book at a time like this, you have everything it takes to turn things around. I guarantee it.

The Least You Need to Know

➤ Make good buying decisions now to avoid credit problems in the future.

➤ Make it easier by reducing your credit cards to one and choosing the card that's right for you.

➤ If you're in trouble, take action. Don't delay—get help now.

➤ Bankruptcy will fix some things and break others—consider your options carefully.

➤ Handle any financial crisis better by taking quick steps to reduce spending and avoid as much debt as possible.

Chapter 7

Oh, Those Taxes!

In This Chapter

➤ Learn to pay as little tax as legally possibly

➤ Explore the basics of the Canadian tax system

➤ Tax tips for employees, employers, and the self-employed

A Little Pain Relief

As I write this, April is just around the corner. One of my favourite seasons—a time of renewal, optimism, blossoms, and ... well, taxes. For many of us, the agony of tax time is relieved by the prospect of a possible tax refund, because we're employees and we've already paid too much. Under any circumstances, though, tax time is a reminder of just how much we pay. Yuck!

Let me begin with a reminder that taxes are not an awful thing in and of themselves. Although I could go on at length, and often do, about inefficient government spending, it is important to remember that we live in what is arguably the most beautiful, comfortable country on the planet. For the most part, we have an absolutely wonderful quality of life, an imperfect but still universally available medical system, and good public schools. Decent roads, heart-stoppingly beautiful park systems, and an excellent police force. As much as we like to complain, most Canadians simply wouldn't want to live anywhere else. This is home, and home is good.

Tip

It is our right and our personal obligation to reduce our tax bill as much as is legally possible.

The point of this section is not to avoid paying taxes, because taxes are our participation in the management and maintenance of this fabulous way of life. The point of tax planning is to avoid paying *more tax than we have to*, which is our legal right.

General Tax Tips

In this chapter, we'll look first at tax-saving tips that apply to everyone, and then more specifically from the perspective of where we are in our life: employed or self-employed. Save the book for future reference, because you never know when things are going to change (she writes with a smile) but for now, you can skip right to those sections that apply to you. If you are in a spousal partnership, be sure to check out the income-splitting tips in Chapter 19, too.

Who Knew?

For information on tax rates or anything else you need to know about taxes in Canada, go straight to the source—Revenue Canada, now known as the Canadian Customs and Revenue Agency. You can find a hotline number for your area in the blue pages of your phone book, or access their Web site at <www.ccra-adrc.gc.ca/menu-e.html>.

In addition to finding tables on tax rates, you can do everything in this site from find out what other Canadians are paying in taxes to downloading and printing pretty well any tax form you'll ever need.

Is It a Tax Credit or a Tax Deduction? Should I Care?

The big little tax mystery—what's the difference between a tax deduction and a tax credit? To put it as simply as possible, a tax deduction reduces your taxable income. A tax credit actually reduces the amount of taxes owing. If we were all taxed at the same rate, it would make very little difference, but because we are not, it does. The personal tax credit, for instance ($6794 times 17 percent in 1999), will actually reduce your tax bill by $1155 (17 percent of $6794), whether your income is $4000 or $400 000. An

RRSP contribution is a tax *deduction,* so if your income is $4000, an RRSP deduction would *save you no money at all.* If it were $400 000, an RRSP deduction of $6794 would save you approximately 50 percent of that amount in taxes, or $3397. Bottom line? A tax credit is better than a tax deduction, and the lower your income, the better it is.

Definition

A **tax deduction**, as the name implies, represents an amount that you subtract from your taxable income. If you get a tax deduction of $50, for example, you subtract it from your taxable income, whether you make $10 000 or $100 000. A tax credit represents an amount that you subtract from your total payable taxes. If you get a tax credit for $50, you subtract it from the tax payable on $10 000 or $100 000.

The Single Most Overlooked Tax Shelter in Canada— the Lowly RRSP

We'll talk a lot more about RRSPs in Chapter 23, but for now, you need to know two things. First, RRSPs are the single most common and effective tax shelters available to Canadians today. If you have earned income, and more than enough income to meet the necessities of life, you should be contributing to an RRSP. *If you aren't, you are paying more taxes than you have to.*

The second thing that you need to know about RRSPs, however, is that allowable RRSP contributions are tax deductions, not tax credits. Therefore, the higher your income, the more you will benefit from the tax deduction. At present, there is no rule stating that you must deduct RRSP contributions in the year that you make the contribution. Therefore, if your income is low, make your RRSP contributions *but do not claim the deduction* until your income is higher. If you can, hold on to those receipts until you're earning more money, and your refund will be much higher. In the meantime, investment returns will be tax-sheltered and benefit from the longer compounding time. For example, if you make an RRSP contribution of $2000 this year, when your income is below $30 000 per year and marginal tax rate is 26 percent, you'll save $520 in taxes. Certainly better than nothing. If your income is likely to increase, however, to $40 000 next year, waiting a year to make the deduction will net you a savings of about $800, or an additional $280.

Charitable Giving—Making It Count in More Ways than One

Give it away. I know—when you feel as if you're being robbed by the government, the last thing you probably want to hear is how you can give more of your money away. However, charitable giving allows you to decide where your money is going to be spent, and let's face it—it feels great. You will receive a federal tax credit of 17 percent of charitable donations for the first $200, and a tax credit of 29 percent on amounts over $200, which also lowers the amount of provincial tax you have to pay. (Remember, tax credits are better.) It makes sense, therefore, to maximize the charitable amount claimed on any given return. If you and your spouse each make charitable contributions of over $200, claim them all on one return, and you'll save an extra $24, or enough for a decent lunch. In addition, you don't have to claim donations in the year they were made—you can get the same effect by claiming for two years at once. But, there are limits. You can't give away more than 75 percent of your net income, except in the year of death and the year prior, and you can't carry donation claims forward for more than five years.

If you have the choice, there are advantages to donating securities rather than cash. If you are thinking about making a substantial gift to charity, it is a good idea to seek the advice of a tax professional.

Planning to Move Within Canada?

If you can plan a move to coincide with the start of a new business, a new job (or an old job at a new location), or full-time attendance at a secondary school, and if your new home is at least 40 kilometres closer to the new office or school, you will qualify for some fabulous deductions. (Keep all your receipts, because you may be asked to provide them.) Among the deductible items are these:

➤ All travel expenses to the new location, including auto expenses, hotel and meals for you and your family, and up to 15 days temporary lodging and meals once there.

➤ All hook-up fees (utilities, cable, telephone).

➤ Costs of transferring any documents (driver's licence, passport, etc.).

➤ Any cancellation costs or penalties on your old lease.

➤ Real estate and legal costs if you're selling your home and/or buying a new one. (If you can't sell your old home right away, you can deduct up to $5000 in interest costs and/or property tax to maintain the cost of two homes.)

➤ The costs of moving and/or storing your furnishings and effects, even large items such as your car or a boat.

Don't go wild, though. There are some things you can't deduct:

➤ Renovations or repairs you did on your old home in order to sell it.

➤ The costs of looking for a job or interviewing in another city.

➤ Costs incurred while looking for a new home.

➤ Cleaning costs at your old home.

➤ Any real estate loss incurred on the sale of your old home.

You can't deduct more than you earned in income at the new location. (If you're a student, remember that grants, bursaries, fellowships, and research grants are considered income.) You also can't claim moving expenses against income earned prior to moving. You can carry moving expenses forward to a subsequent year, however. You'll need to complete a T1-M form.

Venture Capital Investment

If you have a sound financial plan in place, including appropriate life and disability insurance, a cash reserve or credit line in place for emergencies, and you aren't carrying high-interest personal debt, you may want to think about investing in a Labour Sponsored Venture Capital Corporation (LSVCC). These funds invest locally, in small and medium-sized businesses, and the federal government rewards us for taking more risk by granting a credit of 15 percent of up to $5000 per year. Most provinces, with the exception of Alberta, Newfoundland, and New Brunswick, match this credit with an additional 15 percent. These investments are qualified for RRSP investment, so if you make the purchase and contribute it to your RRSP, you will get the tax deduction associated with making the contribution as well.

The bad news about LSVCCs is that they are risky. The V stands for "venture" (read "*ad*venture." However, some of these funds have done very well. If you would consider buying a higher-risk investment without the tax credit (a volatile tech stock or mutual fund, for instance), consider taking advantage of the tax credit and investing locally.

Do remember that you must hold a LSVCC for at least eight years from the date of purchase, except in certain conditions (death, for example).

Filing on Time Saves Money and Trouble

File your return on time. If you're going to get a refund, you want to get it as soon as possible. If you owe money, you'll end up with both penalties and interest if you file late. If you don't have the money you owe by April 30, file your return anyway and wait for Revenue Canada to contact you for payment. You will have to pay interest, but you won't be penalized. The penalty is 5 percent of any amount owing for the year, plus

1 percent per month for each month you are late. (The rate of interest is set by federal tax authorities annually and is compounded daily. Don't think you're going to get a break on the interest rate just because it's your government—you'll pay about the same amount as if you had put your tax payment on your credit card.)

If you filed your return late because of reasons "beyond your control," Revenue Canada may agree to waive this penalty and interest if you include a letter with your return stating the circumstances. For more information, ask your Revenue Canada office for Information Circular 92-2, "Guidelines for the Cancellation and Waiver of Interest and Penalties."

Beware

Your return must be filed by April 30, but if you are self-employed, you have until June 15. However, and this doesn't seem fair at all, if you are self-employed and owe taxes, you still have to pay the tax by April 30, even if you don't file the return until June 15. File it in your memory banks under "stupid but true tax facts."

Tax Avoidance and Tax Evasion—Yes, Virginia, There Is a Big Difference

You have the right to pay as little tax as possible as allowed by law. You do not have the right to reduce your taxes by breaking the law. Although the lines seems fine sometimes, it is really as wide as a highway and just as long if you get caught hiding or falsifying information in order to reduce your taxes. If you are caught, you will pay interest owing from the date you should have paid the tax, and 50 percent of the taxes owing in penalties. If the matter is deemed by Revenue Canada to be a criminal one, the penalties can include five years in jail, and fines of up to 200 percent of the taxes owing.

If you have filed incorrect information, your best course of action is to write Revenue Canada a letter detailing the situation. If you suspect you might be in serious trouble, contact a tax lawyer first. There are real benefits to what the government refers to as "voluntary disclosure," however—no penalties will be applied, and you will not be prosecuted. You will have to pay interest on any money owing, but you'll also be able to start sleeping at night.

Tax Tips for Employees

Let's begin with tax tips for *employers*. One way that employers can make compensation packages more attractive to employees is to find ways to provide nontaxable benefits. Taxable benefits are not so good—take the case of the fellow in Ontario, for instance, who recently received a hefty tax bill because he attended his employer's Christmas party. Yuck! As if a company Christmas party is a *benefit*! Have those Revenue Canada people never attended a company Christmas party? My goodness. But I digress. The following are nontaxable benefits that will enhance your material well-being without increasing your tax bill, if only you can convince your employer to provide them. The next time a round of raises is in order, think about suggesting some of the following instead.

Work at Home

More of us are working at home more of the time, and the cost of getting set up can be significant. However, particularly if you live in a major urban centre, working at home can lower transportation costs dramatically, lower day care costs if you have children, and add hours of leisure to your day. As office politics or coffee talk doesn't distract employees working at home, productivity can be higher, too. (Can you tell I'm a fan?) Rather than negotiating a raise, ask to work at least part of the time at your home office. While you're on a roll, ask your employer to foot the bill for the purchase or lease of the new computer, printer/scanner/fax machine, and office furnishings you'll need. Sign a contract agreeing that this new equipment is property of the company, but that at a stated date, say three years in the future, or at the lease buy-back date, you will buy it from the company at its fair market value at that time. The company doesn't have to worry about investing in you only to have you quit and start your own business, and you have a fully functional home office. Tax ramifications? Your quality of life is higher, your taxes ... not!

Company-Provided Day Care

If you have children, company-provided day care can be a huge benefit. If you are in a 50 percent tax bracket, for instance, a $5000 day care bill (after tax deductions) is equivalent to $10 000 in earned income. If your corporation provides day care at no cost to you, it is the equivalent of a $10 000 raise. Be careful—company-provided day care is different from your corporation paying for or subsidizing external day care. That would be a taxable benefit. Still good, but not as good.

Mortgage or Loan Interest Subsidies

If your corporation lends you money, the interest rate must be at least as high as that prescribed by Revenue Canada, or the difference will be considered a taxable benefit.

However, Revenue Canada's prescribed rate is often lower than the rates available at the banks, and the difference is not considered a taxable benefit.

Taxable Employee Benefits

If your employer is providing a material benefit to you, Revenue Canada regards it as compensation. You don't have to worry too much about this, though. It's up to your employer to report taxable benefits on your T4. The following are examples of some taxable benefits:

➤ Lodging

➤ Rent-free or low-rent housing

➤ Any gifts over $100 (per annum) in value

➤ Life insurance

➤ Provincial healthcare

➤ Stock options

➤ Frequent flyer points earned while travelling on business when used for personal use

➤ Any travel costs for family members accompanying the employee on business travel

➤ Any loans issued at other-than-prescribed rates

➤ Tuition or club memberships when the employee, rather than the employer, is the primary beneficiary

➤ Employer-provided automobile (stand-by charges, etc.)

Not for the Faint of Heart: Tax Strategies for the Self-Employed

I can't say enough about the benefits of self-employment. It isn't for everyone, but for those who are up to letting go of the (often illusory) security of employment, the great benefits, the social benefits, and the regular paycheque—well, self-employment rocks.

You don't have to make an all-or-nothing decision in order to begin reaping some tax benefits either—starting a home-based business in your off-hours can be the segue from the corporate grind into a whole new life.

The important factor from the tax department's perspective is the ultimate possibility of profit. If you begin declaring reasonable losses (the costs of set-up, etc.), Revenue Canada will generally be patient for about three years. Any longer and, well, think of it as an engraved invitation to "audit me!" If that happens, it will be up to you to prove that there was a potential for reasonable profit in a reasonable time frame; otherwise all your deductions will be disallowed and you'll have to pay the tax plus interest.

Are You Really Self-Employed? I Mean, Really?

What about simply deciding to be self-employed and providing your services to your employer on a contract basis?

Well, first, if you decide to become self-employed, think about the benefits you'll be leaving behind—and you must leave them behind. It doesn't really matter what you're called, you must be able to dance to your own drummer or Revenue Canada will decide you are indeed an employee, and disallow those deductions. Belonging to the company benefit plan is a no-no. (The exception to this is membership in a benefit plan available through a professional association, union, etc. If you pay all of the costs, and there are group members who are not associated with the company you're providing service to, you'll be fine.)

Although there is no hard-and-fast test for determining who is and who isn't self-employed, the following criteria will be applied:

➤ The more clients you have, the better. If you provide services to only one company or individual, you must be able to prove that the nature of your work is objective-oriented. That is, you've been contracted to fulfill a specific purpose and your relationship with the company will be terminated, at least temporarily, at the conclusion of that objective.

➤ You must be truly independent. That means being able to decide where and when you work. If you are required to appear at 9:00 a.m. and sit in Cubicle B until 6:00 p.m., you aren't self-employed.

➤ There must be some financial risk inherent in your business—that is, you must be responsible for supplying at least some of the tools you require, and bear some liability for work performed.

➤ How critical are you to the company? If they couldn't "last a day without you" as the song goes, you may be an employee. The less disruptive your absence or departure would be, the most likely it is you will be deemed to be self-employed.

Once you are self-employed, there are quite a few expenses you can deduct. In particular, you can deduct expenses relating to your home office. As long as your home is your principle place of business, or you use a part of your home only for business, you can deduct the costs relating to the space you use. Revenue Canada allows you to calculate a percentage based either on the number of rooms you use solely for business as compared to the number of rooms in the home; or the number of square feet used for business as compared to the number of square feet in the home. Obviously, if your office is in the room that used to be a storage closet, go with the former. Also, if you use a portion of an entryway, hallway, or bathroom for business purposes (I'm laughing) add that to your deduction, as well. Also, if there are portions of your home that are not used (an unfinished basement, for instance), exclude that from your calculations.

Once you've established the percentage you can deduct, you can apply it to the following:

➤ Rent or mortgage interest (but not the mortgage principal)

➤ Property taxes and condo fees

➤ Home insurance

➤ Repairs

➤ Maintenance, landscaping, and snow plowing

You can also deduct these:

➤ Business long-distance costs

➤ Whatever portion of your phone line you use for business

➤ Any interest charges on loans, lines of credit, or credit cards you use solely for business purchases

➤ Your cell phone and usage charges

➤ Your business phone and/or fax line

➤ Any supplies purchased for business (including office supplies, computer supplies, and things like greeting cards you send to your clients)

➤ Research materials, textbooks, or manuals

➤ Service costs such as your Internet service provider or the emergency computer nerd who had to rescue your lost files

➤ Professional fees

➤ 50 percent of meals and entertainment undertaken to generate business

Tip

Under normal circumstances, you are only entitled to 50 percent of the capital cost allowance that you're allowed in subsequent years in the first year you purchase the asset. If at all possible, therefore, make sure your purchase falls before your year end.

➤ Capital cost allowance on any equipment or furniture (your computer, fax machine, printer, office furniture, etc.) used in the course of business. For more details on this relatively complex subject, check out Revenue Canada's *Business and Professional Income Tax Guide* or their Web site at <www.rc.gc.ca>.

Tip

If you're self-employed, you might want to hire your lower-income family members and pay them a reasonable salary—it will be taxed in their hands rather than yours.

➤ The percentage of all automobile costs attributable to business use. You must keep a daily log, and travel to your normal office doesn't count unless you are also seeing clients or doing other business in the course of the trip. (A little creative scheduling can go a long way here.) Some of these costs are gas, oil, maintenance, repairs, detailing, cleaning, insurance, licensing costs, loan interest, and leasing costs.

Note: You are allowed to include a portion of your home as a capital cost allowance. However, according to Tim Cestnick, author of *Winning the Tax Game 2000*, this strategy is a more trouble than it's worth, because you may end up losing your personal residence tax status. If Tim says to avoid it, I'd avoid it. He's a very bright guy when it comes to this stuff.

Your RRSP

The single greatest misapprehension in Canadian financial planning has to be this one. An RRSP is not an investment. An RRSP is a tax-sheltered saving or investment program, created by our federal government to encourage us to save for our retirement. We can purchase two identical investments, but if one of them is an RRSP, the financial institution will advise Revenue Canada of our purchase and we'll get the necessary tax slips to attach to our return.

Why is our government being so generous in the tax collection department on this issue?

Well, if we were to retire at an equivalent age, based on life expectancy, compared to age 65 at the time that old age pensions were introduced, we'd all be retiring at age 79. Instead, thanks to the marketing geniuses at London Life, we're dreaming of retiring at 55. Even if we retire at 65, or even 70, many of us will live another 30 years in retirement. It's enough to make anybody a little nervous, and our government responded to the problem by passing it on to us.

Unfortunately, only the wealthiest Canadians are using their maximum RRSP contribution room. According to Statistics Canada, the average contribution in 1997 was only $4500 for men and $3200 for women (which correlates to women's lower earning power of 73 cents for every dollar earned by a man in equivalent full-time work). Out of a possible $200.4 billion that Canadians were allowed to contribute, they contributed only 12 percent, leaving unused room of $176.4 billion. Just as frightening is the fact that tax filers between the ages of 25 and 64 withdrew $1 for ever $4 that was contributed in the same age group.

If we are not making our maximum RRSP contributions, we are paying more tax than we have to. By reducing our spending, and aggressively paying down consumer debt, we can also reduce our taxes by redirecting the money we save into RRSPs.

Taxes and Investment

The government rewards us for participating in certain types of business development by offering tax breaks as an incentive.

Table 7-1 shows us how different investment income is taxed in different provinces. It assumes the highest marginal tax rate and that only the personal tax credit is available.

As you can see, the rates vary pretty dramatically from investment type to investment type—and from province to province. But before you redeem all your GICs and bonds

Table 7-1
Taxing Investment Income

	Interest/ Employment Income/ Foreign Income	Canadian Dividends	Capital Gains
British Columbia	52.27%	35.30%	39.21%
Alberta	45.17	30.79	33.87
Saskatchewan	50.79	35.73	38.09
Manitoba	48.95	35.35	36.71
Ontario	48.75	32.92	36.57
Quebec	52.18	37.87	39.14
New Brunswick	49.68	33.55	37.26
Nova Scotia	49.23	33.24	36.92
Prince Edward Island	49.55	33.46	37.16
Newfoundland	52.9	35.72	39.67
Yukon	46.11	31.14	34.58
Northwest Territories	43.94	29.67	32.95
Nunavut	43.94	29.67	32.95

and move to Alberta, remember—it's darn cold there in the winter time and there's a lot of cowboys. Also, anything that comes out of a registered plan is taxed at the highest rate, as income, so keep your interest-bearing investments inside your RRSP and dividend and capital-gains-bearing investments outside your RRSP. Obviously, if your entire investment holdings are inside your RRSP, you'll want to hold more than bonds and GICs—the point is to keep bonds and GICs out of your non-registered portfolio if possible.

Investments Outside Your RRSP

If you're investing outside of an RRSP, plan your investments with tax efficiency in mind. The least tax-efficient investments are those that pay interest, such as money market funds, bonds, CSBs, GICs, mortgage funds, bond funds, and international funds that are structured to be 100 percent RRSP eligible. In the middle are balanced funds, which have an interest-earning component, and dividend funds. Although dividends are taxed at a lower rate than capital gains, they are less tax efficient because tax is paid in the year the dividend is paid. Capital gains are sheltered until the asset is actually sold.

Of greatest efficiency are equity funds that provide capital gains, particularly those funds that practise a buy-and-hold strategy, or index funds. Every time a stock is sold within an equity fund, there is a capital gain or loss that must be distributed out to unit holders. The longer the stock is held, the longer its value can increase without triggering taxation. However, you will pay now, or you will pay later. Tax deferral should not be the primary criteria for choosing an equity fund.

Always be aware of the tax implications when selling an asset. What seems like an uneventful shift in your portfolio from one fund to another, for example, can evoke a hefty tax bill. You may want to make the change over a two-calendar-year period, or crystallize a capital loss at the same time.

Beware

Deferring capital gains is not an advantage in a child's trust account. Since up to $6700 can be earned in capital gains without any tax being paid, a buy–and–hold management style is detrimental, creating an unduly large tax burden when the investment is finally sold.

Other Deductible Bits and Pieces

➤ Explore the possibility of a Deferred Leave Plan with your employer. Essentially, this plan allows your employer to contribute the equivalent of a portion of your salary into a registered plan. Tax is deferred until you take a sabbatical and withdraw the money as salary, at which time it is taxed at your usual rate. If you work in an industry in which you have to update your education regularly, or in

Beware

Consider tax shelters only when:
➤ your RRSPs are maxed out,
➤ you're a very sophisticated investor with a high tolerance for risk,
➤ you're in the highest tax bracket,
➤ you have no consumer debt, and
➤ you have trusted professional advice, preferably from more than one source (e.g., both your financial planner and your accountant or tax advisor).

which you take research sabbaticals, you may already be familiar with this arrangement. It works just as well, however, for a year-long sailing trip. Contact Revenue Canada for further details.

➤ Look out for the Alternative Minimum Tax (AMT). Essentially, AMT is in place to ensure that people with high incomes can't deduct themselves into tax invisibility. If you have tax shelters, for instance, you may want to do an AMT calculation before you file. Call Revenue Canada, or visit their web site at <www.ccra-adrc.gc.ca/> to get the AMT calculation form.

➤ Don't assume that everyone who charges to do tax returns is an expert. If you've got the time, energy, skill, and desire to do your own return, invest in a tax help program like QuickTax™ that will walk you through all the possible deductions and common omissions. If you can't, because you don't have a computer, for instance, have your tax return professionally prepared at least once, and then use it as a benchmark for future returns. Be sure to tell your accountant about any investments you have, all property you own, all income you have (on T4s or otherwise), and so on. The accountant's work is only as complete as the information you provide. Sort and add up your receipts before you go in. If it takes you two days to sort that mess, how long do you think it would take someone who has no idea who you took to dinner on February 17 or why?

➤ As mentioned previously, if you are in a marital partnership, deduct all charitable donations together on the highest income earner's return. In addition, deduct any medical, dental, optical, chiropractic, prescribed therapeutic massage, and so on, on the lowest income earner's return, and remember that medical expenses do not have to be claimed according to calendar year, but for any one-year period. There is a long list of deductible health expenses—check it out with Revenue Canada if you think you have expenses that might qualify.

➤ If you receive bonus income, and you have the contribution room, ask your employer to make the bonus payable to your RRSP trustee. That way, unless it's more than $10 000, your employer is not obligated to withhold tax.

➤ Whenever possible, choose tax-deductible investment debt over non-tax-deductible consumer debt. For example, if you have $50 000 in investments outside of your RRSP, and a $50 000 mortgage, consider selling your mutual funds (yes, you will trigger a tax hit), paying off the mortgage, and then borrowing $50 000 to buy back your mutual funds—making the interest you pay tax-deductible. Big warning—do not do this without professional help from someone who is not earning commission on the transaction. There will be tax consequences and the timing of the trades may be tricky as well.

The Least You Need to Know

➤ Sound tax planning offers the same benefit as saving and earning—more money in your pocket.

➤ Let Revenue Canada participate in your future—maximize your RRSP.

➤ If you're employed, or an employer, minimize taxable benefits and maximize tax-free benefits.

➤ Each time you make a change in your financial situation, think about tax implications. Buy a good general tax book, like Tim Cestnick's *Winning the Tax Game,* and refer to it before making investment or employment decisions, or become familiar with Revenue Canada's Web site.

➤ Structure your investment strategy to keep interest-bearing investments in your RRSP and capital-gains-bearing investments outside.

Chapter 8

Hiring Help

In This Chapter

➤ From financial planners to investment strategists to tax professionals, find out who's who

➤ Know what you're looking for before your try to hire someone

➤ Find out what all those lettered designations mean

➤ A word to the wise ...

A sound rule of thumb when hiring help with your finances is to know what it is you need, and to hire neither more nor less expertise than you need.

Need Help with Your Taxes?

If you simply don't want to do your own taxes, it's easy enough to find a "tax preparer." These folks proliferate in the malls in tax season, and will prepare a basic tax return for between $25 and $100, providing a quote in advance. Many of them, particularly those who work for the larger firms like H&R Block, are using tax software not unlike QuickTax. Beware—many tax preparers have been hired for tax season and may know little more than you do about anything more complex than preparing a return. If your return is complex (you are self-employed, for instance, or have extensive investments), you should consider having your taxes done at least intermittently by a CGA or CA.

Beware

Be sure to ask your tax preparer where you can reach him or her if you need help with something like an audit. (Yikes!)

Beware

When hiring a tax professional, remember that you are ultimately responsible for any errors or omissions. Ensure that your preparer has all the relevant information and knows about *all* of your income and assets.

Certified General Accountants (CGAs)

If you are in business for yourself or have a reasonably substantial or complex investment portfolio, hiring a CGA to do your taxes is a good investment. You can cut the costs by doing the legwork yourself—use a good money management system, like Quicken or Microsoft Money during the year to keep track of all expenses, match and total the receipts. At least once, prepare your own return on a software program like QuickTax so that you have a better idea of all of the deductions you might be entitled to. You may even want to do your own tax return and then ask your CGA to review it.

The greatest benefits of using a CGA come from finding one who specializes in situations like yours. Get recommendations from other people in your field—find out who they've used and what they think about the service.

Chartered Accountants (CAs) and Certified Management Accountants (CMAs)

CAs and CMAs both charge from $100 to $150 an hour—and may actually have a junior associate prepare your return for their later review. If you have a very complex return (tax shelters, investments, or assets in a number of countries) it may be worthwhile to hire a CA.

Both CAs and CMAs specialize in business rather than personal financial affairs.

Tax Lawyers

Tax lawyers help with problems—or with complex estate planning. With rare exceptions, they won't prepare your tax return, but they will help you if you are audited, particularly if you plan to challenge the audit, or if you are in tax trouble.

Financial Planning Help

At some point on your personal financial planning journey, you are probably going to consider bringing in some hired guns. Before I address this subject, however, I must recant everything I've ever said previously.

As a financial professional, I strongly believe that professional help can make the difference between doing the right thing and making bad decisions, or just as destructively, doing nothing at all. For that reason, throughout my professional life, and in my last book, *Financial Serenity*, I've waxed eloquent about the need for good financial advice. I've even encouraged readers to invest in "load" mutual funds as opposed to "no load" or index funds, because advice, professional support, and "load" mutual funds came in the same package.

Then, as part of my mission to "enhance quality of life by helping people reduce anxiety and increase joy through effective money management" I became a financial advisor. It seemed clear to me that writing a book was not enough. If it was, the 1.8 billion people who bought and supposedly read *The Wealthy Barber* would all be on their way to being Wealthy Waitresses, Wealthy Dentists, and Wealthy Engineers.

I wanted to help. After working in the financial industry for more than a decade, it seemed clear that the best way to do that was to become an independent financial advisor. In that way, I wouldn't be obligated to recommend only my firm's products, as salaried financial planners are. I wouldn't have a sales quota, or feel pressured to sell the IPOs and other investments my firm was recommending, as is too often the case for advisors employed by brokerage firms. Unlike many fee-for-service financial planners, whose rather astronomical fees put them out of reach of many Canadians, I could choose to work with anyone whose situation I felt I could enhance. What I didn't count on was the unspoken but unrelenting pressure *to sell*.

Tip

Knowing what you need from a financial professional makes it far more likely that you'll get it!

Toxic Environment Warning

The vast majority of financial advisors in Canada are paid on commission (including those known as financial planners, with CFP and/or RFP designations). Almost all of them start out believing, as I did, that providing unbiased, competent advice to their clients will provide them with a good living and the satisfaction of knowing that, at the end of the day, their work has really made a difference. Unfortunately, sooner or later, all financial advisors/planners wake up to the following cold, hard facts:

➤ Financial planning is a time-consuming and complex business. For most Canadian advisors, financial planning is a sales technique, nothing more, nothing less. In the end, financial advisors look around for financial-planning software that can create an impressive-looking document in the shortest time possible. Which, I must add, is a perfectly functional solution for most clients. The point is that financial planning is something that gets squeezed in between cold-calling and sending out prospecting letters—commissioned advisors must at some point decide between being a thorough financial planner or being a successful salesperson. Since one position is paid and the other is not, pragmatism normally wins out.

➤ It is not competent, unbiased advice that expands one's client base and, therefore, one's income. It is determined, effective sales techniques. Commissioned advisors receive income from only one source. Commission. The more product they sell, the more income they earn. Even those advisors who are motivated by a desire to be of service find themselves under excruciating pressure to sell, sell, sell.

➤ The most effective investment sales tool is "past performance." Although most financial advisors are ethical enough to remind their clients that "past performance is not necessarily indicative of future returns," it is almost impossible to resist the temptation of presenting last year's high-flying funds and stocks. We all know, professionals and amateurs alike, that what goes up, goes down, and that buying last year's hot returns is likely to ensure we're "buying high." Unfortunately, the alternative is trying to sell last year's underachievers. It can be done, but boy, it's hard. Before clients are willing to buy an underdog, they must be educated on the benefits of asset allocation, modern portfolio theory, and all sorts of other time-consuming principles. Who has the time? Not someone working on commission.

Whatever gets rewarded gets repeated, and although ethical advisors may commit to and work very hard at doing the right thing, an environment that creates constant pressure to behave in a less than completely ethical fashion is toxic.

Beware

Believe it or not, investment firms in Canada must belong to a self-regulatory organization (SRO) of some kind in order to ensure their business practices are supervised. Rather than regulating professional competence or ethics, SROs work to regulate sales practices and regulatory enforcement. Buyer beware!

So Where Do You Go for Good Help?

I know what you're thinking. "Now that you've got that off your chest, Lori, can you get on with it and tell me how I should go about hiring good financial help?"

Yes. It is still possible to get the service and expertise we need, and the more that Canadians wake up to the situation as it now exists and demand change, the more capable financial professionals will be compelled to change the way they do business. (Why is it taking so long? One of the reasons may be that the regulatory bodies governing financial and investment planning in Canada are almost completely funded by investment firms.) Most financial advisors are ethical and reasonably competent people who want to do the right thing.

You can get the help you need by ensuring that you know what you want.

Do Your Homework—Know What You Need

A lot of people seek out the services of a financial advisor or planner when they know they need to take some kind of action—but they're not sure what kind of action to take. For your sake and that of the person whose office you end up in, it is really important to decide what it is you need.

What exactly are you looking for? Before you start shopping for expertise, think about what kind of service you really need.

Coaching

Even financial advisors need financial advisors, because *knowing* the right thing and *doing* the right thing are two different things. An advisor should be more than just an expert—most of us, rather than needing more information, are seeking help because we're drowning in it. It's often the sheer volume that paralyzes us into inaction, particularly when we start to recognize that the experts, many of whom work for investment firms that want our money, take turns contradicting each other. A good financial coach can help you sort through the dross, and separate the hyperbole from the integral. They can act as a source of emotional support, encouraging you toward your goals—someone that speaks the language, knows the terrain, but also has your best interests at heart.

Education and Mentoring

Once you've read this book, frankly, you're going to know far more than the average Canadian on the subject, and you'll also know more than most advisors have the time to teach you. However, if you bought the book in the hope you'll find time to read it, and are flipping to this section to find out how to hire someone now that it's been laying on your coffee table for three months, you might be better off hiring a mentor. Alternatively, get on the Internet and become familiar with the many great investment sites (check the "Best of the Web" in Appendix A) or go to your local library and check out a new investment book each month.

Mutual Fund or Stock Selection

Once you've educated yourself about what to look for, an investment advisor can help you do the research. This can provide good value, because these advisors have access to software programs and research facilities that you don't. Warning: be sure you're not accepting advice from advisors that are paid a higher commission or are under pressure to sell their "house" products. Again, just ask the questions—"Do you have any in-house products?" and "Are you compensated any differently when you recommend those products?" ("Not really" is not an answer.) As an alternative, or simply to complement what you and your advisor are doing together, begin learning about how to do your own research, and what criteria are worth measuring.

A Personal Financial Manager

Once you have a good understanding of the basics, and some net worth behind you, it's very likely you'll find you just don't have the time or inclination to do all the legwork yourself. At this point, a personal financial manager (PFM) can be just what you need. You know what questions to ask and what your objectives are—they calculate the specifics, do the research, hire the administrators, report back to you regularly with pertinent information, act as an intermediary between any other professionals you need to hire (like tax lawyers, estate specialists, and accountants), and negotiate on your behalf. You should meet with your PFM at least four times a year, for at least an hour, for a progress report. Think about it—if you were the CEO of your own corporation, and you hired a Chief Financial Officer to look after all of the financial affairs of the company, how often do you think you'd want to meet with that person?

Someone to Prepare a Financial Plan, a Retirement Plan, or an Estate Plan

Think about hiring someone on a per-hour basis, or, if your situation is complex and the help you need will be ongoing, find a fee-for-service financial planning firm in your area.

Developing a Prosperous Partnership

Once you decide what you want to achieve by hiring help, think about the person you'd like to hire. Then think about how you're going to do the hiring.

Remember, this is a partnership—and a partnership is a relationship. That's true whether you're hiring a mutual fund advisor, a family doctor, or a dry cleaner. If you are having brain surgery, it's likely that you'll want the most technically competent person available. Their social skills won't be that important, because you'll be unconscious. On the other hand, you may want to know how they get along with their support team. (Every time I read about a gauze pad or instrument being left in someone's body after surgery, I imagine some type-A surgeon yelling, "Hurry up, close her up—I've got to tee off at five!")

My point (and I do have one): When you are engaging professional help, remember that the partnership will only be as effective as the weakest link. Don't hire someone who makes you feel rushed, intimidated, or patronized. Never give money, ever, to someone who does not value your time and chronically keeps you waiting. Rude? Curt? Impossible to reach? Just doesn't seem to care? Move on. This person is not partnership material. It may be that their business has simply reached maximum capacity, or they may have always been rude. Who cares? Not us.

Whatever you do, *do not* fall into the trap of believing that a discourteous person must be really fabulous at the job in order to get away with it. Unfortunately, such people are probably getting away with it because all their energy is committed to toadying to their 20 biggest clients, who represent 80 percent of their income (yes, that's the way it normally works) and are rude to everyone else.

The following list may help you pinpoint some of the specific traits you're looking for in an advisor:

➤ I want a knowledgeable advisor, but someone that doesn't make me feel patronized.

➤ I want an advisor who is prepared to meet with me at least every _____ months.

➤ I don't have time to plow through a ton of information; I'd someone that presents information concisely and gives me only the details I need to know.

➤ I want to be part of the decision-making process.

➤ I don't want to be part of the decision-making process; I just want the bottom line.

➤ I'd like an advisor who is willing to teach me.

➤ I just want someone who will take care of it and report back with the results.

➤ I want someone who speaks my language and is knowledgeable about the field I work in.

➤ I want to work with someone who is interested in all of my financial affairs, not just my investments.

➤ I prefer someone who pays careful attention to the details—I need to know that the t's are crossed and the i's are dotted.

➤ I want a casual, more intimate relationship.

➤ I want to deal with someone who's strictly business.

➤ I really just want someone to implement my instructions. I don't want to sit on hold waiting for a discount broker to finally get to my call, but I don't want advice either.

Now, think about the questions you need to ask. Ultimately, like everything else we've covered, there is no right financial advisor—just the right financial advisor for you, and even that may change over the course of your life.

Once you've decided what you want, ask around. If you have friends who share your values and situation, they may already be working with someone you'd like. Think of the process like any other relationship—it can be a real mistake to commit to a long-term relationship with the first person you date. (You might consider dating someone your friend set you up with, but you wouldn't marry solely on such a recommendation, would you?)

Trust your instincts. You tend to know when it feels right. Don't discount those feelings. On the other hand, if you feel pressured, intimidated, rushed, patronized, or just uncomfortable, don't discount those feelings either.

It's always good to approach an interview with prepared questions. Here are some you might want to ask:

➤ How long have you worked in the financial industry?

➤ Do you have any special designations, and if so, what do they mean? What did you have to do to achieve that designation?

➤ What kind of clients do you most prefer to work with?

➤ What do you feel is the most important aspect of financial planning?

➤ What size is your average client portfolio?

➤ What is your educational background?

➤ Would you describe yourself as conservative, balanced, or somewhat aggressive in terms of investment planning?

➤ How many clients do you currently have?

➤ How often are you in touch with your clients?

➤ Do you send out consolidated statements? If so, how often?

➤ Do you provide newsletters, and if so, may I see copies of some recent ones?

➤ If we work together, will you prepare a financial plan? If so, is there an additional fee?

➤ How often will you review my account, and do you do it in person, over the phone, or by mail?

➤ Are there times that you would prefer me to call you?

➤ How do you get paid? If it is on commission, how does that normally work? How much would I end up paying on a transaction of $10 000?

➤ How long do your client meetings normally last?

➤ What is your career history? Which firms have you been with, and for how long? What was the nature of your work at each firm?

➤ Will you come to my home if I prefer that? Are you ever available weekends and evenings?

➤ Do you tend to recommend a certain type of investments, and if so, what are they?

➤ How do you keep up with all the information out there?

➤ Would you describe yourself mainly as financial planner or mainly as an investment planner?

➤ Do you tend to recommend stocks, bonds, mutual funds, or all of the above?

➤ Where would you recommend I invest my emergency reserve fund?

➤ Do your clients ever move on? If so, why?

➤ Have you ever been involved in any kind of regulatory investigation or proceeding?

➤ Are you involved in any community organizations?

➤ Do you have a minimum account size that you generally work with?

➤ If you work on commission, are there any products you recommend on which you receive higher commissions?

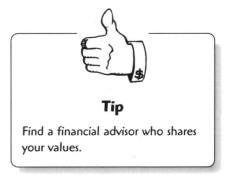

Tip

Find a financial advisor who shares your values.

Warning Signs

There are also a few things that you should look out for, warning signs that should be seen as such and investigated further:

➤ Watch out for potential advisors who try to sell you something on the first date. How do they know what's right for you until they know who you are? What else you own? What your objectives are?

➤ Be concerned if someone is too focused on selling you a specific product as opposed to designing a strategy and then finding the right products within it.

➤ Beware of an advisor who recommends more risk or complexity than you are comfortable with.

➤ Don't tolerate someone who disregards your questions or concerns, or treats them lightly. If you feel as if a client of mine did about her financial advisor—"He talks around my questions for 15 minutes but never actually seems to get to the answer"—it's probably not a good sign.

➤ Watch out for advisors who can't take no for an answer. If you aren't comfortable, you aren't comfortable, and that should be good enough.

➤ Try to avoid advisors who make you feel that your concerns are the result of inexperience or a lack of sophistication. That may be true, but then their job is to educate you—respectfully and patiently.

Beware

There are accountants, tax specialists, financial planners, lawyers, and bankers, among others, who have elevated the old-boy or old-girl network to a science, and who "trade" client recommendations. Some even get paid for referrals. Be aware that there may be more to the referral than just good will.

Beware

Watch out for double dipping. Sometimes a financial planner who charges fees for supposedly unbiased planning also receives commissions on the products they recommend.

Lastly, ask for references. You wouldn't think of hiring a file clerk without checking references—don't put your money in the hands of someone you know by marketing material alone. Unless the person is new to the industry, beware the advisor that gives you the names of people they've been dealing with for a year or less. Everyone's wonderful in the courtship phase—we need to know how they behave when the honeymoon's over.

That brings us to the other half of the partnership. You, the client. Keep looking until you find an advisor you trust and feel comfortable with. Don't compromise if it doesn't feel right. Once it does, stay in touch. Tell the truth, the whole truth, and nothing but the truth. If you have concerns, speak. If you have questions, ask. Be realistic in your expectations.

Now, about that compensation plan. In an environment in which almost everyone we can afford is working on commission, how can we be sure we're getting the range of unbiased advice and service we need?

There are excellent fee-only planners, particularly in major centres. You can find them in the phone book, by calling the Canadian Institute of Financial Planners in your area, or at 1-888-865-2437, or the Canadian Associate of Financial Planners at 1-800-346-2237. Particularly if your net worth, including your home, is more than $500 000, and you haven't done any kind of financial planning before, these fees may turn out to be a bargain. Unfortunately, fee-only planners are generally not allowed to make specific investment recommendations, and there is the possibility they may hand you off to a broker-buddy who then recommends high commission or MER investments. At that point, of course, just say no. Instead, perhaps you could ask your financial planner to prepare a proposal letter like the one in Figure 8-1. Prior to engaging any fee-for-service planner, ask for a written proposal, including the fees that will be charged and exactly what services will be provided. Ask for a clause that states your written approval in advance is required for any additional charges.

Consider Hiring an Advocate

If you have siblings, you probably remember Mom's kitchen table wisdom when dividing the last piece of cake. Remember? One person cut the cake, and the other one picked first? At all costs, avoid manipulations or ploys in relationships, private or professional, but you can still apply Mom's good common sense while being entirely up-front. First of all, call around until you find someone who is willing to provide you with advice on a reasonable hourly basis. What's reasonable? You can expect to pay $65 to $150 per hour, depending on the experience, expertise, and credentials of the person hired. To give you an idea of how much time is involved, in addition to your face-to-face meeting time, here are some rough guidelines:

You can hire an advocate and then place your trades through a discount broker, or, if your situation is somewhat complex or you'd simply rather not do it yourself, ask your advocate to prepare a letter like the one in Figure 8-1.

Basic financial or retirement plan (net worth less than $100 000, excl. residence, no special circumstances)	3 to 6 hours, depending on the quality of the information provided
Investment plan, after providing or completing financial plan	3 to 6 hours if investments are liquid, more if existing investments must be considered. If you add something like an ethical screen, you're probably adding at least an hour.
More complex financial plan (net worth over $100 000 excl. residence, special circumstances such as small business, employee stock options, blended family)	4 to 30 hours. Get an estimate in advance and ensure that you get to pre-approve any extensions to the estimate

Figure 8-1
Sample Letter from a Financial Advocate

May 9, 2000

Humungus Bank Brokerage Firm
Most-Expensive-Rent-in-the-City Tower
Babe Street
Big City, Canada
X0X 0X0

Attention: Lance Sellalot

Dear Lance,

I am a financial advocate for Jim Smith. Jim has enjoyed his relationship with Humungus Bank and the service he has received from you in particular, and would like to continue that relationship, if at all possible, while at the same time meeting his new portfolio requirements.

As you may know, Jim has a portfolio of some $250 000 (including his current holdings at Humungus). Jim and I have designed an asset allocation strategy that he would now like to implement, and we are now in the process of inviting proposals from a number of institutions.

Of particular importance for Jim's requirements are the following:

- Approximately half of Jim's portfolio will be invested in fixed income investments, which may include GICs, high-grade corporate bonds, and government bonds. The allocation between bonds and GICs would depend on the rates available. As 5-year GICs are currently available in the range of 6.5%, we would expect a bond portfolio to exceed that overall. Staggered maturity dates are, of course, important.

- In the equity portion of the portfolio, low management expense ratios and commissions are of the utmost importance. The alternatives that Jim is considering include no-load, low-MER index funds, so our "benchmark" is zero front-end commission, no deferred sales charge commission, and lower-than-average management expense ratios in each fund category. We would consider an individual stock portfolio mirroring an underlying index. In any case where commission will be charged, in any form whatsoever, we would like to be provided with detailed dollar amounts.

- We will provide direction for re-allocation annually, and do not require any "wrap" or similar services.

Following is a chart illustrating Jim's target asset allocation and acceptable range. Currently, Jim has 82.9% of his portfolio in cash equivalents, and 17.1% of his portfolio in the global mutual funds at Humungus. We do not plan to change the global equity portion of the portfolio until the deferred sales charge expires, with the exception of possible switches within the fund families. Therefore, the proposal we are requesting is for the following allocation (approximately $207 500):

	Minimum	Benchmark	Maximum
Cash Equivalents[1]	0%	0%	10%
Fixed Income	45%	50%	55%
Global Equity[2]	0%	5%	10%
Canadian Equity (Large cap value or neutral)	10%	20%	30%
Canadian Equity (Preferred)	0%	5%	10%
Canadian Equity (Large cap growth or neutral)	5%	15%	25%
Canadian Equity (Small to mid-cap neutral)	0%	5%	10%

Fixed Income Portfolio

	Minimum	Benchmark (Approx. Amount)	Maximum
Highest Grade Corporate Bonds	15%	25%	30%
Mid-term Government Bonds[3]	25%	35%	45%
Long-term Government Bonds	25%	35%	45%
MBS or other non-volatile fixed income instruments	0%	5%	10%

[1]Jim currently holds approximately $50 000 in cash equivalents outside of this portfolio, so there is no cash requirement for these funds.

[2]In addition to the existing global equity portfolio.

[3]Municipal, provincial, and utility bonds are acceptable in addition to federal bonds.

As this portfolio is non-registered, tax-advantaged investments are preferable where security will not be diminished as a result. Jim will not require income from this portfolio for the next three years (until January, 2004), but we would like to have cash available in the range of $10 000 (minimum $5000, maximum $15 000) available for withdrawal should that become necessary at the anniversary date of the portfolio each year. Therefore, annual interest bonds would be preferable. During the year, we would like the accumulated interest to be re-invested in a high-yield T-bill fund on which we expect approximate annual interest of 4%. On or about the anniversary date of the portfolio purchases, we would like the portfolio re-allocated to our original benchmarks, and would like to meet with you in that regard.

An annual portfolio review meeting would be sufficient. Monthly statements would be preferable, and online account access would be ideal.

Thank you very much for your consideration. We look forward to hearing from you.

Sincerely,

Lori M. Bamber

Lori M. Bamber

Beware

If the person you're considering also works on commission, let them know that you *will not be buying any investment through them*. Ask them for advice on no-load, low-MER, or low-cost purchase alternatives you can purchase through a discount broker.

Meeting the Alphabet

While you're out shopping for help, you'll probably run into some lettered designations. Be careful. First of all, having a designation does not mean that someone is ethical, experienced, or even particularly bright. It does not guarantee quality of workmanship, service, or advice. As a matter of fact, some of the most horrendous financial devastation has occurred at the hands of very lettered individuals. Consider designations as one aspect of the whole.

Here is a list of what some the current Canadian designations stand for:

CA	Chartered Accountant
CFA	Chartered Financial Analyst
CFP	Certified Financial Planner (granted by Financial Planners Council of Canada)
CFP	Chartered Financial Planner (granted by the Canadian Institute of Financial Planning)
CGA	Certified General Accountant
ChFC	Chartered Financial Consultant (Canadian Assoc. of Insurance and Financial Advisors)
CIM	Certified Investment Manager (Canadian Securities Institute)
CLU	Chartered Life Underwriter (Canadian Assoc. of Insurance and Financial Advisors)
CRFP	Registered Financial Planner (Canadian Assoc. of Financial Planners)
FCSI	Fellow of the Canadian Securities Institute (Canadian Securities Institute)
PFP	Personal Financial Planner (Institute of Canadian Bankers)
PFP	Professional Financial Planner (Canadian Securities Institute)
SFC	Specialist in Financial Counselling (Institute of Canadian Bankers)

As you may note, the confusion here is largely created by the fact that each institute grants its own designation. One thing that you can conclude is that anyone bearing any of these designations has at least met some minimum standard requirement for professional practice. However, because the requirements vary from institute to institute and are changing even as I write, I recommend that you make a practice of asking anyone you may be considering to explain their particular designation and what they had to do to achieve it. I'm thinking, in particular, of an advisor I knew who had an impressive number of framed certificates in his office attesting to his many credentials. Each had been purchased by paying a substantial fee to issuing institutes in the U.S. He had never taken a course in financial planning or passed a single exam.

These are some of the requirements you should expect to hear about. In order to achieve the CFRP designation, for example, this is what your advisor has to do:

➤ Be a practitioner member of the CAFP

➤ Have an academic or professional standing recognized by the CAFP

➤ Be currently practising financial planning

➤ Have two years' experience in financial planning immediately before applying

➤ Have demonstrated competence

➤ Be sponsored by at least one CAFP practitioner member in good standing and provide two professional references

➤ Maintain 30 hours of continuous education each year

➤ Carry "errors and omissions" insurance coverage

➤ Complete the RFP exam (approximately six hours)

➤ Hold current CAFP membership

The bottom line—know what it is you're looking for and don't be afraid to ask tough and direct questions. Work with people you like and who demonstrate that they care about you and your well-being, not you and your chequebook.

The Least You Need to Know

➤ Recognize that the vast majority of financial advisors and planners are commissioned salespeople.

➤ Knowing what you need will help ensure you get it.

➤ Commit to fulfilling your part of the partnership—provide complete and accurate information, stay in touch, define the game plan, and then stick to it.

➤ Don't place too much faith in designations—just as there are great and not-so-great doctors and lawyers, there are great and not-so-great financial planners.

Part 3

Home Sweet Home

I was an anomaly. I'll admit it. I'm not sure where my antisocial tendencies stemmed from—it might have been the result of growing up with four siblings in a house that was less than 700 square feet, or the fact that I was perfectly happy once living in a hotel room for an entire year. (Great swimming pool—and there was a big screen TV in the pub with all the free popcorn you could eat!) Whatever it is, all of my life, I've faced nothing less than incredulity and disbelief when I told people I was happy renting—which makes me aware that the rest of the world, or at least every red-blooded Canadian over the age of 30, wants to own their own home.

"A house can't make you happy," I said in the face of relentless pressure to settle down and buy a place.

Then I fell in love. No, I'm still waiting for Prince Charming—it was a house that captured my heart. And not only does it make me happy, after almost two years of living together, it makes me ecstatic. Which brought me to the realization that this house-buying business has nothing to do with investment, logic, or even common sense—we are talking about nothing less than our heart's desire. Our home represents everything dear to us—a warm hearth, security, a measure of our worth—a safe place in which to raise our families, and an inviting place into which to welcome our friends.

This section takes us home—and looks at the most effective ways of managing our money while we're there.

Chapter 9

All About Mortgages

In This Chapter

➤ It's easy to find a home to love—begin by finding a mortgage to love!

➤ Learn to choose the right mortgage and reduce your interest costs by tens of thousands of dollars

➤ Everything you need to know about features, rates, and shopping around

---

Let me give you a few practical tips that might ease the bumps on the road to Homeowner Heaven and free you from mortgage enslavement a little earlier.

If you've been bitten by the home-buying bug, think about making an appointment with a mortgage officer at your bank or credit union before you do anything else. It doesn't obligate you in any way, and they can answer these burning questions:

➤ What kind of house can I afford?

➤ Will I even qualify for a mortgage?

➤ How much will the monthly mortgage costs be?

Think About Pre-Approval

Pre-approval guarantees your interest rate for the pre-approval period (generally 60 to 90 days). If rates go down, you usually get the lower rate. As well, you'll receive a little pre-approval certificate that's a nice leveraging tool when negotiating with home sellers (the "vendor"). When you find the house of your dreams, you'll still have to provide an appraisal, and your credit will be re-checked. But pre-approval makes for much smoother sailing.

Tip

Instead of a high-ratio insured mortgage, consider a private second mortgage through relatives. It isn't an option for everyone, but it can provide the lender with a secure rate of return on their funds and save you thousands of dollars in fees.

How Much House Can You Afford?

The most basic test is the 2.5 rule—that is, most Canadian families tend to spend about two-and-a-half times their gross annual income on a home. If interest rates are low (less than 9 percent) you've got a bit more breathing room and may wish to multiply your annual family income by 3 or even 3.5. Obviously, this test doesn't take any other debts or circumstances into consideration, but it does give you a ballpark figure.

Potential mortgage lenders will calculate the amount they will allow you to borrow based on the gross debt service ratio and/or the total debt service ratio.

Tip

Pay your mortgage bi-weekly or weekly rather than monthly, and choose a 10- or 15-year amortization schedule.

The Gross Debt Service Ratio

The *gross debt service ratio* (GDS) is calculated by adding your annual mortgage payments or rent, plus property taxes, divided by gross annual family income. It should not exceed 30 percent. For example, if you had payments on a mortgage of $150 000 at 8.25 percent amortized over 25 years, that would be $1169.01 per month, or $14 028.12 per year. Add property taxes of $1000 per year for a total of $15 028.12. Assuming everything else was in order, you would have to earn at least $45 100 per year to qualify.

The Total Debt Service Ratio

The *total debt service ratio* (TDS) is the more important ratio. It is the tougher one, taking into account mortgage and property tax costs (as with the GDS), plus payments on any other debts. To calculate the TDS, it is standard practice to include all consumer credit that has been granted, even if it is not being used. For instance, if you are a collector of credit cards, and have eight of them giving you $50 000 in available credit, a mortgage lender will probably add in the minimum payments on $50 000 (3 percent or $1500)— even if you had never used the cards!

Your total debt service ratio should never exceed 40 percent.

What Is a Mortgage?

This is a much trickier question than you might expect—most people would respond that a mortgage is a loan that you use to buy a home, using the home itself as security, or collateral. Believe it or not, although the word "mortgage" has come to mean a "mortgage loan" with all the attached features, a mortgage is actually just the document that lays out the terms and conditions. You see—I've tricked you already and we haven't even started! Here are some other very important things you need to know about mortgages.

Tip

If your RRSP contributions are up to date, use any found money (gifts, bonuses, inheritances) to pay your mortgage down on the anniversary date. If your RRSP isn't up to date, you should probably contribute first and then use the refund against your mortgage.

A Two-Part Deal—Principal Plus Interest

When you arrange a mortgage, the lender agrees to lend you a stated sum of money to make a home purchase. In return, you agree to repay that sum (the principal) over an agreed period (the amortization period) and to pay interest, or rent, on the principal for the time that you use it. Most potential home buyers are completely in the dark about the significance of that second part—interest. It's bad enough that you're taking on a loan that may be three or four times your annual income—without also acknowledging that you'll pay more than that much again for the privilege of using someone else's money.

Who Knew?

An amortization is the period over which you intend to pay off your entire mortgage loan. The term of your mortgage, on the other hand, is the period for which your mortgage conditions, like interest and payment rates, apply. An amortization may extend over 20 years or more. The term usually extends over five years or less.

Tip

When your mortgage matures, don't assume you have to pay a renewal fee. The mortgage business is very competitive, and another bank may be willing to pay *you* to move your mortgage.

For example, if you buy a home for $200 000, and borrow $150,000 at an average interest rate of 8.25 percent over 25 years, you will be paying $200 703 in interest—in *addition* to the principal of $150 000!

Minimize the Interest— Maximize the Joy!

Next to taxes, your mortgage interest is going to be your single greatest life expenditure, unless you start your own business and turn it into a big business. Therefore, it makes sense that you will do whatever you can to minimize the cost of your mortgage.

The first step, of course, is buying a home within your means. If you are thinking about exceeding your budget, remember that just $10 000 will cost an additional $83 per month on your payment (at 9 percent) and will actually add $24 843 to the cost of the house over a 25-year amortization period.

When you are figuring out how much you can comfortably spend, remember to investigate the following.

Abbreviate That Amortization Period

Consider this tale of two mortgages. They are both for $150 000 at 8.25 percent, paid monthly. One mortgage has a 25-year amortization (that is, the interest payments are calculated on the assumption that you will take 25 years to pay off the loan) and the other, a 15-year amortization period. The payment on the first is lower—by $274.30 per month. Over the life of the mortgage, however, the second mortgage holder, with the 15-year amortization, will save approximately $91,000!

Make Weekly or Semi-Monthly Payments (Rather than Monthly)

Semi-monthly payments make a great deal of sense for those of us that get paid that way, and if you happen to be a two-income family with staggered pay weeks, choose a weekly payment option if possible. The difference? Well, if you choose a 25-year amortization period on the above mortgage ($150 000 at 8.25 percent), you will pay $1169.01 monthly, $583.28 semi-monthly, or $269.22 weekly. It really doesn't make much difference. However, if you can add just $63.12 per week to your weekly mortgage payment, you can shave 10 years and almost $91 000 in interest off your mortgage!

Consider Your Prepayment Options

When you're shopping for a mortgage, look for one that offers prepayment ability—that is, one that allows you to pay off portions of the principal early without penalty. That way, if you find some money (an inheritance, bonus, tax refund, or those ever-elusive lottery winnings) you can pay down the principal and reduce your interest payments overall. For instance, paying down the above mortgage by just $10 000 after one year will save approximately $48 000 over a 25-year amortization period!

Look for These Mortgage Features

➤ *Assumability.* This feature may allow you to take over the last homeowner's mortgage (if the terms are attractive), or alternatively, allow the next buyer of your

Definition

An **interest-rate buy down** is a feature that makes new homes more attractive to buyers. The seller actually "buys down" the going rate of interest; that is, he or she makes a lump-sum payment to the lender to reduce the rate of interest you pay for a stated period. Make sure you know what your payments will be when the period ends—and be sure the seller hasn't just added the buy-down amount to the price you pay for the home!

house to "assume" your mortgage. If your interest rate is lower than the prevailing market rates, this can make your house more attractive to potential buyers.

➤ *Portability*. I know I said never to buy if you're planning on moving in less than 5–10 years—but things happen. Portability allows you to move your mortgage with you, so that you don't have to pay a penalty on one mortgage and then arrange for a new one if you buy a new house. (This is also good if your existing interest rate is attractive and rates at the time of your move are less so.)

➤ *Expandability*. This feature allows you to increase the loan (the principal) at the same rate of interest. Obviously, your intention should be to pay down the principal as fast as possible, not borrow it up—but this is an important feature if you are buying a fixer-upper and need money for future renovations.

The Interest Rate

Obviously, you want the lowest rate of interest for the longest possible term. However, there are usually trade-offs to be made. Experts in this area agree that you should choose a longer term when interest rates are rising and a shorter term when interest rates are decreasing. The problem, of course, is knowing whether interest rates are rising or decreasing, and how much, for how long. Even if interest rates are dropping right now, do you go for the security of knowing exactly what your payments will be for the longest period of time, or pay less, hopefully, and live with the knowledge that rates could be up quite substantially by the time you renew?

Tough decisions. My own feeling is that you can afford to be more adventurous if there is room in your budget. If interest rates look like they are on a downward trend, and there is lots of room in your budget for higher monthly payments on renewal, you may even want to consider a six-month mortgage. If, on the other hand, your family cash flow would be painfully squeezed by even a small increase in your monthly payments, go for a longer term even if it means paying a bit more overall.

Interest rates come in three varieties: fixed, variable, and variable "capped" or "protected." Fixed rates stay the same for the term of the mortgage, variable rates change as interest rates change (which can be an advantage when rates are dropping), and variable capped or protected rates fluctuate but will not go above a certain limit. Variable rates are generally available only to borrowers who have more than 30 percent equity in their homes (that is, their mortgage is less than 70 percent of the home's value).

Kinds of Mortgages

Thought you would just arrange an ordinary, garden-variety mortgage? Well, think again, my friend! There are *all kinds* of mortgages. Luckily for us, the kind of mortgage we get is usually determined by our needs—it isn't something we have to decide on. Here they are!

Conventional Mortgage

This used to be the only kind you could get. In a conventional mortgage, the amount borrowed is not more than the lower of 75 percent of either the appraised value of the property or the purchase price. In order to quality for a conventional mortgage, you need to have, therefore, a down payment of at least 25 percent of the home's value. Conventional mortgages are by far the least expensive way to go, and if there is any way you can scrape together a down payment of 25 percent, you'll be much better off over the long run.

High-Ratio Mortgage

Insurance provided by the Canada Mortgage and Housing Corporation (CMHC), the federal government's housing agency, makes it possible to buy a home with a down payment of as little as 5 percent. However, this insurance costs between 0.5 and 4.25 percent of the value of the mortgage (plus application fees, etc.). It can be paid either up front, in a lump sum, or added to the value of the mortgage, thus dramatically increasing your interest costs.

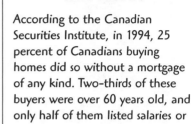

Who Knew?

According to the Canadian Securities Institute, in 1994, 25 percent of Canadians buying homes did so without a mortgage of any kind. Two-thirds of these buyers were over 60 years old, and only half of them listed salaries or wages as their primary source of income.

Second Mortgages

A second mortgage is a higher-interest loan that uses equity in your home as collateral, or security, against default. Once very common for use in home renovations, second mortgages have all but been replaced by home equity lines of credit, which allow you to pay interest on just the money you are actually using.

The Granny Mortgage

There are two kinds of people in the world—those who think that "we should all stand on our own two feet, gall darnit!" and those of us, like me, who believe that life is a whole lot richer when we reach out to do what we can for each other. If you are lucky enough to belong to a family in the second group and that also has assets, you may be able to arrange one of these. A "granny loan" is just an industry term for a family loan that provides a down payment or even the home purchase price, at an attractive rate of interest (hopefully to the lender and the borrower), sometimes with less stringent repayment terms. Whatever you do, however, make sure that there are loan documents drawn up, and that the terms and conditions are spelled out. Remember that there can be benefits to both parties here—the lender earns interest with little risk, and the borrower gets much more attractive terms than would otherwise be available.

Taking Over an Existing Mortgage

It may be that the seller of your new home has an "assumable" mortgage with attractive interest rates and terms that you wish to take over. This can save you the cost of appraisal and legal fees, and may make it faster and easier to qualify, depending on the terms of the previous mortgage.

Definition

A **VTB mortgage** is one where the seller, or vendor, of the house offers to make it more attractive to potential buyers by lending them the money.

The VTB Mortgage

Sounds like a type of virus, doesn't it? Actually, this isn't that complicated. VTB simply stands for "vendor take back," which means that the seller, or vendor, really wants to sell you the house and will therefore lend you money to purchase it. Or, and be careful of this situation—the seller of your home-to-be may be a professional realtor who supplements his or her income by lending money to potential buyers at higher-than-bank rates of interest. All too often, these lenders will lend to you when the banks won't, largely because you shouldn't be borrowing, or borrowing so much. These lenders don't care, but their game plan is that either you will repay the loan or they will foreclose and take back the property—which may be how they got it in the first place.

Open Mortgages

Open mortgages allow you to pay off all or part of the principal without penalty at any time. As interest rates are generally substantially higher for open mortgages, this option

Beware

If a bank won't lend you money for a mortgage, you probably shouldn't be borrowing it. Don't raise the stakes by borrowing from so-called private "mortgage brokers," who charge high rates of interest and would love nothing more than the opportunity to foreclose on your home.

only makes sense if you are in the process of selling your house, or if you are expecting the proceeds of an estate that will enable you to pay down the bulk of your mortgage.

Closed Mortgages

These are the "normal" kind. Closed mortgages may allow some form of prepayment without penalty (for example, allow you to pay off an amount equivalent to three months payment on each anniversary date), but otherwise, you're locked in for the term. Terms generally range from six months to ten years, with the most common being three- and five-year terms.

Shopping for a Mortgage

Begin by either visiting the mortgage officer at your bank or credit union or getting on the Internet and visiting <www.themortgage.com/>, the Online Mortgage Explorer. This site gives you everything from a current rate site to calculators that will tell you which financial institutions want to lend you money, based on your specific circumstances!

It is important to get away from the "hat in hand" mentality. Remember, if you are in the position to buy a home, financial institutions want to lend you the money as much as you want to borrow it, and they often won't offer rate discounts or features unless you ask. If you are in a borderline situation, where you may not qualify, consider waiting a while. You'll be making life a lot easier for yourself, you really will.

Once you know that you qualify, and for how much, consider hiring a mortgage broker, or at least giving one a chance to do some rate shopping on your behalf. Because mortgage brokers may direct many borrowers to a lending institution over the course of time, you may find that the rate offered is as much as 1 percent lower than the one posted in your bank—for the same mortgage, at the same bank. You can find a mortgage broker close to you by checking their Web site at <www.cimbl.ca> or calling 1-888-442-4625.

How to Qualify

First and foremost, know that to qualify for any mortgage, even an insured one, your housing costs—including taxes, maintenance, and utilities—shouldn't exceed 32 percent of your family income. Between 25 and 30 percent is better.

Tip

You have the right to request corrections on your credit bureau report and/or add a short statement of explanation. If you are thinking about applying for a mortgage, call Equifax Canada at 1-800-465-7166 or Trans Union of Canada at 1-800-797-3992.

Obviously, the better your credit rating, the better off you are—and a visit to your mortgage lender will tell you exactly where you stand. If there are problems on your credit report, ask the mortgage officer to tell you exactly what they are, and what might cause them to turn you down. It may be that there are errors on your report that would be easy enough to correct, and the better your credit rating, the greater your negotiating power. If there are errors, call Equifax (1-800-465-7166) or Trans Union of Canada (1-800-797-3992) to request a change.

In addition to having a decent credit rating, a reasonable "total debt ratio" and "gross debt ratio," a good employment record, and sufficient income to make your payments, you will also need to provide a potential lender with some or all of the following:

➤ All your personal details—your age, your marital status, the age and number of your dependants

➤ Employment information and proof of income (your income tax returns, T-4 slips, and/or a letter from your employer stating your position, salary, and time with the company)

➤ Information on any other sources of income—investments, annuities, pensions, rental income, or royalties

➤ Your current banking information, along with proof of the availability of your down payment

➤ Your permission to do a credit bureau investigation

➤ A net worth statement or lists of all assets and liabilities—what you owe and what you own

➤ A list of all your current monthly payments

➤ A copy of the property listing

➤ A copy of the plans and cost estimates for a new home

➤ A copy of the Agreement of Purchase and Sale on a used home

➤ If you are buying a condo, you'll need the condominium financial statements

➤ Either a very recent property appraisal report or a fee to cover the cost of an appraisal

➤ If you are applying for a high-ratio mortgage, you'll need the insurance application fees up front, and you can either pay the insurance premiums or have them added to the mortgage

➤ If you're buying in a rural area, you'll need a certificate.

The Least You Need to Know

➤ Consider applying for a pre-approved mortgage—it will provide peace of mind, help you stay within your housing budget, and give you some leverage in sale negotiations.

➤ Choosing the right features can save you tens of thousands of dollars in interest payments.

➤ Negotiate and shop around—remember, the lender wants to lend you money as much as you want to borrow it.

➤ Avoid a high-ratio, insured mortgage if at all possible.

Chapter 10

We Came, We Saw, We Bought

> **In This Chapter**
>
> ➤ Your mortgage is pre-approved and, you know exactly what you can afford—now it's time to find the house
>
> ➤ How to get the most house for your money
>
> ➤ Putting together your "home team" to provide the help you need
>
> ➤ Offers, counteroffers, and closing—what it's all going to look like
>
> ➤ Best practices for reducing the costs of home sweet home

According to the Web site for the Canada Mortgage and Housing Corporation (CMHC), at <www.cmhc-chl.gc.ca/cmhc.html>, prospective home buyers have to balance three primary factors: location, style, and cost.

This is where dream building meets compromise—and it may also be the point at which you decide to rent for another year or two until the house you can afford is more like the house you want to live in. If you live in an urban area and work downtown, you may also discover that buying a house is going to add an hour or more to your commuting time. Let's assume, however, that you're undaunted. You are going to buy—you just don't know when or where.

Finding the House of Your Dreams in the Size of Your Payment

If you're going to buy a house, nothing makes more sense that getting the most house for your money.

Real estate experts suggest window shopping for two to three years prior to actually making a buying decision to get an idea of price trends in your area. In general, you can count on the old truisms to apply: try to buy in a recession, buy when interest rates are going up (particularly if you have a significant down payment), and buy during December, January, or February. (Unless you live in Vancouver or Victoria, where the winter syndrome doesn't make a dent in housing prices.)

A private transaction can shave 5 percent off the house price and, in hot markets, can save even more by keeping you out of bidding wars. Watch the real estate section of the paper, look through classified Web sites, and check for signs in the neighbourhood you're looking at—but put the word out, too. Let everyone know you're looking—according the "degree of six" principle, you are at most six acquaintances away from the person you'll buy your next house from.

Tip

Before buying, always contact your municipal office to inquire about zoning by-laws and development planning in the area. A new elementary school can be a good thing—a new high school or highway may be not-so-good.

The key to home value is still "location, location, location." Never buy the biggest house on the block, and try to buy the smallest, most run-down home you can stand and improve in the nicest location you can afford. Before deciding on a home, spend a few days touring the neighbourhood at different times of the day and night. Just one harmless-looking Hell's Angels club can have an irritating effect on resale prices. Even if you aren't interested in things like schools, parks, transit systems, and recreation centres, you may want to consider them anyway—they may make a difference to the next buyer of your home.

Thinking About Buying a Condominium?

If you are buying a condominium or townhouse, the condition of the development property is as important to your home value as the condition of the unit you are buying. Remember, too, that a condominium association is a democracy in which the people with the most time on their hands will end up with the most power over your home. If you decide to make an offer, make it conditional upon receiving an "estoppel certificate," which gives you information on the development's financial situation, including reserves and insurance, and a copy of the council meeting minutes for the last year or two. Be sure to review all by-laws and regulations. Meet the people running the council and talk to some of your potential neighbours.

Hiring Your Home Team

Don't start looking until you've decided on an affordable price range and done your research on qualifying for the necessary mortgage. Once that's done, resist the urge to view homes outside of your negotiating range. You'll save a lot of time and avoid the temptation to spend more than you can afford.

Consider Hiring a Buyer's Agent

These fine folks generally split the realty commission with the selling agent, but act solely on your behalf. There are even realtors who specialize in working as buyer's agents—you can find them by calling your local realty association. Ask in advance about fees you may be asked to pay directly, and look for someone who specializes in both the area and the kind of home you're looking for.

Once you've found someone you'd like to work with, provide him or her with the tools necessary to help you. It can be both fun and practical to spend some time putting together a "Dream Home" journal. Buy a scrapbook, and divide it into sections. Keep a centralized record of any features you'd like to see in your new home, along with clippings from newspapers or magazines. Create a "bottom line" section—your new home *must* not be above this price, must be in this general location, must have three bedrooms, and so on. When you start looking, record the houses you've seen, what you did and didn't like, and anything you might want to take a look at if the price was reduced. (This can save trips back to homes that you didn't really like anyway when you see a price reduction advertised.) Being clear both on what you want and what you can live with will save everyone a lot of time.

Tip

If you've already found a home you'd love to have and find yourself dealing with the seller's agent, ask him or her to sign a buyer's agent agreement. It won't cost you anything, but it will obligate the selling agent to act in your best interests as well as those of the seller, and advise you of any bad news you may need to know.

An experienced realtor can make the job of buying a home much easier for you. They can give you information on pricing in the neighbourhood in which you're looking, and will help you prepare an offer if you decide to make one. Remember that realtors don't usually investigate the quality of the properties themselves, and they do have an inherent conflict of interest in that they don't get paid until you actually buy something.

Hiring a Home Inspector

Make a satisfactory home inspection a condition on any offer you decide to make—and be sure to hire a reputable home inspector who carries errors and omissions insurance. If the inspector overlooks something, you may be on the hook for thousands of dollars in repair costs, so your well-being rests in that person's hands. Check with the Better Business Bureau for a record of any complaints, and ask for references from both recent clients and those from past years. You can often get a listing of inspectors from your local home association or real estate board.

A good home inspector will provide you with a comprehensive report of the home's general condition, any problems that need or may potentially need repairs, and an estimate of costs for doing so. In older homes, they should also be checking for things like termites, foundation problems, wiring, plumbing, roofing, any air quality or moisture problems, leaded paint, and asbestos.

If you're buying in a rural area, you'll want to have the water quality checked, and ensure the septic system is in good working order.

Your Lawyer or Notary

Even your first offer on a home is a legally binding document, so you are going to need a lawyer or a notary to review them for you. In addition, when you finally buy, they will handle the "closing," the transaction in which the money changes hands and you get both the keys and the deed. Again, call your local real estate association for recommendations. Since many lawyers have their paralegals (highly trained legal assistants) prepare and review all documents anyway, you may be able to save a few hundred dollars by using a notary public that specializes in real estate transactions. If you dealt with a mortgage broker, ask for recommendations.

Making an Offer

You came, you saw ... you want. Now it's time to make an offer. An offer has two parts: the actual document and a deposit, normally 10 percent of the purchase price. If your offer is accepted, the deposit is used against the final purchase price on closing day, and if it's rejected, your deposit is returned.

As your offer is legally binding, you may want to have it reviewed by your lawyer or notary. He or she will then present it to the vendor or the vendor's agent. Alternatively, you or your realtor may make the offer to the seller's realtor or to the sellers themselves.

Clean vs. Conditional

A *clean* offer has no conditions. It simply states the basics: Your name, the vendor's name, the legal and civic address of the property, the price you are willing to pay, the date on which you wish to close, and financial details like the amount of your deposit, mortgage arrangements, and whether or not you wish to receive interest on the deposit prior to closing. If you are shopping in a very hot market and you really want this home, be aware that the simplicity of a clean offer is more attractive to the vendor. Remember that the price on a first offer is negotiable, so you may want to offer less than your absolute top price.

A *conditional* offer essentially says that you want the home, and provides the basic details above, but it also says you will only buy if certain conditions are met. Although you can add almost any conditions, some of the more common are these:

➤ Your current home must sell prior to a certain date.

➤ A satisfactory home inspection must be made.

➤ Certain "chattels" (stuff in the home, like drapes, carpets, appliances, etc.) must be part of the deal.

➤ The vendor must provide a current land survey and/or property appraisal.

➤ Certain repairs, cleaning, or painting upgrades must be made prior to the closing date.

Don't forget the expiration date, the day on which the offer is no longer valid.

Who Knew?

When making an offer, don't be afraid to include conditions that are on your wish list. One of my friends just sold her house. The buyer asked for the usual things, like appliances and carpets, but she also insisted on keeping one of the shower curtains. My friend didn't need it in her new home and was happy to throw it in.

The Vendor's Response

The vendor will respond to your offer in one of three ways: (1) accept it, (2) ignore it, or (3) make a *counteroffer*.

Once a counteroffer is made, your first offer becomes void, and you will have to agree to the counteroffer, make a second offer by revising the counteroffer, or step out of the bidding.

In a counteroffer, the vendor may decline to meet some of your conditions (you can't have the gardening equipment, but you can have the dog). More often, the counteroffer concerns the price—you've offered $175 000, $5 000 less than the asking price, and the vendor counteroffers with a price of $178 500.

Closing Day

Wow. Your offer has been accepted, and today's the day.

By this time, your lawyer or notary has received copies of your final signed offer and has done a title search on the property to ensure that there are no outstanding liens and that the home, land, and chattels can actually be sold by the vendor without encumbrances. Any conditions have been met. Your lender has received all the necessary documentation, including a current land survey and a copy of the title search. The lender will provide a certified cheque to your lawyer in trust, and you will have to provide the down payment along with payment for any fees or disbursement charged by the lawyer. Your lawyer will then arrange to register the property in your name and get you the keys.

Definition

Just as it sounds, an **encumbrance** is a legally binding impediment to the sale of a house. It might take the form of a lien by a contractor who hasn't received payment for installing a new furnace. Or it may take the form of a lawsuit by a neighbour who disputes the placement of a new fence in the backyard. If an encumbrance exists, you'll have difficulty obtaining clear title to the property.

Tip

When it's time, consider selling your home yourself. You can buy self-help books to guide you through the process and, with the Internet, advertising to a broad audience is much less expensive than it used to be. On a $250 000 home, you can save up to $15 000 after-tax dollars—the equivalent of $30 000 in employment or investment income!

You or your lawyer should ensure that all property taxes are up to date, and you should arrange to have all utilities and services switched over to your new address. Closing day may also be moving day, but if you can arrange it otherwise, you'll save yourself a great deal of stress.

The Least You Need to Know

➤ Don't shop outside of your negotiating range.

➤ Planning prior to viewing can save a lot of time and money.

➤ Hire reputable, experienced professionals that specialize in the area and kinds of homes you're looking for.

➤ When making an offer, don't be afraid to ask for what you want.

Chapter 11

Reduce Your Utility Bills

In This Chapter

➤ How to make a house a home, economically

➤ There are simple ways to reduce your expenses and have fun, too

➤ Make sure your house runs at peak efficiency

Now that you're a homeowner, it's more important than ever to cut expenses without diminishing your quality of life. And now more than ever, you're going to need an emergency fund to rely on during those inevitable days, so begin by having $50 to $100 debited from your chequing account into a money market mutual fund each month. Not only will it make you feel a lot better when something happens, but you will avoid

Definition

In the Canadian money market, borrowers and lenders trade short-term instruments like corporate and government loans. There are hundreds of these instruments. Money market mutual funds invest in them. Your money's pretty safe, and you can get access to it almost immediately. You'll earn a return that's higher than a savings account, but not much.

credit-card interest in the aftermath and earn decent returns on your savings. (Don't let your emergency fund grow larger than six months of your net income. It can be tempting to just watch the numbers get larger, but once you've met your crisis needs, look for a longer-term investment vehicle. Keep your money working for you!)

10 Tips for Reducing Home Expenses

Here are 10 easy ways to save some money when you move into your new home:

1. If you're single, think about sharing your home.
2. Now that you're in a new neighbourhood, try the local transit system a few times to get a sense of whether or not it works for you as an alternative to taking your car.
3. If you must have pets, don't buy designer pet food. Check out the ingredient list—you'll find they're virtually the same.
4. On the other hand, if you feel you spend too much on entertainment and dinners out because you're lonely, a pet can provide real value and much love.
5. Buy soap, toilet paper, cleansers, etc., in bulk.
6. Stop buying paper towels. Use newspapers to clean mirrors and glass, and cloth for everything else.
7. Stop buying paper napkins. Use cloth. (You'll feel royal.)
8. Buy furniture at discount centres, auctions, consignment stores, and second-hand stores.
9. When buying wood furniture, in particular, check the antique stores and estate sales. Both price and quality are often superior.

Tip

New home? You must have a house-warming party, I know. Ours cost in the range of $500, and in the preparation, cooking, greeting, serving, and cleaning up, I don't think I had a conversation that lasted more than five minutes with anyone. Instead, fire up the barbecue and have a pot luck—ask everyone to bring something to barbecue and a side dish, make up pitchers of lemonade, and relax and enjoy the company of friends and family. If it's winter, or you don't have a barbecue, just do a simple potluck in which everyone brings a dish.

Beware

Think before buying or adopting a pet. People with pets are measurably happier than those without, but animals can be expensive. We faced a $2000 vet bill when our dog was hurt, after we very frugally adopted her from the animal shelter for an $80 fee, naively assuming that the highest costs we would ever face were inoculations and pet food. The same dog destroyed our drapes, all our upholstered furniture, and a number of our carpets before we realized that she just wasn't getting enough exercise.

10. Spend a few afternoons at your local library reading *Architectural Digest* and other decorating magazines. A little bit of decorating know-how can save you thousands of dollars in not-quite-right purchases, and will give you the confidence you need to mix-and-match used furnishings creatively.

Home Décor on a Shoestring

After you've lived for a while in your new home, you'll get a sense of how traffic moves through it and how you can use each room most effectively. Then you can start applying some of these tips to decorating the place:

➤ Never buy anything that you can't use. Make "comfortable, beautiful, and durable" your bottom line.

➤ Avoid trendy décor colours, and choose paint and painted effects over wallpaper if you can. Neutral walls and colourful accents create a much more soothing and long-lasting effect. Remember, neutral doesn't have to be beige or white.

➤ Let at least one colour continue throughout the whole house.

➤ Be a minimalist. Less truly is more. Include "white space" in your home design—areas in which the eye is soothed by nothingness.

Tip

Buy linens at bargain centres, and stick with white bed linens and towels. You can bleach and interchange them, and they always look great.

Tip

A single compact fluorescent light (CFL) saves $25–$50 in bulb and electricity costs over its life! And of course the planet wins too, because that one bulb prevents the emissions of 8 to 16 pounds of acid-rain-causing sulfur dioxide and 1000 to 2000 pounds of carbon dioxide (a greenhouse gas).

Reduce Your Utility Bills

Once you own your own house, you can do a few things to ensure that it works efficiently. For example, your utility service provider can inspect your home (at no cost) to make recommendations on decreasing your consumption of electricity, gas, and water. Here are a few other things you can do to keep your house shipshape:

Who Knew?

Residential water use can be broken down as follows: 40 percent for toilets, 35 percent for showers and baths, 20 percent for laundry and dishes, and only 5 percent for cooking and drinking.

➤ Install weather-stripping around doors and windows, and try to keep them closed unless your heating is off.

➤ Fill an empty one-litre plastic drink bottle with water and sink it in the tank of your toilet.

➤ Install a water-saving showerhead. You'll notice a difference in your hydro bill.

➤ Install a timer on your heating system so that the temperature is automatically reduced to 16 degrees Celsius after you go to bed and increased to 18 or 20 degrees just before you get up.

➤ Keep some cozy afghans (you can find lovely used ones at thrift stores) in the family room or living room to wrap yourself up in while watching TV or reading.

➤ In the summertime, set a few bowls of ice in front of your electric fans, and keep all windows and blinds closed between 10 a.m. and 8 p.m.

➤ Get rid of energy-guzzling appliances, like old refrigerators and freezers.

➤ Rinse your dishes and run the dishwasher only when it's full. Air dry rather than heat dry.

➤ What would you do if you didn't have cable? Why not try it for six months?

The Least You Need to Know

➤ Creativity can cut your home care costs enormously.

➤ Use more of your imagination and less of your money to decorate your home.

➤ Utility companies will gladly help you reduce your utility bills.

Part 4

Savvy Investing

We're all looking for a bit of magic in our lives, something to give us hope that tomorrow, or next year, will be a little easier than today. Take Lily, for instance, a 64-year-old woman who asked me to prepare a financial plan for her and her husband. The two of them were rapidly depleting their savings on a lifestyle that was far beyond their means; they knew they needed help. (She'd already invested more than 25 percent of their life savings in a dot-com company.) When I presented the plan, which was, in essence, about reducing their expenditures and investing in a conservative, diversified portfolio, she tossed it back on my desk and said, "This is boring."

Yep. Boring. Unfortunately, a lot of the stuff we need to know about investing might be described as boring. (Come to think of it, so can most of the world's richest people. The only thing that's really exciting about them is—they're loaded!)

As Bill Schultheis states in his brilliant book, The Coffeehouse Investor, *the three fundamental principles of investing are*

> ➤ *Asset allocation*
>
> ➤ *Approximating the stock market average*
>
> ➤ *Saving*

Can't get much more boring than that. Or, depending on one's perspective, more simple, sophisticated, or sublime.

As you move through Chapters 12 to 18, bear in mind that most of what you may now know about investing is propaganda—information disseminated by institutions that want you to be intimidated because they need your commissions and fees. Is it possible that it's all much less complex than you've been led to believe?

Eleven Integral Investment Principles

For those of us who are dizzy from trying to figure out why all those experts are out being paid huge salaries to contradict each other, and why no one seems to get it right over the long run, it's great to finally hear the voice of reason and relax.

As I mentioned earlier, Bill Schultheis thinks that the three fundamental principles of investing are: asset allocation, approximating the stock market average, and saving.

So let's skip right to that third thing—saving. It doesn't get much more boring than this. Once more, we're reminded that our financial well-being depends on us, saving for the future what we could be gleefully spending today. Sound saving behaviour will save us from the most common errors in *investing* behaviour:

➤ Buying too-risky investments in an attempt to compensate for a lack of foresight and discipline.

➤ Choosing financial advisors who make extravagant promises. (You can do a lot worse than to find a financial advisor who is boring. Dead dull is particularly good.)

➤ Impatience, which results in a tendency to chase last year's hot performers. (Yes, so your neighbour's tech fund did 149 percent last year, and your dull little balanced portfolio returned a measly 7 percent. That was last year!)

Past performance is not only "not indicative of future returns" as the ubiquitous disclaimer states, it is just as likely that the opposite will be true. Performance on any given investment tends to "revert to the mean." In English, that means, simply, that what has gone up will come down and what is down will go up. In a well-diversified portfolio, invested for the long term, you can expect to "approximate the stock market average"—which is not a bad thing at all!

How can you avoid these costly errors? Ensure you have an adequate savings plan in place. Then, when you are grappling with an investment decision, take a few minutes to check out what your stomach is doing. Ask yourself, "Am I acting out of fear? Out of greed? Do I feel I somehow need to do better than everybody else? Have I lost sight of the goal in the fervour of playing the game?" If you have the fortitude to be honest with yourself at that moment, you have what it takes to be a successful investor. If the answer to any of these questions is yes, don't do anything. Wait until you *know* you are making the decision according to sound investment principles.

What are those sound investment principles? Let me offer you the CIG's expanded investment principles for Canadians.

Investment Principle #1: Save Your Money

The single greatest influence on your investment returns is your own saving behaviour.

Do not look to investment products to make up for your inability to save. If an investment sounds too good to be true, it surely is, and you are likely to end up moving in the opposite direction of your intended goal. If you're not saving money on a monthly basis, that's where you must put your energy first. I'm sorry—but it's the undeniable truth.

If you are reading this book, it is probable that you are not living below the poverty line. (If you are, and you are reading this book to change your situation, I commend you.) You've got enough income coming in to pay for the essentials and a few extras. If that's the case, I'm hoping you've already set up an Automatic Investment Plan, but if you haven't, now is the time. If you're not sure how to do it, check out the Web sites and 1-800 numbers listed in Appendix A.

Investment Principle #2: When Hiring Help, Know What You're Buying

When hiring help, be sure you know what you're buying. The vast majority of financial advisors and financial planners in Canada today receive their income in the form of

Beware

If a financial advisor tells you he will get you higher equity returns than the long-term stock market averages or cut kazillions from your tax bill, or if he directs you to fixed-income investments that pay more than 3 percent above the current rate on a 5-year GIC (check with your bank) ... Be afraid. Be very, very afraid—now is the time for a second opinion.

commissions on product sales. Whatever their title, their professional designations, the size of their office, or the quality of their suits, they are salespeople.

Think about it for a minute. Even the most ethical, competent commissioned advisor feeds his or her family by selling you investment products. Not by helping you to save, not by doing financial planning, not by encouraging you to apply sound investment principles—but by selling you investment products. Period.

What gets rewarded get repeated—it's an accepted management principle and a fact of life. You should know that the average "load" mutual fund pays 5 percent in commission (that's $500 on a $10 000 purchase) on a deferred sales charge basis (plus 0.5 percent per year in "trailers"). The average bond or GIC pays less than 1 percent (with no trailers). Limited partnerships pay up to 10 percent. Most importantly, low-cost no-load managed and index funds do not pay commission to your advisor. Therefore, if they recommend these funds, they are not getting paid for their service.

Beware

Limited partnerships are risky endeavours. Michael Nairn, of the Equion Group, once wisely said, "Limited partner *(the investor)* starts out with the money and the general partner *(the project manager and promoter)* starts out with the experience. At the end of the project, the general partner has the money and the limited partner has the experience."

Obviously, this situation creates an inexorable bias toward those products that pay commission. It also means that advisors are pressured to target their services toward those that may need it the least and neglect very important areas of financial planning like debt reduction.

It's Your Money

There's also sometimes a tendency to recommend a higher percentage of equities since these pay more commissions. Some planners even suggest taking out a mortgage and using the money to invest. This strategy may work for you, but it is terribly important to be aware that the planner may be earning a commission that increases with the amount you invest. Never forget that it's your money, and ultimately, your responsibility to invest it wisely.

When you need financial help, shop around for "unbundled" advice—advice separate from investment products. It is far more likely you'll get the range and depth of unbiased expertise that you need by paying an hourly rate. It may be as easy as approaching the advisor you're already working with and saying, "I no longer want to pay commissions. Instead, I'd be happy to pay you a reasonable hourly rate for your service and expertise."

The world is changing, and the financial services industry is no exception. Think about it this way: How would you feel if your doctor received a 5 percent commission on all surgical procedures, a 1 percent commission on prescriptions, and absolutely nothing when his or her advice was "take two days off and get some rest"?

For more information on the types of help available, and how to sort the good from the bad and the ugly, see Chapter 8, "Hiring Help."

Beware

A "wrap account" is a service intended to put your broker on your side. Rather than paying commissions, you'll be charged an annual fee of 2–4 percent of your portfolio for complete investment management. No relentless grinding pressure to buy and sell—for only 2–4 percent of your portfolio! There's something about this that just doesn't smell right ...

Investment Principle #3: Watch Those Fees

Taxes, fees, commissions, and management fees do make a difference. In Chapter 14, we are going to take a hard look at what mutual fund managers actually do, and what we pay them for. In other parts of this section, we'll look at costs like administration fees, commissions, wrap account fees, etc. For now, be aware of the impact on your bottom line.

According to *The Coffeehouse Investor*, if we invest $500 per month in investments earning 11 percent annually, the difference between investing in index funds (with an annual fee of 0.25 percent) rather than managed mutual funds (with an annual fee of 1.5%) over 25 years of investing is a mind-blowing $147 000. That's a lot of sweet retirement!

Definition

An **index fund** is a mutual fund that invests in the companies that make up an index. An index is a benchmark made of a "basket" of representative stocks on a particular exchange. Index funds are sometimes referred to as "passive" because no active stock-picking takes place.

Is It Worth the Fee?

What is even more astonishing is that although 1.5 percent is considered a reasonable management fee in the United States, you can expect to pay close to twice that in management costs (the management expense ratio, or MER) here in Canada. (Index fund fees are also higher, at about 0.5 percent.)

Does that mean you should avoid management fees, and therefore managed mutual funds? Sometimes. The answer is sometimes. Bill Schultheis, author of *The Coffeehouse Investor*, lives and writes in the U.S., home of the largest, most efficient stock market in the world. We live in Canada, home of less than 3 percent of the world's equity market. If you were to buy a Canadian index fund (reflecting the TSE 300) on March 31, 2000, more than 33 percent of your investment would be in two companies, BCE (13.7 percent) and Nortel Networks (19.5 percent). Both are worthy companies, to be sure, but in light of their huge share price growth over the last few years, it is unlikely they are undervalued and much more likely that they are overvalued.

The bottom line is that we must recognize that cutting costs can make a significant difference over the long term, and then shop for the best value. Most mutual fund managers do not beat the index most of the time. Some of them do, and if we could just predict the ones that would do so *in the future*, which is when it will make a difference to us, it would be well worth paying for their expertise. (Assuming, too, that these star managers wouldn't leave our fund and move to another company, which they have a disconcerting habit of doing.) Unfortunately, we can't. Therefore, where we can get the same diversification from a low-cost index fund, we should consider that alternative.

Investment Principle #4: Accept Underperformance

Effective diversification means that some of your assets will be underperforming all of the time—and the least effective investment strategy is attempting to forecast the next hot performer.

Bill Schultheis writes:

> Once you remove yourself from Wall Street's complete and total obsession with trying to beat the stock market average and accept the fact that approximating the stock market average is a rather sophisticated approach to the whole thing, building a common stock portfolio becomes an immensely gratifying experience.

> Wall Street has conclusively proven to us that pursuit of performance above a benchmark is an unproductive use of our time, our talent and our money. By trying to beat the stock market average, it's easy to forget that the stock market has historically provided an excellent investment return, and by trying to beat an already good thing, investors are virtually guaranteed to end up below it.

Who Knew?

According to Oxbridge Communications, in 1998 we had access to 187 financial publications, 5 financial television stations, and 162 financial Internet sites.

I know what you're saying to yourself: "Well, I can't pick the star funds, but surely my financial advisor can—or at least those mutual fund gurus who write mutual fund books—they must know."

Financial advisors can help. They can't tell you which mutual fund is going to be this year's star performer, or even score in the top 25 percent of the field, but they can help you minimize costs and avoid the stinkers. Indeed, you should try to read at least one of the mutual fund tomes out there to get a sense of what to look for—what to compare to what. But if you think the experts are able to predict what will do best over the short term, you're wrong. According to "Bylo Selhi," the revelatory online mutual fund guru:

> Last year [1999] no fund was given the highest rating by all seven [top-selling mutual fund] books. Bissett Canadian Equity, however, was recommended by 6 of 7. This fund has a long track record of 1st or 2nd quartile returns. Sounds like a "sure bet" doesn't it? In 1999, it was a 4th quartile fund." [Meaning that it underperformed more than 75 percent of similar funds!]

You can visit the Bylo Selhi Web site at <members.xoom.com/bylo_selhi/index.html>.

Does all this mean the books aren't worth reading? Not at all. As a matter of fact, I'd recommend you not buy a mutual fund without one. As some wise soul once said, it is much better to be "approximately right than completely wrong." These books, with or without the additional help of a trustworthy financial advisor, can ensure you avoid the bad funds, those funds that aren't suitable for your investment personality or objectives, and help you do the right thing when fear raises its ugly head. But what they can't do is predict the next big winners. Let's face it—all of us will get lucky some of the time, and financial advisors are prone to loudly proclaim our genius when that happens. (Just like everyone else, when it doesn't work out, we compile a complicated list of reasons why it wasn't our fault.)

We'll talk more about this in Chapter 14. For now, though, know this: you cannot pick next year's star investment, but you can reduce the costs you pay.

Be aware too, that anything you buy and then sell outside of your RRSP will create tax consequences. Always take these consequences into consideration when making a sell decision.

Whenever possible, be wisely passive when it comes to your investment decisions. Warren Buffet, the "Sage of Omaha" and the world's wealthiest investor (even after a couple of years of laggard investment performance), says his favourite holding period is "forever." Most of us will need the money a little earlier than that, but his principles put things in perspective. The world's most successful investors are not day traders, or even year traders. They buy businesses and hold them for the long run.

To take things to the next level of efficiency, you don't even have to buy specific businesses—you can buy them all in an index fund.

Definition

Quartile means the applicable 25 percent. If a fund is in the "top quartile," its performance is in the top 25 percent of all similar funds. Conversely, if it is the third quartile, its performance is in the range of the bottom 50 percent but higher than the bottom 25 percent.

Tip

Duff Young, columnist for *The Globe and Mail* and author of *Fund Monitor 2000*, says that we ask the wrong questions when buying mutual funds. Instead of asking "which fund should we buy?" we should be asking "which fund can we hold for the long term?"

Investment Principle #5: Look Beyond Canada

Act locally, invest globally.

Most Canadians are under the misapprehension that it is less risky to invest only in Canadian companies. Not true. As a matter of fact, Canada represents less than 3 percent of the world's equity markets. How can you seek diversification in such an exclusive investment arena? The answer is—you can't possibly have a well-diversified Canadian portfolio. The two terms are mutually exclusive.

According to research conducted by Ibbotson & Associates, published by Fidelity Investments, the optimum internationally balanced portfolio (that is, the one most likely to produce the highest returns with the lowest amount of additional risk) is approximately 68 percent global, 32 percent Canadian.

For RRSPs, you are limited to a maximum of 25 percent in non-Canadian assets in the year 2000, rising to 30 percent in 2001. You can increase your global exposure through the use of "clone funds," which qualify as Canadian investments but behave more like foreign-based funds.

What difference can this make? How about this? The TSE 300, Canada's leading index, has returned an average of 10.5 percent annually since its inception in January 1956. Not bad, not bad at all. However, a similar U.S. index, the S&P 500, has returned an average of 13.4 percent annually since its inception in 1966. If you're investing $500 per month over 25 years, just a 2 percent difference in annual returns will cost you (drum roll, please) $230 525! Ouch!

Bottom line—diversify outside of Canadian borders. It's important.

Investment Principle #6: Buy Low, Sell High

It's worth repeating: Buy low, sell high. The technical term for this is *contrarian investing*, moving at odds with the lemming mentality that normally drives the marketplace. You may have heard the tuna analogy: When the price of a can of tuna drops from $3 to $1.50, tuna-lovers race out and stock up. Conversely, when our mutual fund drops from $10 to $5, we sell as fast as we can and buy some more of whatever has just risen from $10 to $20. (If you work in the financial industry, you've heard this analogy so many times you can't enjoy a tuna melt anymore.)

Why do we do this? It's the herd mentality, I'm afraid. There's no more flattering way to describe it. We are genetically programmed to stay with our tribe, doing whatever it is our tribe is doing. In the misty beginnings of human history, going our own way usually had a very bad ending. Today, although the world has changed a great deal, we still get extremely anxious when we dance to a different drummer. Particularly when it comes to something as naturally anxiety-provoking as our money and future. We want to buy what our tribe is buying and sell what our tribe is selling, ensuring that we do poorly on our investments.

The most effective antidotes for this tendency are dollar cost averaging, a buy-and-hold strategy, and disciplined asset allocation. Stay tuned.

Investment Principle #7: Buy and Hold

Practise a buy-and-hold strategy. Simply, do not trade stocks. Buy good companies that have excellent management, strong potential for growth under all economic conditions and in all competitive environments, good cash flow, and little or no debt. (To find out how to identify these so-called good companies, see Chapter 17.) Own them for at least five years or until you need the money.

Alternatively, do not pick stocks or companies at all, but buy into a broad-based index that allows you to own all the companies, all the time. Now, if you do this, there is a chance the entire index will be overvalued at the time you buy in, so in times like these, practise caution and buy through a dollar-cost-averaging program. (See Chapter 13 for more information on dollar cost averaging.)

Investment Principle #8: Understand Inflation

Recognize the risk of inflation. Inflation was the bogeyman that we all got to know pretty well in the '70s and '80s. Things have changed a great deal since those wild and woolly times, and our government inflation-fighters (Gordon Thiessen at the Bank of Canada and Alan Greenspan in the U.S.) have done a good job of controlling inflation over the past decade. We can reasonably expect them to continue to do so, and it is difficult to imagine that inflation will increase above the Bank of Canada's targeted

Who Knew?

To determine how long it will take something to double in price or value, use the "Rule of 72." Divide the annual increase or return into 72 to get the number of years required. For example, if your mutual fund is earning returns of 10 percent per year, the equation is 72 ÷ 10 = 7.2. In 7.2 years, your investment will have doubled.

range of 1 to 3 percent. As a matter of fact, the benchmark, the Canadian Price Index, has increased an average of 2.8 percent over the last 15 years, and just 2 percent over the last 10 years. However, even with inflation of 2 percent, the cost of a loaf of bread doubles every 36 years. (At 6 percent, it doubles in price every 12 years.)

Investment Principle #9: Diversification

This is my favourite. Otherwise known as "not keeping all of your eggs in one basket," this may be the most important concept in investment and financial planning. There are many levels of diversification, which must be examined and applied individually:

➤ Diversification of asset type, or "asset allocation" (stocks, bonds, GICs, real estate, "hard" assets such as oil, gas, and gold).

➤ Diversification of industry (stocks and/or bonds issued by corporations in banking, technology, utilities, healthcare, communications, etc.).

➤ Diversification of geographical location (Canada, U.S., global, Europe, or more speculative investment in defined "growth" locales such as Asia or Latin America).

➤ Diversification of time horizon—the very essence of financial planning. Short-term (less than five years) cash flow needs must be met through income-producing investments in which there is virtual certainty that capital will not be diminished. Therefore, GICs and short-term bonds are most suitable but produce a low return and unfavourable taxation. Medium-term cash flow requirements (five to 10 years) are most appropriately met through a balanced combination of secure investments (five-year bonds, for instance) and blue-chip or value-style mutual funds with low volatility. (If you are a conservative investor, avoid equities altogether if your time horizon is less than 10 years.) Long-term investment requirements may be met with a diversified portfolio of equity investments—with a foundation of globally diversified blue-chip equity investments. It is in the long-term investment portion of your holdings (over 10 years) that you can take advantage of diversified growth-style investment opportunities, trusting that history will repeat itself and provide occasions to sell at a substantial profit.

➤ Diversification of maturity dates. In the '80s, this was usually as complicated as investment planning ever got. High-interest yields on guaranteed products allowed investors to avoid the higher risk/volatility of the equity markets altogether. Sound financial planning was regarded as the process of staggering maturity dates to ensure that cash was available when needed and/or that rising interest rates could be accessed through investment of maturing funds. Further protection was offered against falling interest rates, as only a portion of an investor's portfolio would require re-investment at a given time. In today's vastly different financial universe, it is still important to diversify the bond and GIC portion of your portfolio.

The one element of diversification that is chronically overlooked, mentioned in Principle #4, is that effective diversification means that at least one of your asset types is going to be doing poorly at any given time. For some reason, we seem to be under the impression that the opposite should be true—if our portfolio is well diversified, everything will be doing just grand. No, no, no. To be a successful investor, learn to view your portfolio and its performance as a whole, not by the strongest or weakest performance of the underlying assets.

Investment Principle #10: The Market Knows

Give the market credit.

We've heard it at least a million times—self-proclaimed market specialists telling anyone who will listen why this industry sector or this country's stocks or this company is going to be the next hot item. They may be right. The problem with any and all of these arguments is this: by the time you hear about it, you can be reasonably sure *the party is over*. Why? Large institutional investors who employ well-funded research teams to know this kind of stuff in the early stages of the cycle drive the market. As a matter of fact, Fidelity, the mutual fund/research company, accounts for over 10 percent of the trading on any given day on the Dow Jones. Therefore, by the time that we're all talking about "it" (whatever the latest "it" is), we can be reasonably sure that it's already priced into the market. Therefore, if we treat this as a buy signal, we're paying the already-inflated price.

Investment Principle #11: Understand Risk and Return

Risk and return are inextricably linked. Diversification and time decrease risk.

There are many very complicated theories about ways in which we can decrease risk and increase return, and I for one have lain awake and night wondering which particular theory may be more accurate in the current economic conditions. Well, no, I haven't. But I could have.

There is so much *noise* devoted to theories about risk and risk reduction, and all of them are founded on research, statistics, and the work of some very bright people. To be useful, however, we have to understand how these theories play out in our world, in our portfolio, and therein lays the gaping flaw. We aren't a controlled study group. We are women and men with jobs, families, and angst about our futures.

The Least You Need to Know

➤ Your savings behaviour is the foundation of your investment plan.

➤ Fees, commissions, and taxes do make a difference

➤ Reduce risk by respecting the efficiency of the market, your own time horizon, and practising sound investment principles.

Chapter 13

An Exercise in Risk Tolerance

In This Chapter

➤ The issues to consider when designing your own investment portfolio

➤ Time horizon

➤ Dollar cost averaging

➤ Asset allocation

➤ Your risk tolerance

Now that you've become familiar with the principles of investing in general, let's look at the ways in which they may apply to you, and your efforts to create financial well-being in the years to come.

Recognize and Honour Your Time Horizon

Do not invest in equities (stocks or equity mutual funds) with money that you will need in less than five years. Sure, it might go to the moon. And it might be worth half of what you invested when you need the money, too. To be safe, avoid equity investments with any money you're going to need within 10 years.

If you invest for one year, there is a significant chance that your investment will not only *not* have made money for you, but it will have gone down in value, as well. Cash in now, and you've lost your very hard-earned money. However, the chances of your portfolio being down in value over a 10-year period are much lower.

I don't know about you, but I care very little what the TSE 300 or the S&P 500 does over any period of time. On the other hand, I care very, very, very much about what *my* investments do over any period of time. If I invest a lump sum into the market, say, tomorrow—in the second decade of the greatest bull market in the history of the world—there is a good chance that I may pay too much for my investments, particularly if my buying criterion is past performance.

Will You Need Your Money in the Next Three Years?

If you'll need the money in the next three years, stick with short-term savings-style investments. Even in a well-diversified, blue-chip equity portfolio anything can happen in a three-year period. This isn't investment money—it's savings. Your objective, then, is to get the highest rate of interest or income on your savings without risk. Consider these:

➤ Canada Savings Bonds or Provincial Savings Bonds.

➤ Money market funds offered by mutual fund companies.

➤ T-bills, or T-bill funds offered by financial institutions.

➤ Short-term bonds. If you are talking about a fair amount of money, you may want to talk to a fixed-income specialist at a brokerage firm about short-term bonds. As long as the maturity dates fall within your time frame, you can count on at least the yield you'll be quoted.

➤ GICs that mature within your time frame.

Beware

Bond funds are not the same as bonds (see Chapter 18). As a matter of fact, they are significantly riskier.

Will You Need Your Money in the Next 10 Years?

Depending on your risk tolerance level (that is, the way you *feel* if your investments drop in value), you may wish to consider any of the above (very safe, very predictable, generally less rewarding in terms of returns) or the following:

➤ Longer-term bonds.

➤ Strip coupons maturing within your time frame.

➤ A diversified portfolio including up to 25 percent in blue-chip or preferred equity (dividend income) funds.

➤ Bond funds (see the section on bond funds in Chapter 18 before considering these).

Don't Need the Money for at Least 10 Years?

If you won't be needing the money for over 10 years, you should consider a diversified portfolio of bonds and equities. Read on ...

Use Dollar Cost Averaging

Have you been experiencing the recent gas price wars in your part of Canada? If so, you may very well have practised a form of dollar cost averaging. When a litre of gasoline is 75 cents, and you put $25 worth in the tank, you're buying 33.33 litres. When gas drops to 65 cents a litre, the same $25 buys you 38.46 litres. In times of price volatility, always buying $25 worth of gas means that you buy more when prices are low, and less when prices are high, reducing your overall cost of fuel.

In a marketplace that is always somewhat volatile, like the stock market, this can make a tremendous difference in your gains over the long haul. The key is to begin investing in the equity market as soon as you begin investing. Many people save monthly but wait until they've accumulated a relatively substantial sum prior to actually investing the money. (In the meantime, it's sitting in their savings account earning 1 percent before taxation of 50 percent and inflation of 2 percent. That's not a kind thing to do to a perfectly nice dollar.) Then, after we've accumulated an amount that we won't be embarrassed taking into a financial advisor's office, we again do the opposite of what logic would dictate. We put our lump sum into equities, usually at the worst time—when we cannot stand listening to our co-workers talk about their hot stocks for one more day. When said hot stock plummets, we call our hapless broker in a panic, tell him or her to sell everything and put our vastly diminished nest egg back into the savings account.

No, no, no. As soon as you have taken care of your emergency fund and your risk management needs, set up a Monthly Automatic Purchase Plan. This serves two

Tip

To invest successfully using dollar cost averaging, you have to commit yourself to investing for the long term. Once you start, you can't cash in your chips after a month or two because you want the money for a trip to Acapulco or a hot date with your former music teacher. Nor can you cash in when the market starts to fall. You have to stick with it.

purposes—you pay yourself first, and you buy *more* when the price is low than you do when the price is high—the opposite of usual investor behaviour. You can do this with either stocks or mutual funds, believe it or not.

Dollar cost averaging with large lump sums of money over a short period (a year, for instance) does mitigate risk to some degree, although it works better with small amounts over the long term. In extremely volatile markets, if you have your heart set on moving into an equity investment with lump sums, dollar cost averaging is unquestionably a good idea. If you're buying a mutual fund, you can usually arrange to put the entire amount into a money market fund and have the fund company transfer a stated amount (say, a twelfth) on a designated date each month. This is going to be a bit frustrating if the fund you're moving into is going up in leaps and bounds and your money market fund is returning a ho-hum 3.8 percent. However, it means that, if you've got the fortitude, and the stock market (or your particular fund) drops 15 percent in a month, you are buying more units than you would have if you had invested the lump sum.

Beware

Does your investment advisor seem resistant to the idea of dollar cost averaging? It's time to remind yourself how he or she gets paid—that is, on commission. How would you rather get paid? A hundred percent today or 1/12 of 100 percent each month for 12 months?

Apply Asset Allocation

The returns on investments can be attributed to four different factors:

1. Market timing decisions (and it's been proven, time and again, that even the gurus can't get this one right)
2. The choice of specific investments (i.e., *which* mutual funds, stocks, or bonds we choose)
3. The choice of asset *types* (i.e., stocks, bonds, mutual funds, T-bills, etc.) or "asset allocation"
4. The luck of the draw

Definition

Treasury bills (or **T-bills**) are actually very short-term bonds. The Canadian government regularly needs to borrow enormous amounts of money for short periods. Once a week, it sells T-bills in an auction to banks and other large financial institutions. They mature in three months, six months, or one year.

According to a number of studies, asset allocation, is responsible for 80 to 90 percent of the variability of total returns. Now, what does that statement mean, exactly? Without delving too deeply into the technicalities of the studies concerned, this becomes much easier to understand when we recognize that equities have consistently outperformed other forms of investment (bonds, T-bills or other "cash equivalents") over the long term—but not always over the short term. From 1968 to 1982, for instance, U.S. T-bills outperformed the U.S. equity market, and people who had a large portion of their portfolio in T-bills were very happy with their wise planning. For the last ten years, however, the average annual return on U.S. 91-day T-bills was 4.8 percent, while the S&P 500 returned an annual average of 21.4 percent over the same period. You can imagine the self-congratulating going on among those with the "foresight" to be heavily invested in equities during this period!

The Four Basic Asset Types

At its essence, asset allocation can be reduced to diversification between the four fundamental asset types:

1. *Cash.* In this category, we have savings accounts, GICs, Treasury bills (or T-bills), and bonds that will mature in the near future, usually within 180 days. In the mutual fund world, we have money market funds (sometimes known as T-bill funds or cash funds). This is where we keep our emergency reserve money, as well as any money that doesn't yet have a home. Cash provides a stable base for our portfolio. It won't provide for our retirement, but it will never go down in value, either.

2. *Fixed income investments (sometimes called "debt securities").* This category includes bonds, mortgages, and other investments that pay a "fixed" rate of income. Obviously, fixed-income investments work well for those of us who rely on our investments for our income, but they also provide a stable component to our overall portfolio. In times when the stock market seems to be a temperamental

cousin of the Energizer bunny, fixed-income investments don't get the respect they deserve. We need to remind ourselves that interest rates aren't the whole story—real returns are the whole story. First, interest is taxed at a higher rate than capital gains or dividends, but if your interest-bearing investments are in your RRSP, that doesn't matter. Second, with five-year GIC rates at more than 6 percent and inflation at less than 2 percent, real returns are higher now than they were in the '80s—when Canada Savings Bonds paid 15 percent and inflation was 12 percent.

The fixed income category also includes mortgages and mortgage funds. Preferred share and dividend funds (which generally invest in preferred shares or dividend-paying common shares) are also sometimes referred to as "fixed income." They are really equities, although they can meet income requirements in your portfolio. High-quality preferred shares have become rather rare in Canada, so buyer beware—some dividend funds have a heavy weighting in common shares, which are more volatile and whose dividends are obviously not "preferred."

Who Knew?

Guaranteed investment certificates—called **GICs**—are similar to term deposits. But GICs usually have longer terms, maturing in one year or more. Most GICs lock up your money for the duration of the contract. Some financial institutions, however, will allow you to cash in a GIC early if you pay a penalty. So make sure you understand the terms of the contract.

3. *Equities.* Equities are financial instruments that give you partial ownership of a public company. (When you buy bonds, on the other hand, you're actually lending money to a company, and you don't have any ownership interest in the business at all. As a common shareholder, you can participate in the company's growth by electing its board of directors, voting on corporate policies, and attending its annual meetings. Preferred stock also represents part ownership, but investors in preferred shares participate in the company's growth in only a limited way. For example, owners of preferred shares often cannot vote on corporate policies.

4. *Hard assets.* Hard assets include precious metals, oil and gas, and real estate. The premise for holding hard assets is that they will always rise in value with rising inflation, and they tend to do well when both stocks and bonds are not. The

Who Knew?

Even though they're bought and sold just like common shares, preferred shares are different in several significant ways:

➤ Preferred shares carry a fixed dividend rate that's higher than the common stock.

➤ If the company that issues preferred shares goes belly-up, any money left after its creditors are paid must go to the preferred shareholders first, then to the common shareholders. That's why they're called preferred shares.

➤ Preferred shareholders often do not enjoy the same voting rights as common shareholders. But because they receive higher dividends, they're not supposed to care.

disadvantage with hard assets is that they rarely provide income, and in times of low inflation, these assets tend to do nothing for returns.

Bottom line? Own some T-bills (or equivalents), own some equities, and own some bonds. Then no matter what's going on, you can congratulate yourself on being at least a partial genius. Again, "better approximately right than completely wrong."

Tip

If you want to know everything there is to know about this asset allocation business, read George Hartman's first book, *Risk Is a Four Letter Word*.

Time to Start Allocating

Now, how do you decide exactly how to allocate your assets? That's a little tricky, but this is one area in which it is important not to get caught up in the complexity. According to many very astute investment professionals, the key is not so much how you allocate your assets but that you do, and that you re-allocate once a year to adjust for the growth that's occurred in the prior 12-month period.

Asset allocation usually only becomes complicated if you haven't taken care of your financial planning basics first. Before you worry about designing an allocation for your portfolio, you should do the following:

➤ Ensure you have an adequate emergency reserve.

➤ Set money aside (in money market funds, T-bills, or a high-yield savings account) for anything you plan to spend money on over the next five to ten years.

➤ Make sure you have adequate disability, unemployment, and life insurance in place.

Once your emergency reserve and five-year cash flow needs are taken care of with cash equivalents, a simple method is to subtract your age from 100 (for a conservative portfolio), your age from 110 (for a moderate portfolio), or your age from 120 (for an aggressive portfolio) to determine how much of your portfolio should be in equities. If, for example, you are 45 and a moderate investor, you will then invest 65 percent of your portfolio in equities, with the balance (35 percent) going into fixed-income investments.

Definition

A **fixed-income investment** is something like a bond or GIC that returns a "fixed" rate of return. That is, you know when you buy one that if you hold it to maturity, the "yield" or amount you receive in income will be a certain percentage of your initial investment.

Again, it is fundamentally important that you rebalance your portfolio each year to compensate for growth. For instance, the growth of equities will usually outpace the income from fixed-income investments, so what began as 60 percent in equities this year may become 70 percent in equities a year from now. Therefore, you'll need to sell some of your equity investments and invest the proceeds in fixed income to get back to your original allocation. It can sometimes be difficult to do this, because if your bonds are down 5 percent and your equities are up 20 percent, it's really hard to convince yourself that you want more in bonds and less in equities. Therein lies the beauty and effectiveness of asset allocation—it forces you, or at least strongly encourages you, to buy low and sell high, and therefore become a successful investor!

Recognize Your Risk Tolerance Level

Risk tolerance is the measure of your ability to emotionally withstand a threat to your financial well-being. Unfortunately, after more than a decade of living beside a booming bull market, most of us have no idea whatsoever of our own tolerance level.

As investors, we tend to talk with our heads and make decisions with our hearts and stomachs (rationalizing those decisions later, of course). I find that we tend to be overoptimistic about the way we will react to bad news—not only when our portfolio, or a portion of it, is dropping in value, but when it is underperforming other investments. Often we view underperformance not as an indication that we are adequately diversified, but as a failure—either ours or our financial advisor's.

It is important to separate your investment needs from your feelings of self-worth. It is this tangle of unrelated issues that too often leads people to overaggressive investment behaviour and short-sighted decision making.

There are literally dozens of risk tolerance questionnaires out there. If you are online, check out Appendix A for some good ones or simply stop in at your favourite financial institution and request one.

Critical Issues About Risk and Planning

In the meantime, however, consider the following issues in assessing your risk tolerance:

➤ Do you have a sound financial plan in place and a clear vision of your future? If so, you have removed some of the gravest risks to your investment portfolio. You will not have to sell your investments in a down market because you need the money. You have an emergency reserve fund, disability, property, and life insurance, and if you are going to build a new house in five years or take a year off to do Europe, you've already built those needs into your financial plan. Most importantly, you are not "investing" money that you need to meet daily or even annual cash flow needs. You see investment as a long-term venture.

➤ Do you make investment decisions after careful research and consideration? If so, you are avoiding the risk of second-guessing yourself, second-guessing your financial advisor, or acting out of greed and regretting it "at leisure."

➤ Do you ever allow others to pressure you into making decisions that don't feel right for you?

➤ How did you react to past economic threats or crises? Prior to Y2K (yes, remember that?) did you take any protective measures? In particular, did you make any decisions that you now regret, like making expensive purchases or taking all of your money out of the market?

➤ Are you a risk-taker by nature, or do you usually choose the safest road? When it comes to money, would you consider yourself entrepreneurial and enterprising—or cautious and pragmatic?

An Exercise in Risk Tolerance

I'm now going to ask you to close your eyes and use your imagination. I'd like you to imagine that you've invested $100 000 in the stock market. You won't need the money for at least 10 years, but it is your retirement fund. If you lose it, or part of it, your retirement is going to be a lot less comfortable.

Now. The stock market is crashing. It has dropped 30 percent in the past week, and the media is full of reports about how experts are saying this is it—the big crash. They're comparing it to 1929, and dot-com investors are being interviewed on TV, talking about losing their homes, being tens of thousands of dollars in debt, even about considering suicide. At your office, the depression is thick. "Have you sold out yet?" says your colleague at the water cooler. "I sold everything yesterday. I took a huge loss, but it's better than losing everything."

Close your eyes. Imagine it—really think about this scenario. What would you do?

When you are designing an asset allocation, always operate within your comfort zone. It may be that you are nervous because you don't understand the stock market or don't have adequate experience. Fine. Accept that—work with it. As time passes, educate yourself, gain experience. As you do, increase your portfolio exposure to equities.

Never feel obligated to take more risk with your money than you feel comfortable with. If you're torn, and feel that you *should* invest in the market even though it causes you a great deal of anxiety, do some work on that before you move ahead. Educate yourself. Revisit your childhood issues around money. Think about your relationships with your financial advisors. Is there enough trust there?

It's your money. Investing it should feel good.

A Note on Socially Responsible Investing

Speaking of feeling good about investment ... I have to confess to be profoundly confused about this business of socially responsible, "ethical" investment. I envy people who are more black and white about this—either "I want to make as much money as possible, so man the torpedoes!" or "No one in his right mind would want to profit from the avails of tobacco companies, arms dealers, auto manufacturers, sugar refineries, etc."

The problem, for me, is where to draw that ever-troublesome line. An example of my dilemma is the Ethical Growth Fund, a well-managed fund that has taken some of the wind out of the sails of those who said a fund can't succeed with ethical limitations. That's not my problem. It seems to me that companies that are socially responsible will ultimately fare better, and therefore profit more, than those that aren't. My problem is the Royal Bank, which is one of the largest holdings within the Ethical Growth Fund. Not that the Royal Bank isn't an ethical company—it does a lot of very socially responsible things. However, in 1999, almost immediately following its announcement of record profits, in the billions of dollars, the Royal Bank, which operates in a highly regulated and therefore protected industry, announced that it would eliminate 8000 jobs from its payroll. Hello? I have a problem with that. Am I comparing the Royal Bank to Rothmans Tobacco Company? No. Do I agree with its methods? No again.

A second issue for me is the "best of" practice. That is, the Ethical Group will invest in environmentally invasive industries like oil and gas, for instance, but they invest only in the company that has the best record for responsible practices. I think this is probably a good idea, but again, where is the line to be drawn?

My Ethical Compromise

The moral compromise I've come to on ethical investing is this. I make the best investment decisions for myself, and socially responsible business practices are certainly one of the criteria I apply. However, in my opinion, the single greatest way to invest is in index funds, which do indirectly profit from tobacco companies, arms manufacturers, and banks. (Don't forget, though, that until the day they are shut down, we all profit from tobacco and arms manufacturers through their considerable tax contributions.) It may be rank rationalization, but I choose to see my investment not as a vote for one kind of business practice or another, but as a means to allow me to then live the socially responsible life I choose. There will always be people willing to invest in tobacco companies if that will bring the greatest profits—the tobacco company will not suffer in any way because we refuse to participate. (I mean, more than 30 percent of Canadians still smoke, for heaven's sake! I certainly participate in *paying* for the public health care that must be provided to cope with some of the ravages of tobacco. But then, I also pay for the ravages of the automobile, which maim and injure thousands of people every year.)

Financial freedom, however, allows me to contribute 10 percent of my earnings to the charities of my choice, donate 10 percent of my working hours to people who couldn't otherwise afford my services, and live in direct reflection of my principles and values.

It's Your Choice

Obviously, we all have to decide what's right for ourselves. If you do decide that you are most comfortable with the more traditional ethical screens, you have two choices in Canada—the Ethical Funds or the new Universal Global Ethics Fund offered by Mackenzie Financial. Alternatively, you can devise your own stock portfolio by joining the Canadian Shareholders Association (see Chapter 17).

The Ethical Funds can be reached at <www.ethicalfunds.com/index.html> or you can purchase these no-load funds through your local credit union or your discount brokerage.

Mackenzie Financial's Web site is at <www.mackenziefinancial.com>. The Global Ethics Fund, like all Mackenzie funds, is sold on a load basis through financial advisors or through your discount broker.

The Least You Need to Know

➤ Your time horizon and risk tolerance determine your portfolio allocation.

➤ Review your portfolio annually, and if necessary, rebalance to your original asset allocation.

➤ The importance of asset allocation is twofold—it helps you achieve effective diversification and forces you to do the right thing by pruning "hot" assets and buying more underperforming assets.

➤ Be realistic about your risk tolerance, and act within your comfort zone. To do otherwise is to risk reactive decisions during periods of market volatility.

Chapter 14

Mutual Fund Basics

In This Chapter

➤ Mutual funds: their benefits and their costs

➤ Managed vs. index funds

➤ Open vs. closed-end funds

➤ The disappearing investor

Now that we've covered the basics of investment planning, let's get down to the nitty gritty. What do we buy, exactly? Let's look at the options.

What Is a Mutual Fund?

A mutual fund is simply a pool of investor dollars, all of which is then invested in a diversified portfolio of investments by the institution managing the fund. When you invest in a mutual fund, you are, in essence, throwing your money in the pool with that of other investors in order to share in their profits. (You may also end up sharing in their losses.)

The primary advantage that you get from a mutual fund is diversification. With $500 to invest, an individual investor can buy only a limited number of shares of a company or bonds or T-bills or other types of investment. Put 500 investors together, each with $500, and they can buy lots of shares or T-bills and diversify their investments.

Who Knew?

Mutual funds can be classified in several ways: growth, income, balanced, money market, global, sector, index, and so on. Within each of these categories, you'll find a wide variety of funds investing in domestic and foreign stocks, bonds and other related investments. You'll also find a wide range of short- and long-term performance records. *Growth funds*, for example, aim for short- and long-term growth through capital gains rather than dividends or interest payments. They primarily invest in stocks, or equities, issued by companies with better than average potential for growth. *Income funds* seek investments that will generate annual income in predictable amounts. They invest a large percentage of their money in government and corporate bonds, mortgage-backed securities, and other income-producing investments such as dividends. *Balanced funds* pursue an investment strategy that seeks to balance their portfolios in general, between growth and income. *Money market funds* invest primarily in low-risk, short-term, government-backed treasury bills. *Index funds* invest in the same equities and with the same weighting as a particular index such as the TSE 300 or the S&P 500.

Definition

Stocks, shares, and **equities** are interchangeable words used to mean a unit of investment in a corporation or business.

Basic Types of Fund

There are two basic types of mutual fund—managed (or active) and index (or passive). In a managed mutual fund, the investment decisions are made by professional investment managers and their team of researchers. In an index fund, investor dollars are simply invested in accordance with the index the fund reflects. If the index fund mirrored the TSE 300, for instance, each investor dollar would be invested in the 300 companies that make up the index, in exactly proportionate measures. That is, if ABC Co. makes up 10 percent of the index, 10 cents of each investor dollar will be used to buy ABC Co.

Although we tend to associate the term "mutual fund" with the stock market, mutual funds can actually invest in anything from T-bills (these are known as money market funds) to mortgages (you guessed it—mortgage funds). An equity mutual fund invests in equities, and balanced mutual funds invest in a balance of equities and fixed-income investments like bonds.

Net Asset Value

Mutual funds are purchased in *units*. Unit value fluctuates with the total value of the securities in the fund. Mutual funds are valued daily and reported in the financial sections of most newspapers. A fund's *net asset value* (NAV) is the total value of its assets minus fund expenses. The *net asset value per share* (NAVPS) represents the value of one unit in the fund, based on the NAV. The value of the NAVPS is determined by dividing the total value of the mutual fund's portfolio on a particular day by the number of units outstanding. The NAVPS is calculated daily and will fluctuate with the overall value of the fund.

Open vs. Closed-End Funds

The majority of mutual funds are open, which means that the pool can grow to infinity unless the manager decides to cap or close it. Closed-end funds sell a limited number of units, which generally trade on a stock exchange.

If you own shares in an open-ended mutual fund, you'll almost never have trouble finding someone to buy your shares or sell you more shares, at the current NAV. If investors don't want to deal with you, the fund itself will.

Most mutual funds currently traded in Canada are open-ended. There are also a few closed-end mutual funds. These funds issue a limited number of shares when they're first set up. Once they sell all the shares and there are none left to sell, the fund is closed. At that point, no new shares are issued, and the fund company will no longer redeem your shares.

That's where the stock exchange comes in. You can still buy and sell shares in a closed-end fund on the stock exchange. The price will fluctuate up and down, just like shares in other companies. Sometimes the price per share will be higher than the NAV—selling at a premium. Sometimes it will be less—selling at a discount.

Definition

A **closed-end mutual fund** is one with a limited number of units. These units trade on a stock exchange, and their value moves up and down in relation to their popularity with investors as well as their underlying value. When more people want to buy than sell the closed-end fund, the market price will rise above the NAV, and vice versa.

Why Buy Mutual Funds?

There are six basic reasons to buy a mutual fund:

1. Professional investment management
2. Reduced volatility through portfolio diversification
3. Access to a broad range of investments with even a small contribution
4. Broad choice of funds to meet virtually any investment objective
5. Easily bought and sold
6. Flexible payment options

For these reasons, I've always weighed in heavily on the side of mutual funds as opposed to individual stocks, and I've even stated a preference for managed mutual funds as opposed to index funds (sometimes referred to as "passive funds"). To some degree, it was because the average 2.25 percent expense ratio paid on the average Canadian equity fund seemed like a steal to me if it could let me participate in the equity market *and* not have to spend hours each week going through annual reports. In addition, I felt that fund managers can offer a degree of protection from loss in bear markets.

But not so fast ... Then I read *The Coffeehouse Investor*, by Bill Schultheis, and I was enlightened as to the true impact of that 2.25 percent over time and the real alternative to managed funds—index funds.

The other flaw in the theory on which I based my preference for managed mutual funds was this: There are as many mutual funds available in Canada today as there are stocks. My experience as a financial advisor convinced me that many investors are making the same mistakes with their mutual funds as individual stock owners do with their stocks! That measure of protection and expertise may be there, but sadly, investors aren't getting the benefits.

Who Knew?

Can't remember what "bulls" and "bears" represent in the stock market? Just think of a charging bull—a bull market is one that is going up in value. Or, think of bears hibernating—in a bear market prices are sluggish and in decline.

Where Did That Mutual Fund Investor Go?

In 1998 and 1999, mutual fund sales in Canada dropped dramatically, from $51.9 billion in 1997 to $17.7 billion dollars in 1999.

It's a mystery that no one seems able to explain, but some of the answers may lie in research that was done in the 1990s about where all the mutual fund investment money was coming from. It was discovered that although some of the new mutual fund investors were the so-called "GIC refugees," people who had formerly never invested in the stock markets, a great deal was also shifting from individual stock portfolios. Investors were giving up on attempting to do it themselves, or allowing their stockbrokers to do it for them.

Today, with many discount brokerage options available, we may be seeing a shift in the opposite direction. It's too early to tell.

Having said that, mutual funds, particularly passive (or index) mutual funds, are still a great option. Just watch the fees—they will make a difference.

Who Knew?

Of the 114 Canadian mutual funds that Morningstar Rating Service assigned their highest, five-star rating on March 31, 2000, 53 were no-load funds. Management expense ratios on the 114 five-star funds ranged from 3.65 percent to a low of 0.3 percent. It's worth shopping around.

The Least You Need to Know

➤ Mutual funds come in two basic versions: open and closed.

➤ As an alternative to managed funds, an index fund costs less to own.

➤ The number of mutual fund investors in Canada is falling.

Chapter 15

The Way Funds Are Sold

In This Chapter

➤ Load vs. no-load funds

➤ MERs, trailer fees, and DSCs

What do you really get when you buy a unit of a mutual fund? Read on and get the gory details.

No-Load Funds

A "load" is a sales commission that is paid to somebody for selling you a fund. A no-load fund is one that doesn't pay a sales commission.

However, the person who sells you a no-load fund is not doing so out of goodwill. On the contrary, he or she is receiving a salary, often a salary plus bonus package that relates to the amount sold. Rather than being paid by any number of fund companies, this person is paid by one, limiting the number of options he or she is likely to recommend. In addition, because no-load fund companies do not pay commissions to an independent sales force of financial advisors, they must market their funds somehow, and TV advertising is not inexpensive. These costs, like the commissions that are paid on "load" funds, come out of your investment returns.

The great thing about no-load funds is that they offer more of an opportunity to lower the cost of annual management expenses, which over time will have a much greater impact on your returns than the initial commission.

The bottom line? When choosing between load and no-load funds, do so on the merits of the fund, not on the way it's sold.

Now I'm going to share a very valuable little secret with you: You don't always have to pay the "load" on load funds, either. Let's take a brief look at load mutual funds, and I'll explain.

Tip

You can usually check whether you've paid on a deferred basis for your mutual fund by looking at your statement. You'll see the letters DSC beside the name of your fund.

Beware

Whether or not you pay a deferred sales charge, a front-end load, or neither, you are paying your advisor through the management expense ratio. Advertising, commissions, those funky-looking marketing materials—it all comes out of your profits.

Load Mutual Funds

If you deal with a financial advisor, you probably own load mutual funds, because that is probably the way your advisor gets paid. There are two ways to purchase load mutual funds. It is likely that you are one of the 75 percent of Canadian purchasers who pays with a "deferred sales charge" (DSC).

A deferred sales charge means that, if you make a $10 000 fund purchase, $10 000 goes into the fund. If you purchase on a front-end basis, the alternative to DSC, you will pay an up-front commission of up to 5 percent. If you're paying a front-end commission of 5 percent, only $9500 will go into your investment, which therefore has to increase in value by a full 5 percent before you get back to square one.

The tricky bit with a deferred sales charge is that once you're in, you're in. That is, you must stay within the same fund family for a stated period (generally six or seven years) or you'll get whacked with a nasty penalty on your way out. The penalty, which generally decreases from 6 percent in the first two years to 2.5 percent in year five, is based either on your initial purchase or the redemption amount, depending on the fund company you're dealing with.

As a financial advisor, I generally sold funds on a deferred sales charge basis, in part because most clients were far more open to a commission they would probably never "pay."

Researchers in the U.S. have shown that investors in deferred sales charge funds actually do better because they are less likely to sell when things get rocky. However, there are some concepts you must know and understand before you purchase mutual funds on a load basis.

Trailer Fees

Are you still waiting for me to get to the part about not paying any commissions on load mutual funds? Here we are. Your financial advisor receives what are called "trailer fees" on every dollar you have invested with a load mutual fund company, with the exception of some money market funds. If you purchased an equity fund on a deferred sales charge basis, he or she receives 0.5 percent per year, or $50 on every $10 000 investment. If you purchased the same fund on a front-end basis, your advisor would receive 1 percent per year, or $100 on a $10 000 investment. Remember all the Canada Trust advertisements for free mutual fund purchases? That was the deal—you purchased load mutual funds at *zero percent front end*, and Canada Trust received a trailer fee of 1 percent per year on all assets "under administration," that is, registered to them. The same is true of mutual funds purchased through some discount brokerages or discount mutual fund services. You don't necessarily have to move your account to get these "free" (say it with me people—nothing is free!) purchases, however—here's the key.

Your financial advisor wants your business, particularly if you aren't a difficult or demanding client and you have a relatively substantial portfolio. (I know it seems like a lot of money, but anything under $50 000 is not a substantial portfolio.)

Why? Trailer fees. One percent per year doesn't sound like much, but for an advisor with 300 clients and an average account size of $100 000 (which is not at all unusual) that's $300 000 per year!

If you are one of those clients with the $100 000 account, therefore, the next time you meet with your advisor, say something like this: "I've really enjoyed working with you, Joe, but I've recently learned about trailer fees. From now on, I only want to purchase funds on a zero percent front-end basis. I know you'll get the trailer fees, and I don't think you provide more than $1000 in service to me each year. Are you okay with that?"

I can guarantee Joe is going to be a bit taken aback, but if he understands that you're willing to take your business elsewhere, I'm sure he'll be open to the idea.

Free Units and Fund Switches

Is there any hope for us if we're already knee-deep in deferred mutual funds that we want out of?

Well, first of all, you should know that you can switch from fund to fund within any fund family without incurring further costs. But, beware: your financial advisor has the right to charge up to 2 percent for processing a switch within a fund family. Unless your advisor also provides regular Swedish massages and feeds your cat when you're away, I would advise moving your account to another advisor if he or she does.

It costs next to nothing to process this kind of switch, and it should be part of the service package that's covered by trailer fees and any initial commission your advisor was paid. (If you are a pain-in-the-neck client, however, who is forever waffling about objectives, taking up your advisor's time by arguing with him or her on the basis of your cousin the taxi driver's new theory on e-com, being rude to the receptionist, and complaining about your returns—just pay the 2 percent.)

Stay Invested

Remember, the key to investment success is to get invested and stay invested.

Flopping around from fund to fund or stock to stock may seem to be of benefit over the short term, but ultimately, all the research that has ever been done on this proves you're better off to stay where you are and catch the updraft when it comes. Don't switch just because you can, but know that you do have the option. It sure beats paying a big penalty by redeeming and moving to another fund company.

DSC Advantages

Then there are "free units." When you purchase on a deferred sales charge basis, the mutual fund company allows you to redeem up to 10 percent of your units each year without penalty. This makes the DSC option viable for people who are living off of their investments, but it also makes it possible to rebalance your asset allocation and/or simply prepare for the day you might want to move your funds.

Tip

Here's a great idea from Bylo Selhi: "Instead of having distributions reinvested in more DSC units, ask your mutual fund company to invest them in the front-end fund equivalent of your DSC fund. If they can't help you, have them pay the dividends in cash, and use the cash to buy front-end load or index fund units. Often funds pay out 5% to 10% or more in annual distributions. This effectively doubles the rate at which you can escape from 'DSC jail.'"

Note however that some companies won't allow an investor to get cash distributions and take out 10% penalty-free. As always, it pays to read the prospectus, or ask your adviser to translate it into English.

Your financial advisor can help you either redeem your 10 percent, if there is something you want to do with the money, or simply move your free units into the equivalent front-end fund to make it available down the road. The reason this is a good idea is that your 10 percent free amount does not accumulate. Whatever you don't use in the calendar year disappears.

Management Costs and Management Expense Ratios

In a study done by Toronto's Marketing Solutions Inc. in the late '90s, more than 60 percent of mutual fund investors surveyed did not know they were paying a management fee. Obviously, they weren't thinking too deeply. Why, might I ask, would anyone think that these fund companies would manage this money for nothing? How would it even be possible? There are substantial costs involved in conducting all of that research and administering those great pools of money. Your management company is charging a fee—and so they should be. The question, of course, is how much? What are they providing in terms of value per fee dollar? As we reviewed in Chapter 12, fees and costs really do make a difference, so it's important to give consideration to this issue.

There are two factors to be considered—management fees and the management expense ratio (MER). Duff Young, author of *Fund Monitor 2000*, says this:

> My advice is to disregard management fees and focus instead on the management expense ratio. That's the total of all management fees plus other expenses, divided by the number of units. It includes legal, accounting, custodial, and safekeeping costs, as well as the costs of providing prospectuses and other reporting materials.

Very sound advice. The management expense ratio can almost always be found in the fund's prospectus in the "costs and fees" section. If you can't find it or don't yet have the prospectus, just ask whoever is selling you the fund to provide the information.

Definition

A **prospectus** is a lengthy document prepared by a mutual fund or other investment company to inform investors and potential investors about the investment. Subjects covered are operations, costs and fees, risks, etc. As a minimum, read the sections on fees and risks.

The Least You Need to Know

➤ Don't assume that mutual fund "loads" and financial advice have to come in the same package—look for advice that's sold by the hour and funds that are sold without commission.

➤ If you are stuck in DSC funds now, take advantage of your 10 percent free unit switches.

➤ The management expense ratio can have a big effect on a fund's annual return.

Index or Managed Funds?

Now that you know how funds work and how you pay for them, let's take a closer look at your options for reducing expenses without necessarily limiting your returns.

Index Funds in Detail

How do we reduce the management expenses we pay? No-load funds can offer lower costs funds, perhaps because most no-loads usually pay a much lower trailer fee (the ongoing annual fees paid to financial advisors), an off-the-top expense of one-half to one percent for load funds.

Index funds, in particular, have dramatically lower management expenses because they don't pay fund managers and there's no research team. They simply buy whatever's in the underlying index the fund represents, in the same weightings.

How Index Funds Perform

Ted Cadsby, author of *The Power of Index Funds*, gives us some Canadian figures: "The TSE 300 beat 68% of active Canadian equity funds over the 10-year period ended December 1999, and 83% over five years." Beware: These Canadian figures are heavily skewed by the performance of Nortel Networks and BCE Inc. For example, in 1999, the TSE 300 was up over 30 percent—but if we were to remove the returns on three tech-oriented stocks, BCE, Nortel, and JDS Uniphase, the remainder of the index was up roughly 7 percent. This is important because only the most aggressive fund managers or investors would bet that heavily on just three stocks. However, even if we take this caution into account, it's difficult to deny the bottom line—index funds do better, and cost a lot less to own.

I asked the manager of one of Canada's top global mutual funds (who shall remain unnamed for obvious reasons) his opinion on indexing and passive investment. I expected a strong defence of active management (that's an industry term for non-index funds). I was surprised by his response. He said he believes that in most cases, an investor's core equity portfolio should be invested in low-cost index funds, with the addition of one or two proven managed global or international funds.

If that's the feeling of one of the world's top active managers, I think we should probably heed it and at least consider index funds as an option when we are shopping for a fund.

An Example

One of the lowest-cost funds in Canada today is Greenline U.S. Index, a Morningstar 5-Star fund with an average annual return of 26.5 percent over five years. This fund has a management expense ratio of only 0.64 percent. As a comparison, actively managed U.S. funds have MERs in the range of 2.5 percent.

Beware

In efficient markets, such as those in the U.S., research shows that active management creates better-than-index returns less than 20 percent of the time—not good odds on which to bet the extra 2 percent (on average) that you pay in fees annually.

Tip

You can buy exchange-traded index funds through the Canadian Shareowners Association. See Chapter 17 for further information on joining.

Definition

A **basis point** is 1/100 of one percent. Fifty basis points, therefore, is half a percent.

That's a huge difference—which would be worth paying if active management could create higher returns by at least 2 percent annually. Unfortunately, that doesn't seem to be the case. For the five years ending March 31, 2000, of over 271 U.S. funds available in Canada, only 11 outperformed Greenline U.S. Index. The other 260 charged management expense fees of approximately 2.5 percent per year to *underperform* the index.

Table 16-1 (from Bylo Selhi) provides information on the lowest-cost index funds available in Canada today, along with their MERs and performance data. The table shows only low-MER, no-load index funds. Low-MER means 0.50 percent (50 basis points) or less. Each cell in the table shows the index that the fund tracks and the MER.

Tip

Index funds may offer a tax advantage if you own them outside of your RRSP or RRIF. Since there's no stock-picking, there's far less trading; and since there's less trading, the capital gains created on which to pay tax are much lower.

Tip

If you own investments outside of your RRSP, investigate tax-advantaged and index funds. Index funds trade less because of passive management; tax-advantaged funds are generally buy-and-hold-style funds that trade as little as possible without sacrificing gains.

Who Knew?

It is important to know that fund returns are always quoted net of management expenses, so if your fund returned 14 percent last year and has an MER of 3 percent, the fund actually earned 17 percent. Obviously, the less generous the market is, the more important management expenses become.

Table 16-1
Low-MER, No-Load Index Funds Available in Canada

	Altamira Precision		CIBC Index[1]		Royal Index[2]		TD eFunds3	
	Regular[4]	RRSP[3]	Regular	RRSP	Regular	RRSP	Regular	RRSP
Canadian Bond			SCM Universe 0.30	SCM Universe 0.30			SCM Gov't 0.45	SCM Gov't 0.45
Canadian ST Bond			SCM Short Term 0.30	SCM Short Term 0.30				
Global Gov't Bond			JP Morgan Glbl Gov't 0.30	JP Morgan Glbl Gov't 0.30				
Canadian Equity	S&P/ TSE 60 0.50	S&P/ TSE 60 0.50	TSE 300 0.30	TSE 300 0.30	TSE 300 0.52/0.30	TSE 300 0.52/0.30	TSE 300 0.29	TSE 300 0.29
US General Equity		S&P 500 0.50	Wilshire 5000 0.30	S&P 500 0.30	S&P 500 0.52/0.30	S&P 500 0.52	S&P 500 0.29	S&P 500 0.45
US Large Cap	DJIA 30 0.50						DJIA 30 0.29	
US Technology				NASDAQ 100 0.30				NASDAQ 100 0.45
US Mid Cap	S&P 400							
International		MSCI EAFE 0.50	MSCI EAFE 0.30	MSCI EAFE 0.30		MSCI EAFE 0.52		MSCI EAFE 0.45

	Altamira Precision		CIBC Index[1]		Royal Index[2]		TD eFunds3	
	Regular[4]	RRSP[3]	Regular	RRSP	Regular	RRSP	Regular	RRSP
Europe	MSCI Europe 0.70	Eurotop 100 0.50	MSCI Europe 0.30	MSCI Europe 0.30			MSCI Europe 0.45	
Pacific	MSCI Pacific 0.70							
Japan				Nikkei 225 0.30			MSCI Japan 0.45	

Notes:

1. The normal MER for CIBC index funds is 0.90%, however, this is reduced to 0.30% (or even 0.25%) under their MER rebate program for accounts that hold more than $150 000 (or $500 000) in CIBC index funds.

2. The normal MER for Royal index funds is 0.50%, however, this is reduced to 0.30% when at least $250 000 is held in a specific fund.

3. TD eFunds are only available directly from TD. The higher-MER (approx. 1%) Class A funds are available from other brokers/dealers.

4. All funds that invest in Canadian asset classes are fully RRSP eligible. Funds that invest in foreign asset classes may be fully RRSP eligible ("RRSP") or may only be eligible as foreign content ("regular"), i.e. up to 20% of the plan's book value.

5. Other fund companies that offer index funds with MERs under 1% include Canada Trust, Scotia Bank and National Bank.

6. Other low-cost "index funds" include Index Participation Units (e.g., XIUs, TIPs) and Exchange Traded Funds (e.g., SPDRs, QQQs).

7. This chart was accurate at the date published (26 Feb 2000). However, index fund fees are very competitive and may have changed. Please check with the companies involved for updated information. You'll find their Web sites in Appendix A.

Tip

If you have access to the Internet, you owe it to yourself to spend some time at the Bylo Selhi site at <www.bylo.org>.

The Least You Need to Know

➤ Commissions are negotiable—don't pay more than you have to, and understand what you're buying.

➤ If you're buying a fund that focuses on one country or index, consider a low-cost index fund first.

Chapter 17

Full Service Brokerage Firms

In This Chapter

➤ Want something a little more exciting than a mutual fund? Yearn for the action of stock trading?

➤ How to tell a "great" stock from a "grief" stock, courtesy of the Canadian Shareowners Association

➤ The best and worst of the discount brokerage services

If you want to make your own investment decisions, maybe you should try investing in equities. There are simple ways to stay informed as you invest.

Confessions of an Automatic Transmission Fan

The thing I've found most challenging (and, I have to admit, most rewarding) about writing books and attempting to share my experience of the financial industry is continually tripping over my own prejudices.

As I was thinking about what to write in this chapter, it occurred to me that I'm simply not fond of individual stocks. For most of the 12 years that I've worked in financial services, I was clear on the following:

➤ Individual investors do not have the time to do the necessary research on stock selection.

➤ Even investors who have time to do the research tend to use it only to justify their emotion-based decisions.

➤ Stock brokers are no better at selecting stocks than the average investor with time to do the research, and they charge outrageous commissions to provide their own biased recommendations.

➤ Most Canadian investors do not have enough money in the equity portion of their portfolio to get the diversification they need in stocks without paying too much in commissions.

I Was ... Wrong

Well, I'm ready to admit that I was w...w...wrong. Or rather, not wrong, exactly—just deluded.

First of all, there are a lot of investors now doing with mutual funds the very thing I believed mutual funds were created to avoid. Instead of choosing good funds and letting the fund managers do their job, investors are flopping from mutual fund to mutual fund like they did from VSE mining company to VSE mining company in the 1980s. Buy high, sell low. And independent financial advisors are making money the same way stockbrokers did back then—on commission. Not a lot of incentive there to encourage investors to buy and hold for the long term, which has been scientifically and indisputably proven to create better returns than chasing performance.

Sins of Commission

The second thing I didn't like about stocks and stockbrokers was those darn commissions. Bad enough paying an annual management fee to a mutual fund company—I was astounded when I found that I had to pay a commission to buy a stock on my broker's

Who Knew?

Stocks come in two essential formats—common and preferred. Preferred shareholders are only preferred when it comes to receiving dividends, or sharing in the company's profits. They don't normally get to vote on the company's affairs, a privilege generally restricted to common shareholders.

advice and then I had to pay another commission when the company went south and I sold it. Talk about adding insult to injury!

Then there were discount brokers, who for much lower commissions, threw you right into the shark tank by yourself.

In the fall of 1999, after my book *Financial Serenity* was released, I was invited to take part in a expert round table discussion for *Maclean's Magazine Annual Personal Financial Edition*. The subject was "Stocks or Mutual Funds" and the gentleman who sat in on the side of stocks was Dr. John Bart, founder of the Canadian Shareowners Association.

Until I was invited to participate in the event, I'd never heard of the Shareowners Association, but I immediately got on the Internet and did some research. Though I still found myself weighing in on the side of managed mutual funds in the debate (what can I say?), I was very heartened by what I found.

Stock Basics

Let's look first at the basics of stocks and investment in individual stocks, and then I'll tell you about the Canadian Shareowners Association and why it's overcome so many of my objections to stock ownership for the average Canadian.

Off the top, you should know that the terms, "stock," "shares," "equity," and "equities," are used interchangeably to refer to partial ownership of a publicly traded company. In the old days (when we were walking to school in our bare feet, uphill both ways), stock ownership was represented by a certificate stating the number of shares owned in the underlying company. These days, ownership is normally indicated only by a number on a brokerage statement.

Owning a share of a company also entitles you to a share of its profits. Losses of a company, on the other hand, are generally reflected in a stock's declining share price. You can lose the money you've invested, but you cannot lose more than that. Because public companies are corporations, legal entities unto themselves, shareholders are never asked to pull additional money out of their pockets to subsidize corporate losses or shortfalls.

Corporations issue shares in order to raise "working capital"—money to expand, create new projects, and in some cases, to return capital to the original owners. When a company "goes public," it is allowing the public to buy portions of itself that were previously privately owned, that is, owned by a small group of private shareholders.

Who Knew?

Shares, equities, and stocks—they're all the same. Literally, these words are all used interchangeably to mean the same thing—partial ownership in a corporation.

The Value of a Share

Once, when I was young and very naïve, I realized that the company I worked for had a "book value" of $2 per share. That means that when the shares were originally issued, a business evaluator determined that the value of its assets, were they sold off in parts and bits, would be worth $2 times the number of shares outstanding. Luckily, I didn't have any money at the time. The shares were trading at $1.50 (their "market value") and I foolishly believed that I had brilliantly figured out what everyone else was missing and, therefore, if I bought the shares at $1.50, I would make a 50-cent profit on each share when the rest of the world inevitably came to its senses.

Beware

The first rule of survival is—when you're as naïve and uninformed as I was, don't do anything with real money. Stick to books and online trading games until you figure out how little you actually know about the way the investment world works. A little information is a dangerous thing.

When you're investing in stocks, the second rule of survival is this: A share's value is not determined by the underlying value or profitability, but by the esteem in which stock buyers hold that particular company. There is not always a logical relationship between a stock's price and the intrinsic value or even potential value of the underlying company. *The stock market is not a store—it is an auction.* Even the most brilliant analysis of a company's value or potential value may not serve you well as an investor, particularly over the short term. Profiting on stock requires that you evaluate the company's value and then the share's price. Paying too much for even a great company means you may wait a very long time to reap any rewards for your astute analysis.

Kinds of Stocks

If you've been through Chapter 13, you'll know how relieved I am to advise that there are two kinds of stocks—common and preferred. Common shares are the ones we normally hear about. Their price is determined by the market's affection for the underlying company and the general state of the market.

Preferred shares, on the other hand, tend to be less volatile in price movements because they pay "preferred dividends." That is, they pay a stated, or "fixed" dividend at a stated date on a regular basis. The reason they are called "preferred shares" is because as a preferred shareholder, you get first dibs on any profits. If a company goes through a difficult time and cannot pay its dividends, it must make up any dividend payment it owes its preferred shareholders prior to paying any dividends to any of those poor common shareholders.

Tip

Canadian dividends receive favourable tax treatment as opposed to interest or employment income (see Chapter 7 for details).

Therefore, although preferred shares are still equities, their price tends to correlate more to interest rates. If a preferred shareholder receives preferred dividends equaling 7 percent of an investment, and corporate bonds were paying 6 percent, buyers would be willing to pay a premium (an increased price) for the preferred shares.

How to Buy Stock

The alternatives are:

➤ Full-service brokerage firms

➤ Discount brokerage firms

➤ Online brokerage services (provided by discount brokerage firms)

Who Knew?

With a dividend re-investment plan (DRIP), your dividends are automatically invested in more shares at whatever price the shares are trading at the time. With a stock purchase plan (SPP), shareholders have the privilege of buying more shares directly from the corporation. Unfortunately, you can take advantage of these commission-free direct stock purchase plans only if you already own shares of the company. If you are an owner of one of Canada's blue-chip corporations, however, and want to buy more shares, inquire as to the availability of these plans.

➤ Direct purchases plans, otherwise known as "DRIPs" (dividend re-investment plans) and SPPs (stock purchase plans)

➤ The Canadian Shareowners Association Low Cost Investment Program

Full-Service Brokerage Firms

Full-service brokerage firms are the ones we're all familiar with, and they've been around for a long time. They play a unique role in the Canadian market place, using the stock markets to bring buyers and sellers together, and to access capital for business development. Our economy would suffer greatly without them, as corporations would have much more difficulty raising money for development.

Brokerage firms make money a few ways. They make money by bringing new offerings, or IPOs (initial public offerings), to market. On top of the commissions they earn selling the shares to you, they receive a fee from the public company, sometimes as much as 10 percent of the selling price.

Increasingly, brokerage firms are also investing on their own behalf. On one hand, that's reassuring, because it means that the brokerage firm is putting "its money where its mouth is," betting on the same recommendations it makes to its clients. On the other, it is a scary trend, because there is a significant conflict of interest—the more investors are interested in buying a stock, the higher the price will be. The higher the price, the higher the brokerage firm's profits, thus casting grave doubts on the supposedly objective research reports issued by the firm to its brokers and clients.

On the other hand, full service brokerage firms do a bang-up job of creating bond portfolios—more on that in Chapter 18.

The Canadian Shareowners Association

The Canadian Shareowners Association (CSA) is a nonprofit organization dedicated to bringing the benefits of stock ownership to ordinary Canadians. According to its membership material, the CSA's strategy is as follows:

➤ Principle #1: Invest only in the highest-quality common stocks.

➤ Principle #2: Invest in these quality stocks, regularly, over the longer term—don't try to "time" yourself in and out of the stock's short-term ups and downs.

➤ Principle #3: Re-invest the dividends and gains from these quality stocks over the longer term to get compounding working for you.

➤ Principle #4: Diversify your portfolio to minimize unavoidable risks by including quality stocks from different businesses.

Their methods seem to produce positive results. According to data on the CSA Web site (at <www.shareowner.ca>), comparing performance of its index to the S&P/TSE 60, the

CSA's portfolio outperformed the S&P/TSE 60 consistently between January 1999 and May 2000.

My Beefs and How the CSA Addresses Them

The CSA, frankly, has blown away many of my objections to stock picking, but I'll go over my objections anyway, for your benefit, and how the CSA addresses them.

First, the average Canadian investor, who has less than $25 000 in the equity portion of his or her portfolio, cannot afford to get the kind of diversification needed in a stock portfolio.

The Shareowners' Solution: The Low Cost Investing Program (the Trust Company of the Bank of Montreal is the Trustee and Custodian), which we will refer to as the CSA does, as the LCIP. For shockingly low fees, investors can become a Shareowner ($89 per year), open both an RRSP and a non-registered plan, and buy stock for as little as $4 per trade (after an initial set-up fee of $8 per company). All dividends are re-invested at no cost. Annual RSP fees are $36—compare that to the usual self-directed RSP fee of $125. There is no minimum purchase, so for a relatively small amount monthly, investors can invest in a diversified stock portfolio.

There are investment pundits who believe that it is possible to mirror the returns of an index by owning as few as 12 of the major companies within that index. If this is true (and their arguments sound reasonable to me) then it should also be possible to achieve the necessary diversification through the LCIP program. Frankly, I'd still lean toward the simplicity of just buying the index, but for those of you who want to own stocks, this is a great service.

Beware

Although your first account set-up fee of $8 is waived on automatic purchases, a $4 fee on a monthly purchase of $100 is still 4 percent. Therefore, you may be better off subscribing to the quarterly service and investing $400 each time, for a 1 percent fee. There is also a one-time $8 set-up fee for each new stock you decide to buy. And any time your purchase exceeds $1000, the transaction fee decreases to 4/10 of 1 percent.

Second, mutual funds allow investors unparalleled ease of investment, with monthly purchase plans, free switches between funds, monthly withdrawal plans, and free monthly RRIF payments.

The Shareowners' Solution: If you're in a RRIF, the LCIP can't help, and if you need to make monthly withdrawals, this service isn't for you. Which makes sense—it's an investor service, not an income service. However, you can set up monthly or quarterly pre-authorized withdrawals from your bank account to purchase any of the participating Canadian or U.S. stocks of your choice. (For the list of securities, see Appendix D.) The transaction fee of $4 is automatically taken off your purchase.

Third, researching individual stocks takes a tremendous amount of time, and a certain level of expertise—not just once, when making the buying decision, but regularly, to ensure this company still belongs in your portfolio.

The Shareowners' Solution: Dr. Bart teaches potential investors to pick well-managed growth companies that are likely to be around for the long term. And he makes it relatively easy. It still takes some time, but we spend a lot of time making money to invest—it makes sense that we would also invest some time making it work for us.

Basically, the CSA teaches people how to use its *Stock Study Guide* to decide if a stock is a great one or not. The guide comes in two formats: (1) a single sheet of paper with a growth chart on the front and space for some simple calculations on the back, and (2) a software program. You can download a demo version of the software at <www.shareowner.com/guide.htm>.

The CSA Evaluation

The CSA's guide to choosing a great stock works as follows:

1. First you review a company's history of growing its revenues; then you make your best judgment about the revenue growth rate during the next five years.

2. Next you review a company's history of growing its *earnings per share* (EPS); then you make your best judgment about the EPS growth rate during the next five years.

3. Next, you review the history of the prices that investors have paid for $1 of the company's EPS; then you make your best judgment about the price that investors will pay for $1 of the company's EPS in five years.

   After you make these judgments (and a couple of easy calculations), the guide identifies the potential reward (i.e., rate of return) from owning the stock during the next five years. Then you make your best judgment about the stock's risk (based on a low price for the stock during the next five years) and compare that risk to the earlier-projected reward. At this point, the guide identifies the stock's "buy," "maybe" and "sell" zones.

Who Knew?

Investors look more closely at a company's earnings per share than at any other financial figure. A business calculates its earnings per share by dividing the company's net earnings by the number of shares outstanding. For example, if a company has net earnings of $100 million, and it has 20 million shares outstanding, then the earnings per share are $5 ($100 million ÷ 20 million = $5).

4. Next, you identify the potential reward (and rate of return) from owning the stock during the next five years.

5. Last, you make your best judgment about the stock's risk (based on a low price for the stock during the next five years) and you compare that risk to the earlier-projected reward.

This software, which costs $99, will actually take you through each of these processes in an amazingly pain-free way, and do all the relevant calculations for you—almost as good as having an automatic transmission.

The CSA makes it crystal clear that they do not provide investment advice, but simply provide education and the tools for Canadians to make their own sound investment decisions. And as "great" as the stocks in their list may be (see Appendix D), you should never ever buy a stock without doing your own analysis of its vices and virtues, but if you insist on doing so, you could do worse than beginning with a list like this one. (As opposed to acting on the advice of your co-worker—who was a Dungeons and Dragons expert in the '80s, an Age of Empires champion in the '90s, and is now an online trader.)

Discount Brokerage Services and Online Trading

In my totally biased view, most people who buy stocks through discount brokerage services are woefully unprepared to do so. Having said that, too many brokers make stock recommendations on the basis of self-interest, flimsy research, and ill-founded attempts at market timing—so, if you're going to buy through a brokerage firm, it makes sense to pay the lowest commissions possible.

Discount brokerage has opened a whole new world to the Canadian investor. If you are going to buy individual stocks, and you're willing to do the research or buy "unbundled" investment advice, discount brokerage services can dramatically reduce your costs. Likewise, discount brokerage services are a first-rate way to buy index funds and put together low-cost bond portfolios.

For a list of major discount brokerages in Canada, see Appendix C.

The Least You Need to Know

➤ Trying to choose the stocks that will do well is challenging—it makes more sense to own a little bit of all the companies on an exchange (through an index fund) than to try and identify those 10 or 15 stocks that are going to do the best.

➤ If you are intent on owning stocks, however, you can't afford to do so without doing research on the underlying companies, and the easiest way to do that is with the tools provided by the Canadian Shareowners Association.

➤ Whatever you invest in, keep your costs low.

Chapter 18

Fixed Income and Investment Esoterica

In This Chapter

➤ Fixed income investments—what they are and the different varieties

➤ How to buy bonds, and what purpose they serve in your investment portfolio

➤ Options, futures, and commodities—the stuff of speculation rather than investment

➤ A brief word on employee options

From the cozy security of fixed-income investments to the wild and woolly frontier of futures and options, this chapter takes you for a dizzy ride. So hang on ...

Fixed Income

Fixed-income investments are the Volvos of the investment world. Reliable, steady, safe. Not too exciting. Unless you're possessed by the Evil Greed Monster, you'll never regret owning fixed-income investments. You can't count on these to fund your retirement by themselves, unless you start very early or are an awesome saver, but they are a fundamentally important part of a diversified portfolio.

Let's take a look at the different types of fixed-income investments available.

Guaranteed Investment Certificates and Term Deposits

Guaranteed investment certificates (GICs) and term deposits are issued by banks and credit unions. Like bonds, which we'll get to later, your GIC is actually a loan you make to the bank. They pay you a stated rate of interest and return the principal to you on the maturity date. The bank or credit union then invests your money and keeps "the spread"—the difference between what they earn and what they pay you. Bank deposits, including GICs, are guaranteed by the Canadian Depository Insurance Corporation (CDIC) for up to $60 000 per account holder per institution; credit union deposits are guaranteed to $100 000 per account holder per institution.

When buying GICs, remember that rates are negotiable. If you are purchasing short- or longer-term GICs in amounts larger than $25 000, your branch probably has the ability to increase the rate by 0.5 to 1 percent over the posted rates. They won't offer if you don't ask. (It helps to shop around and then go in with rates from other institutions—they will probably match a higher rate rather than see you transfer the money.) As deposits are guaranteed, feel free to shop around—often smaller credit unions offer excellent rates even on smaller deposits. If you have access to the Internet, you can find current rates at <www.cannex.com>.

Beware of the gimmicky GICs—you know, the "escalators" or "step ups," the ones that pay 4 percent in the first year, 4.25 percent in the second, and so on. Pick the interest rate in the middle year—that's approximately the rate you'll earn overall. If it's higher than the rate available for a regular term, great; if not, forget it.

GICs are locked in, which means you can't get your hands on the money until the maturity date.

Who Knew?

When interest rates are on their way up, GICs can offer an attractive alternative to bonds as their rates tend to move up with mortgage rates—which increase in anticipation of rising rates.

Beware

If you're buying GICs at smaller financial institutions, be aware that your deposits, including GICs, are only guaranteed to $60 000 (banks) or $100 000 (credit unions) per account holder. In addition, your interest is never guaranteed—only the principal.

Stock-Indexed GICs

Boy, what you can't come up with if your marketing budget is big enough! In an effort to stem the flow of money out of GICs and into mutual funds, Canadian banks have introduced stock-indexed GICs. With these, your principal is guaranteed, and you receive a lower guaranteed rate of return in order to "participate" in the stock market. Using rather complex formulas, you receive a "bonus" based on the performance of a specified index. Your returns are taxed at the highest rate, as income. There's no magic here, and no great deal either.

Bonds

A *bond* is also a loan, but one that is made either to a government or a corporation (called the "issuer"). In return, the issuer provides you with regular interest payments (sometimes referred to as "coupons" because the bond actually comes with interest coupons attached. Prior to the date the interest payment is due, usually every six months, your trustee will submit the coupon for payment on your behalf).

Beware

Perhaps the most common misunderstanding about bonds and bond funds is that they will be worth more if interest rates rise. The opposite is true—bond values go down when interest rates rise, because buyers want the new, higher-rate bonds rather than the old, lower-rate bonds. To take the risk out of bonds, don't buy bond funds and plan to hold government bonds to maturity.

Bond prices go up when interest rates go down, and their prices go down when interest rates go up. This is simply an effect of buyer response—if you can get 5 percent on a new bond, you're not going to buy the old one that pays 4.5 percent, unless you can get it for a discount.

You can purchase bonds from the bond trading or fixed income desk of most brokerage firms. Firms generally buy bonds as "principals"—which means they buy the bonds and sell them to you. (Unlike most equity transactions in which stocks are purchased out of the open market on your behalf.)

Government of Canada Bonds

In 1996, there were $450 billion of Canadian bonds in the market, ranging in maturity from 1 month to 30 years. All Government of Canada bonds pay interest semi-annually and are non-callable, which means the government will never redeem them prior to maturity. Government of Canada bonds, like most modern bonds, are not secured by actual assets but by the "full faith and credit" of the issuer, in this case, the federal government.

Provincial Bonds

As these bonds are backed only by the more restricted taxation powers of the individual provinces, their risk rating is somewhat less attractive and their yields, therefore, somewhat higher. They still offer a high degree of security, and like federal bonds, are usually non-callable.

Tip

Don't confuse *provincial savings bonds* with *provincial bonds*. Savings bonds can be redeemed at a stated date or within a stated period. Regular bonds cannot be redeemed until maturity. Although they can be sold in the bond market, the price will depend on interest rates at the time of the sale.

Corporate Bonds

Corporate bonds are issued by Canada's largest corporations, and their safety rating is by the Canada Bond Rating Agency and other agencies like Standard and Poor's. Corporate bonds may also be

➤ *Convertible* (meaning they can be converted into common stock at a certain date or within a certain period),

➤ *Subordinated* (which means other bond holders get first dibs on any assets if something bad happens), or

➤ *Floating* (this refers to the rate of interest, which is not fixed but "floats" in relation to some other benchmark, usually the performance of the underlying company).

Tip

Most bond desks sell bonds in denominations of $10 000 and upward; savings bonds are available in advertised periods through most financial institutions in denominations of as low as $100, with a usual maximum of $75 000; and GIC minimums are normally $1000 (long term) and $2500 (short term).

Savings Bonds

Issued by the Government of Canada and some provinces, savings bonds come in much smaller denominations than bonds (as low as $100) and are redeemable at stated dates for full principal value.

Canada Savings Bonds are not really ... bonds. They're savings bonds, which are different. For instance, if you own Government of Canada bonds and you wish to sell them, you'll have to do so in the bond market, through a broker. If you wish to "sell" your Canada Savings Bonds, you just have to take them to your nearest bank and have them redeemed for cash. (Wait until the first of the month, when you'll receive interest for the last month—otherwise you'll lose it.) The other thing that is different about savings bonds is that the rates may change during the period you own the bond.

All in all, savings bonds are more like a really good savings account in certificate form than a true bond. These are ideal for your emergency savings money, and your employer may even offer a monthly CSB purchase plan.

Mortgage-Backed Securities (MBSs)

Introduced in Canada in 1986, *mortgage-backed securities* (MBSs) provide investors with a diversified portfolio of high-quality residential first mortgages. These mortgages are "pooled" and then sold to investors in minimum denominations of $5000. The Canada Mortgage and Housing Corporation

Definition

MBSs are **mortgage-backed securities**—sort of a mutual fund of Canada Mortgage and Housing-issued mortgages that pays the investor monthly interest and principal on the outstanding mortgages.

(CMHC), a Government of Canada corporation, insures both principal and interest, as well as guaranteeing the monthly payments. Mortgage-backed securities come in two basic types: pre-payable (or "open"), where the mortgagor (the person that has the mortgage) can prepay principal at any time; and non-pre-payable (or "closed"). Open or pre-payable mortgages create uncertainty of cash flow, and therefore normally provide a higher yield.

Foreign Currency Bonds

Bonds are issued by governments all over the world, and may act as a hedge against devaluation of the Canadian dollar. Foreign bonds generally pay interest annually, and the minimum purchase amount is usually $35 000.

Zero Coupon Bonds

More commonly known as "stripped bonds" or "strips," zero coupon bonds were hugely popular in the late 1980s for RRSP investments. In this case, a bond is separated from its interest coupons, which are sold separately. The bond and coupons are then all sold at discounts from their face value. For instance, a new $100 000, ten-year Government of Canada bond paying 8.75 percent would originally come with 20 semi-annual interest payment coupons valued at $4375 each. The bond itself would have a maturity value of $100 000.

A strip purchaser would buy one of these components at a discount and simply hold it until the maturity or due date.

Strip coupons gained in popularity largely because they can be purchased in small increments and have a wide range of maturity, from one month to 40 years. Like the bonds from which they are stripped, they are issued by federal, provincial, and (occasionally) municipal governments.

Beware

Interest must be declared as income each year, even if it is not received until maturity. Aim to hold your long-term GICs and strip coupons in your RRSP.

Creating a Bond or Fixed-Income Portfolio

Diversification is as important in a bond portfolio as it is in an equity portfolio. Here, however, we look for diversification by

➤ Credit rating (or safety)—a balance of federal, provincial, municipal, and corporate issues,

➤ Maturity dates—holding periods ranging from short to long term, and

➤ If appropriate, by currency.

Bonds vs. Bond Funds

When you purchase a bond, you have the option of eventually selling it in the bond market or holding it to maturity. If interest rates go down, and the value of your bond therefore goes up, you might choose to sell it at a premium—that is, the higher price that a buyer would be willing to pay. If interest rates went up, and no buyer was interested in your bond except at a discount, then you would presumably hold it to maturity. Therefore, your total investment return is not going to be lower than the yield of which you were advised when you purchased the bond.

With a bond fund, you have no control of the underlying maturity dates, and if interest rates go up, your bond fund will go down in value. If bonds are getting beaten up because of a significant rise in interest rates, it is also possible that other fund holders will redeem some or all of their bond fund holdings. In order to access cash to cover these redemptions, the bond fund manager is then forced to sell some of the bond holdings—at a discount. Bond fund returns are not guaranteed; nor are they "fixed." They will fluctuate, generally not as dramatically as equities, but their value can rise and fall.

Yield to Maturity

When buying a fixed income investment, the purchaser is quoted a *yield to maturity*. Although bonds are issued at a stated rate of interest, the secondary market means that the capital value of the bond may fluctuate. Therefore, the yield must then be calculated by incorporating the increase or decrease in the bond's principal price.

Esoterica

Options. Puts, calls, LEAPS. Yikes, we say.

For the advanced investor who likes action, these can either serve as purely speculative plays (you're betting on the price of a particular stock on a future date) or can be used as a "hedge" to protect you from too great a loss if things don't go your way. Either way, these aren't strategies for the faint of heart—and they don't belong in a book on the basics of personal financial planning. If you're intent on moving in this direction, there are a number of good advanced investment books available that can give you the information you need. However, just to give you something interesting to say at cocktail parties if the topic comes up—or if, you lucky dog, your employer has given you options on your company's stock as part of your remuneration package—here are the fundamentals.

Definition

Derivatives are so-called because they derive their value from an underlying security rather than having value in themselves. Options and futures are also referred to as derivatives.

Puts and Calls

Options trade on exchanges just like stock. They come in two formats—*puts*, which enable their owner to sell a certain stock at a stated price within a stated period of time, and *calls*, which allow the owner to "call for" (or buy) a stated stock within a stated period. The price at which you can buy or sell is called the "strike price" or the "exercise price." Remember that options give you the right to buy or sell at a stated price within a stated period—but not the *obligation* to do so. If things don't go your way, you simply let the option expire, and you're only out the amount that you paid for the options themselves.

The attribute that makes options so attractive to speculators is that they can be bought quite cheaply as compared to actually buying and selling the stock on which they're issued.

Don't confuse this with investing. It isn't. It is pure speculation—you are betting that the price of a stock is going up or going down. A lot of speculators do this because they've heard news about a particular company that they believe will drive the stock up or down in price. However, unless you are an insider, in which case this activity is illegal, know that the market is very intelligent—and that thousands of people know what you know. It is very likely that the news is already reflected in the price of the stock, and that the formal announcement is going to have the dead-opposite effect of the one you expect. It happens every day.

The other purpose for buying options is to limit your losses. I'm all for limiting your losses by sticking to sound investment principles and buying and holding a well-diversified portfolio—but hey, if you must walk on the wild side, it can't hurt to take a net. In this case, if you own 1000 shares of Wildhorses.com for which you paid $50 per share, you may want to purchase a put option that allows you to sell them within a three-month period for $40. This will probably cost you a few hundred dollars, but it means that if the price drops to $25, you'll limit your losses to the $10 per share between $50 (the price you paid) and $40 (the strike or exercise price on your option).

You can buy options on the stock of most large index-traded companies, or you can buy options on the entire index—that is, you're betting that the whole index will either go up or down.

LEAPS

LEAPS are "long-term equity anticipation securities"! Unlike options, which have a maximum expiration period, normally nine months, LEAPS are issued with an expiration date of up to three years from issuance. They also cost less and come in smaller denominations—which may be why there aren't as many of them.

Employee Options

These are becoming a far more common part of remuneration packages, particularly in the tech sector—so much so that the 2000 federal budget recognized the need for tax reform.

Employee options are invariably calls—that is, you are given a number of options that allow you to buy your company's stock at a given price within a stated period. With the latest tax change, you no longer have to pay tax on your profits as soon as you exercise your option and buy the stock. As of February 2000, you will only be liable for capital gains tax once you've exercised the options and sold the underlying stock. As long as you hold the stock, your profit is sheltered from tax and can continue to grow.

The danger with employee options is the danger faced by every under-diversified portfolio. Remember that the stock market is an auction, not a store—the price is set according to the popularity of a company with investors, not its underlying value. Therefore, your company may be growing in leaps and bounds, exceeding all its targets—and still find its stock price in the toilet. The good news, of course, is that you didn't pay for the options. Still, tread carefully and don't be afraid to take profits by selling stock that is up in value. The only thing worse than paying tax on capital gains is not having capital gains to pay tax on.

The Least You Need to Know

➤ Buy savings bonds or short-term GICs for your short-term cash needs (anything under three years).

➤ Buy longer-term bonds for your three- to ten-year cash needs.

➤ Bond funds and bonds are not the same thing. Bond funds are riskier.

➤ Advanced "investments" like options and futures aren't really investments at all, but speculative market-timing ploys. If you go there, do so as a hobby—don't put your retirement or family well-being at risk.

➤ Employee options, on the other hand, are a lovely thing—but remember your integral investment principles from Chapter 12 and don't sacrifice portfolio diversification.

Part 5

Family Planning— The Money Kind

I probably don't have to tell you that most married people fight more about money than any other subject.

Well, I have a secret to share with you: It isn't about money. It's about everything we attach to money—self-esteem, security, freedom, choices, our image, control, independence, dependence, fear, love, affection, and our dreams.

To add to this melting pot of highly charged emotion, we tend to be attracted to whatever we are not. If we tend to overspend, we admire and esteem those who pinch pennies. If our greatest pleasure is watching the total in our savings passbook go up, we may find ourselves terribly enchanted with someone who spends "like there's no tomorrow."

Once married to them, of course, we may spend years badgering each other to be more like we are.

The best way to avoid all of this, or as much as possible, is to first know ourselves very well, to communicate our needs and desires clearly, and to approach the business of money partnership consciously, with our eyes wide open.

The next three chapters will focus on how money fits in to our relationships, and how changes in family status can affect our finances.

From "Me" to "Us"

Whether you are currently in a partnership or thinking about entering in to one, make a date with your partner to discuss some of these issues. (Note: I'll use the words "marriage" and "partnership" interchangeably, and mean them both to include common-law and same-sex relationships.)

It is fundamentally important that you treat the occasion as an information-sharing session, not as a debate. We usually believe that our opinions and perceptions are inalienable truths—the reality is that they are simply our opinions and perceptions. We should neither have to defend our right to hold them or convince others to give up their own in order to adopt ours.

The objective in this exercise is to find a process that will honour both partners' dreams, desires, and even foibles, while creating a plan that recognizes your differences and uses your money skills in the most creative way.

Beware

Depending on where you are in your relationship, you may find yourself tempted to simply agree with everything your partner says. If you're doing this exercise because you're going through a rough patch either financially or in your relationship, on the other hand, you may find yourself arguing for the sake of arguing. In either case, write your individual answers down and then come together to discuss them. If your discussion becomes heated and emotions take over, try again another day.

Money Myths and Misunderstandings

Complete the following statements. Take turns going first, allow each partner to finish speaking, and practise "reflective listening" (i.e., summarize what you believe your partner just said back to him or her, and allow your partner time to restate anything you may have missed or misinterpreted).

Beware

Opposites do attract when it comes to money styles. Remember that anger and conflict are an invitation into the pain of your beloved—true intimacy and strong relationships result from staying calm, staying clear, and allowing your partner to express anxiety without making it about you.

1. The thing I hated most about the way my parents were with money when I was growing up was _____.

2. My mom was _____ with money.

3. My dad was _____ with money.

4. When my parents fought about money, it was usually because _____.

5. When I was a child, my greatest fear about money was _____.

6. The most important thing about having enough money to me is _____.

7. The thing that scares me most about not having money is _____.

8. The thing I think it is most important for children to know about money is _____.

9. When I die, I want to leave _____ for _____.

Now discuss your feelings on each of the following subjects:

1. Ethical investing
2. Allowances for children
3. Giving money to adult children for education, to buy a home, or if they are simply in financial difficulty
4. Driving a newer car
5. Saving regularly
6. Vacation spending
7. Riskier investments
8. Life insurance
9. Having to borrow money from family
10. Lending money to family or friends.
11. Expensive gifts
12. Spousal RRSP contributions
13. One partner staying home to look after young children
14. One partner taking a second job to make ends meet
15. How you feel your assets and debts should be divided in the event you separate
16. Child support

Now rate yourselves in each of the following categories below using these ratings:

E = Excellent   C= Competent
I = I'd rather not and probably shouldn't   A = Awful

1. Taking care of the details—recording expenditures, tracking our spending plan, keeping receipts in order.
   Partner A _____ Partner B _____

2. Negotiating—mortgage rates, car prices, commissions, etc.
   Partner A _____ Partner B _____

3. Investment planning—asset allocation, keeping our portfolio well diversified, tracking returns, etc.
   Partner A _____ Partner B _____

4. Communicating with advisors.
   Partner A _____ Partner B _____

5. Controlling spending.
   Partner A _____ Partner B _____

6. Saving.
   Partner A _____ Partner B _____

7. Finding tax breaks.
   Partner A _____ Partner B _____

8. Finding bargains.
   Partner A _____ Partner B _____

9. Avoiding impulse purchases.
   Partner A _____ Partner B _____

10. Keeping track of insurance requirements, terms, and policies.
    Partner A _____ Partner B _____

11. Planning for the future.
    Partner A _____ Partner B _____

12. Getting full enjoyment out of the moment.
    Partner A _____ Partner B _____

You will probably find that you have opposing opinions on a number of things, and complementary abilities—that is, what one of you is good at, the other is awful at. If that isn't the case, you agree on everything and you are good at the same things, you will probably have a low-conflict relationship. You may also need to hire someone with some knowledge of financial planning.

Divide Responsibilities—But Share Knowledge and Decision Making

Once you've clarified your feelings and identified your skill sets, the next objective is to set up a plan that will utilize your strengths while minimizing conflict. For instance, if Partner A is a great saver, while the other is a great bargain hunter (no, they sure aren't the same thing), decide on a monthly savings amount and a spending plan for expenses. Partner A can be in charge of setting up and tracking the savings plan, and Partner B can be allotted the designated amount with which to fulfill lifestyle needs.

Whatever plan you come up with, make sure you do things together—even if one partner is more skilled at communicating with financial advisors, for instance, make sure you both attend the meetings. As some wise (if somewhat sexist) financial planner put it, "Many of the wives of my clients don't care about their husbands' investments, but all the widows do."

By this point, hopefully, you've done all of the exercises in the first section, and you know where you stand financially. Now it's time to decide, as a family unit, on the following:

1. How much will we save and invest each month?

2. Will we have life insurance on each other, and if so, how much?

3. How will we handle it if one of us is unemployed or disabled?

4. Is there anything we should be doing now that we aren't?

5. What are our top three saving/investing priorities?

6. What are our top three spending priorities?

How Will We Handle the Money, Honey?

If you're just coming together as a couple, now is a good time to decide how you will handle the money. Three options are:

1. Keep your money entirely separate, and have one partner in charge of paying joint expenditures (like rent and groceries) and collecting from the other.

2. Create "yours," "mine," and "ours" accounts. Divide common expenses either in half or by a percentage of income, and transfer each partner's contribution to the joint account each payday. If you desire, you can also set up joint savings and investment accounts. Keep a portion of earnings as discretionary spending money.

3. Pool everything.

In between each of these options, of course, are a hundred degrees of blending and keeping separate. Any one of them can work for you if you have a plan set up in advance.

For Married Folks: Spousal RRSPs and Income Splitting

Income splitting is the practice of dividing income-producing assets so that each spouse will be taxed at the lowest possible rate in retirement. Unfortunately, Revenue Canada is fussy about this—you can't just give your partner money and have him or her go out and invest it. If you can't reasonably prove that your spouse earned the money, any income on the investment will be taxed to you no matter whose name it's in.

There are a number of ways to plan your financial affairs well while staying in Revenue Canada's good graces.

Definition

Income splitting *is the practice of arranging income so that both partners are in a lower tax bracket, as opposed to having one partner in a high tax bracket and the other in a very low tax bracket, with no joint benefit.*

The Corporate Spouse

If you own your own business and one partner works at home with hearth and children, hire someone to do some of the household domestic work and have your spouse do paid work within the business instead. If you hire someone to clean your house, your spouse can receive an income (which may be taxed at a lower rate) even if he or she is just cleaning your business offices. Your business can then deduct the cost as an expense. Stupid but true. Likewise, you can't pay a spouse to care for your children, but you can, theoretically, pay him or her to run a company day care that then provides free day care to employees of the company.

One Buys, the Other Invests

Plan your investment buying wisely. The higher income earner should pay for living expenses, allowing the lower income earner to invest his or her income. That way, the investment earnings will be taxed at the lower tax rate.

Tip

Your RRSP contribution room is limited to your allowable contribution whether you contribute to your own or your spouse's RRSP. If you both can't make your maximum contribution, begin by making the contribution to the lower income earner's RRSP out of the income of the higher income earner.

The Spousal RRSP

Then there are spousal RRSP contributions. This simply means that either spouse can contribute to an RRSP owned by the other spouse. Your contribution room does not increase—that is, your total contributions, regular and spousal, cannot exceed your allowable maximum contribution. And once it's in, it's in. It doesn't belong to the contributor anymore, but to the annuitant, the spouse whose name the RRSP is in. You can't transfer it back and forth. If you withdraw the money, it will be taxed in the hands of the contributor for three calendar years following the date of the contribution. After the third calendar year, withdrawals are taxed in the hands of the annuitant.

If one partner is giving up income in order to provide more of the child care or domestic support, a spousal RRSP contribution can be an extremely fair and pragmatic way of showing appreciation.

Juggle Ownership of Assets

Try to arrange ownership so that the higher-earning spouse owns non-income-producing assets, like furniture and the house, and the lower-earning spouse owns the investments. Remember that family and tax law are different—just because one partner "owns" the house in title doesn't mean he or she will be entitled to it if there is a marriage breakdown, and the same is true of any RRSPs or investments. This can even work if one spouse brought family heirlooms into the partnership—by "selling" items of value to the higher-earning spouse, creating a bill of sale, and receiving a cheque, the lower income earner now has money to invest. The income on this investment will, therefore, be taxable in lower-earning spouse's hands.

Honey, Lend Me a Dime

As long as the lower-income-earning spouse pays interest at Revenue Canada's prescribed rate or current commercial rates, the HIE (higher income earner) can provide a loan that is then invested. Interest must be paid, by cheque, by the LIE (lower income earner—an unfortunate acronym) at least annually, by January 30 of any year the loan is outstanding. The LIE can pay the interest with income earned on the investment— but remember, the money must belong to the LIE or the whole thing doesn't work. The interest income to the HIE is taxable to him or her. Obviously, this whole thing only makes sense if the investment will earn income higher than the interest paid.

Pension Time

When it's time to start collecting CPP, ensure that you choose to split both CPP pensions. That is, Spouse A will receive half of Spouse B's pension, and Spouse B will receive half of Spouse A's pension. That way, if Spouse A worked full time for 40 years and Spouse B took 15 years off to raise the children, you'll both still receive and be taxed on the same amount.

The Least You Need to Know

➤ As far as money styles are concerned, opposites attract. Make it work for you rather than against you.

➤ Enhance your relationship by sharing your money stories—not only will it help you understand each other better, but it will make it so much easier to see the inevitable conflict as coming out of childhood issues rather than being about your relationship.

➤ Divide responsibilities, but share information and decision making.

➤ Split income for maximum tax benefits.

Chapter 20

Baby Makes Three

In This Chapter

➤ The financial considerations of having children

➤ Preparing yourself for going from two incomes and no dependants to one income and one dependant

➤ The government programs you need to know about—maternity leave, parental leave, the Child Tax Benefit, and the CESG

➤ The high cost of secondary education and ways to make it a little more manageable

---

Thinking About Having a Child?

My opinion is that if money is a consideration, you're probably not really ready to have a baby. The urge to procreate (and I'm not talking about the early stages here) is a kind of divine madness, and if you're deciding on the basis of whether or not the Visa is paid off, you're not really there yet.

I think there are two great reasons to have a child. One of them is that you're pregnant (or your partner is), and the other is that you'd rather have a child than anything else on earth.

Having said that, know that having a child is the greatest financial sacrifice you will ever make in your life. I have two children, aged 22 and 12 years old. Many of my conversations go like this:

"Do you have your MBA, Lori?"

"No, I have a 22-year-old."

"What's your favourite European city?"

"I don't know. I've never been to Europe—I have children."

"Do you make your maximum RRSP contribution every year, Lori?"

"No, I do contribute what I can, but my children plan on looking after me when I'm old."

Oh, I crack myself up!

Who Knew?

According to the Centre for International Statistics at the Canadian Council for Social Development, it costs approximately $159 927 to raise a boy to age 18 and $158 826 to raise a girl to age 18.

Actually, I'm only half kidding about that last part. Unlike many financial advisors who will tell you that you must put your retirement planning first and your kids' needs second, I believe the opposite is true. That's what families are for—I will do whatever I can to give my kids the best possible start in life, and if I need their help down the road, there is no question they will be there for me. It saddens me a great deal to see how disconnected many families have become, both emotionally and financially: fifty-something parents sit with hundreds of thousands of dollars in interest-bearing investments, while their adult children pay for insurance in order to qualify for a low-equity mortgage; an elderly woman lives alone in poverty, completely out of touch with well-off children and grandchildren.

Let's get back to this business of family planning.

According to the Centre for International Statistics at the Canadian Council for Social Development, as quoted by Ann Douglas in her wonderful book *Family Finance*, it costs approximately $159 927 to raise a boy to age 18 and $158 826 to raise a girl to 18. As Ann notes, however, these statistics don't consider the difference in costs for a second or third child, and perhaps most importantly, are averages. Some parents are spending a lot more on child-rearing and others, by necessity, are spending a lot less.

Whichever way you cut it, though, it's a lot of money—and a lot of personal sacrifice. But like most personal sacrifices of great magnitude, you will find the rewards exceed the price a thousand-fold.

Preparing Financially for Parenthood

As with any life transition, the shift from two to three goes much better with planning and preparation.

After "Will we or won't we?" the second question is probably, "Who will stay home and for how long and can we afford it?" (Yes, that's three questions, but since they invariably are spoken in the same breath I thought I'd do the same.)

It's time to go back to Chapter 2 and revisit your spending plan. No matter how wildly in love you fall with that baby (and you will), you're still going to have to feed it and yourselves. Too many parents get into real financial trouble by just deciding to "do it." As in, "I can't go back to work and leave Emma in day care. We'll just have to find some way to *do it*."

I feel for you, I really do, but having been there myself, I know that if you can't afford diapers and Pablum, you'll find a way to go back to work. On the other hand, "doing it" may very well be possible. It is doing it and maintaining the standard of living you enjoyed with two incomes and no dependants that is not. If you are going to sacrifice income in order to be home with the baby, then you're going to have to sacrifice expenditures, too.

Tip

As soon as you're expecting, begin an accelerated savings plan. Do whatever you have to in order to pay off any consumer debt you may be carrying.

Make a plan. Think about which expenses you can reduce. You won't need work clothes, vacations, travel, or dinners out. Your entertainment budget will probably be restricted to the occasional video and pizza night. Friends and family will understand if you reduce your gift budget.

If it's going to be tight, but manageable, you've come to decision number three—are you going to be a designer parent or a pragmatic parent?

Designer parents shop at the Gap. Pragmatic parents shop at Value Village. Until your little one heads off to school, they don't need new anything unless it is going in their mouth or it's a car seat. Designer parents enroll their budding prodigy in circus camp at $1500 a week; pragmatic parents sign their kids up for Gymboree at the local community centre. You get the picture. Just know this—if you choose to be a designer parent, it's for you, not for them. You might want to save your money until they're teenagers, when it really will matter to them, and you find out that riding lessons are $25 an hour.

Tax Matters

Particularly if you're at the lower end of the income scale, there are a number of government programs that are there to help.

A Little Help from the Government—Maternity and Family Leave

Whether you give birth to or adopt a child, your family is currently entitled to 10 weeks of parental leave, which can be taken by either parent or split between both parents. If you give birth, you are also entitled to 15 weeks of maternity leave, meant to facilitate the physical recovery of the mother after delivery. (If you are ill during pregnancy or are incapacitated due to complications, you may be eligible for an additional 15 weeks of benefits.) Unfortunately, these benefits are not available for the self-employed. In order to qualify, you must have accumulated 700 hours of insurable employment.

Definition

Maternity leave is for biological moms only—this 15-week leave is meant to provide a period in which the mother's body can recover from the stresses of pregnancy and delivery.

During the benefit period, the stay-at-home parent will receive 55 percent of his or her normal employment income to a maximum of $413 a week. (Yes, that's before tax.) In addition, you should know that if your income in the year of parental leave is higher than $48 750, there are significant claw-backs. That's a consideration when you're deciding who's going to stay home-it isn't automatically Mom anymore. Many couples are dividing their parental leave—Mom stays home for the first four months and then Dad takes leave for two months to have some bonding time with the baby while Mom gets back to work. Or vice versa. (The dads are always going to have a harder time with breast-feeding, which is not only important for the health and development of the baby but is much less expensive than formulas.) There is a two-week waiting period before any benefits are received, and if parents split the leave, both must wait two weeks.

There are changes in the works. If the proposed amendments go through as expected, as of December 31, 2000, only 600 hours of insurable employment will be required to qualify for benefits, and the period of parental leave will be extended to 35 weeks from 10. With the 15 weeks of maternal leave, that would provide almost a year (50 weeks) of benefits, and the Canada Labour Code will be amended so that the period of job protection under the parental leave provisions will be the same. In addition, only one two-week waiting period would be applied even if parents decide to split the leave. (Can you imagine the anxiety this is going to cause for parents expecting on or around December 31, 2000? It appears that HRDC is dead serious about this hard and fast time line, too—if your baby is born at 11 p.m. on December 30, you get a total of 35 weeks of combined parental benefit. An hour and one minute later, you're qualified for 50 weeks!)

These changes also allow for a part-time return to work—parents on leave can earn the great sum of $50 or 25 percent of their weekly benefits without any deduction being made from the benefit amount.

Tip

Split your parental leave to provide Dad with some bonding time, too. As long as your little one is expected on December 31, 2000, or later, the waiting period of two weeks will only be applied once. Not only does it make sense from a parenting point of view—it is good economic planning, too, as Mom's employer will get the message that both parents are raising this baby and she can still be counted on to get the job done.

For more information on proposed or current benefits, contact HRDC either by calling the number listed in your blue pages or check out their Web site at <www.hrdc-drhc.gc.ca>.

Child Care Deductions

Some day we will live in a world in which raising children is our single highest priority. In that world, children will be raised by whoever is best at raising them. In the meantime, however, we live in a world in which staying home with our kids is a privilege that many of us cannot afford.

There is at least some financial relief—the child care tax deduction. This deduction must be claimed by the lower-income parent (presumably, the one who would otherwise be staying home). The maximum deduction is $7000 for children under age seven or who are disabled, and $4000 for children aged seven to 16.

The Canadian Child Tax Benefit

This new program provides benefits to lower-income families with children at home. As benefits are calculated using the family income, you'll want to consider this when you're deciding whether or not to stay home and for how long. It can make quite a difference.

The basic benefits are combined with the National Child Benefit Supplement to provide the following:

➤ $85 a month for each child under age 18 (except in Alberta[1]); in addition to

➤ $6.25 a month for your third and each additional child; in addition to

---

[1]In Alberta, the rates are a basic monthly benefit of $77.91 for children under seven; $83.66 for children ages seven to 11; $94.41 for children 12 to 15; and $100.41 for children 16 or 17.

➤ $17.75 a month for each child under the age of seven. (If you have claimed child care expenses, this last amount will be reduced by 25 percent of the amount you or your spouse deducted).

If your net family income is higher than $25 921, the total amount will be reduced by 2.5 percent for a family with one child and by 5 percent for families with more than one child.

Add to these amounts the National Child Benefit Supplement, which provides the following additional benefits to families with net incomes of $20 921 or less. If your net income as a family is more than $20 921, benefits will be reduced by 11.5 percent for a family with one child, 20.1 percent for families with two children, and 27.5 percent for families of three or more children. Maximum monthly benefits are:

➤ $65.41 a month for one child;

➤ $48.75 a month for the second child; and

➤ $42.50 a month for each additional child.

Education Planning

You have a baby, you bring it home from the hospital. And the moment you stop worrying about whether or not the navel is going to heal properly, you start worrying about how you are going to put this beautiful little thing through university.

Who Knew?

Unlike the Canada Price Index, which has averaged an annual increase of just 2 percent over the past ten years, tuition costs have increased an average of 8.7 percent annually across Canada.

We live in interesting times. The Internet truly is revolutionizing the way the world works, in the same way railroads and the automobile did in the last century, the way the printing press did centuries before. We live in the Age of Information. It has been theorized that much of what one learns in a standard MBA program today will be obsolete less than seven years after graduation.

Clearly, our children need tools with which to flourish in this brave new world, and it is our responsibility as parents to provide them with as many of those tools as possible.

Secondary education is transforming from an after-high-school endeavour to one of a lifetime. By the time your children graduate from high school, they may not only be entering the first of a number of degree programs they'll study throughout their lives, but they may do so in a virtual university.

RESPs: What You Need to Know

RESPs (Registered Education Savings Plans) are not new, but 1997 brought a number of significant legislation changes that made these tax-deferral devices more attractive.

These are the answers to some of the questions you may have:

How Much Can I Contribute?

You can contribute up to $4000 per child per year, with a lifetime limit of $42 000 per child.

Who Can Contribute?

Anyone. There is no tax deduction for contributing, so any family member or friend (a godparent, for instance) can contribute to an RESP for any child. The only restriction applies to family plans, in which case all beneficiaries (the children) must be related by blood or adoption to any contributors.

If Contributions Aren't Tax Deductible, How Can They Call This a Tax-Deferral Plan?

RESPs provide a way to shelter investment income within the plan. If I was to deposit $4000 in Canada Savings Bonds for my daughter, for instance, I would have to pay tax on the interest earned every year. If the interest rate was 5 percent, I would have to pay $125 of $250 earned to Revenue Canada. Therefore, that $125 could not be invested on her behalf—it's gone forever. If we earned the same income in an RESP, however, she keeps the entire $250, which is then re-invested, presumably, putting the power of compound returns to work. Later, when she withdraws the income, assuming she has little or no other income at the time, it will be taxable in her hands at the much lower rate.

(Capital gains are always taxed in the hands of the child. Therefore, if you have already taken advantage of the CESG and/or have made the maximum RESP contribution for a given year, you may want to investigate the possibility of opening an "In-Trust" account holding a growth-oriented equity mutual fund. Before opening any trust account, it's a good idea to seek professional advice.)

How Do I Apply for the CESG?

The Canada Education Savings Grant matches 20 percent of contributions made to an RESP to a yearly maximum of $400 and a total lifetime maximum of $7200. If you were to contribute $2000 a year ($167 per month) beginning at the birth of your child to

age 18, the total contribution amount would be $36 000. With the full CESG amount of $7200, and an average annual return of 8 percent, your child's education fund will top the $90 000 mark. If that sounds like a ridiculous amount of money, you may be surprised to hear that economists are predicting that the cost of a university education will be in that ballpark in 18 years. I am more optimistic—I believe that the Internet is going to decrease the cost of education even as our government offloads costs and inflation increases. However, it's better to be safe than sorry. If your child or children don't need all the money for university, there are a number of alternative ways to use it that we'll talk about later.

When you open an RESP, the trustee will require your child's date of birth and Social Insurance Number. To apply for the SIN, pick up an application at the Resources Canada branch nearest you. (You'll need a copy of your child's birth certificate.) Once this information is supplied, the trustee will apply for the grant on your behalf.

Are There Any Age Restrictions?

Yes. Children aged 16 and 17 are only eligible if contributions of at least $100 per year have been made in any four years before the age of 16; or alternatively, if a minimum contribution of at least $2000 has been made prior to age 16.

Is There a Deadline for Contributing?

The deadline for RESP contributions in a calendar year is December 31. You can't currently carry contribution room forward as you may with an RRSP, so if you contribute nothing in 2000, your maximum contribution in 2001 is still $4000. You can, however, carry forward the CESG. If you contribute nothing in 2000, for instance, but contribute $4000 in 2001, the CESG will be $800 (20 percent of $2000 × 2).

What Kind of Investments Can Be Held Within an RESP?

As with an RRSP, qualified investments include mutual funds; segregated funds; GICs; shares listed on a prescribed stock exchange; bonds and other debt obligations issued by governments, Crown corporations, or corporations listed on prescribed stock exchanges.

Who Knew?

Although RESP room can't be carried forward, the CESG can. If you can't contribute anything one year, you can contribute up to $4000 the next, and the CESG will be applied as if you had contributed $2000 in each of two years, for a total grant of $800.

Any RESP investments made prior to October 28, 1998, are considered qualified. As to what kind of investments *should* be held in an RESP, it's important to balance safety with the effects of inflation. A balanced portfolio with both equities and fixed-income investments can be re-allocated toward greater fixed-income investment as the child gets closer to university age.

Is There Anything Else I Should Know About RESPs?

The new RESP and CESG legislation provides much greater flexibility than the old-style RESP, and provides a longer time frame before the plan has to be collapsed—25 years from inception. If you open an RESP for your newborn, it doesn't have to be collapsed until he or she is 25—but there is no reason you can't have more than one RESP, so it may be a good idea to open a new one every five years or so. In that way, if your child doesn't go to university right away, or goes over a longer period of time, you won't have to collapse everything at the same time.

Tip

As each RESP must be collapsed within 25 years of being opened, open a new RESP every five to ten years to extend the length of time the later plans can continue to grow sheltered from tax.

Is Full-Time University Attendance Required?

No. Funds can now be applied to tuition and living expenses required by any post-secondary program, as long as the course is more than 10 hours per week for three weeks.

What Happens If My Child Decides Not to Go to University at All?

If the plan has been open for more than 10 years, and all beneficiaries are over 21 and are not in secondary education programs, you can transfer up to $50 000 to your RRSP, assuming you have contribution room. You can also transfer the RESP plan to another child, or apply the funds to upgrading your own education. Contributions are returned without penalty or taxation, because they were made in after-tax dollars. Since up to $50 000 can be transferred to the contributor's RRSP, ensure that both you and your spouse are shown as contributors. Alternatively, register the child or children as both contributors and beneficiaries, so that they can transfer the income to their RRSPs once they've built up contribution room. (If it isn't applied to secondary education, any CESG will be reclaimed.)

Evelyn Jacks, of the Jacks Institute, recommends this advanced strategy. Rather than naming a parent as contributor and the child as beneficiary, "gift" the money to the child and name the child as both contributor and beneficiary. In that way, if the child doesn't go to university, he or she can use the contributions for a small business venture, for instance, and move the income into an RRSP (assuming the child has built up the contribution room.) The child can then use the RRSP and the Lifelong Learning Plan to fund any post-secondary education programs he or she decides to participate in later in life.

When some clients of mine tried to implement this strategy, they ran into a problem with the RESP trustee. Unfortunately, the account must have an adult on file as the account holder, and many trustees don't have the capacity to record an adult account holder in addition to the beneficiary and contributor. However, this is a administrative issue, and if you keep looking, you'll find a trustee that can accommodate you.

How Do I Open an RESP?

You can purchase an RESP through most financial institutions. Like RRSPs, the kind you buy will depend on the investments you want to put in it. Do set up a monthly automatic purchase plan—you'll be able to take advantage of dollar cost averaging (if you're investing in mutual funds or other equities) and it's so much less painful than trying to come up with lump sums.

Is There Ever a Time When an "In Trust" Account Would Be Better?

Yes. If you're one of those lucky few who can save for your own future and contribute more than $2000 a year to an RESP for your child—don't do it. Well, not unless you want to invest only in interest-bearing investments. Any capital gains are taxed in the hands of your child, who can earn up to $4441 in taxable income (or $6700 in capital gains, which are taxed on only two thirds of the gain) without paying any tax or creating any consequences to you. (Don't do this if you're a single parent and your child is also deemed as equivalent-to-spouse—your credit will be reduced by anything the child earns over $572.)

An "in trust" account can also provide funding for non-educational purposes—the down payment on a first home or a start-up fund for a new business. As well, as long as the money is used by the child for whom it is in trust, there are no restrictions on withdrawals, transfers, and so on.

The Least You Need to Know

➤ Having a child demands a lifestyle change on every level, including the financial one.

➤ Don't attempt to reduce your income while maintaining your expenditures.

➤ Learn the ins and outs of parental and maternity leave as soon as possible—it may provide more time, but way less money, than you are expecting.

➤ If you are in a lower-income bracket, know that the Child Tax Benefit may provide some relief.

➤ Are you a designer parent or a pragmatic parent? If you are the former, know that it's for you, not for the kids—they want your love, not your money.

➤ Our government is slowly but steadily shifting the costs of secondary education onto us—be prepared by taking advantage of the RESP and CESP programs.

Chapter 21

Separation, Divorce, and Single Parenting

In This Chapter

➤ The challenge of separation

➤ Creating a spending plan

➤ Child support

➤ Crisis control

So. It didn't work out. Or it's not working out. Not that it eases the pain at all, but it often doesn't work out, and you may find some comfort in knowing that because it happens so often, there are tried-and-true methods of making things a little easier.

Separation

The way you and your partner handle the situation now will have ramifications on your children, and your finances, for the rest of your life. No matter how hurt, angry, disappointed, and devastated you are, you have the strength and ability to take the high road here.

I have a great deal of experience with both separation and single parenting, and boy, is it tough. That isn't just my opinion or a statement of experience—it's a fact borne out by the statistics. In research conducted by Statistics Canada, lone-parent families headed by women have the lowest income of all family groups, with 52 percent living below Statistics Canada's Low Income Cut-Off line. Believe it or not, 23 percent of all families

Tip

Here's a tip from Gail Vaz Oxlade's *Women of Independent Means*: If you're considering separation, photocopy every financial record you can get your hands on. Gather information on insurance, medical plans, tax returns, investments, etc. This isn't a war, or it shouldn't be—but it will help keep everybody honest and up-front even when pain might cause them to be otherwise.

with children at home fit in this category, meaning that almost 12 percent of Canadian families with children are living in poverty. (Men who head single parent families tend to have higher incomes, although that's no recipe for ease.)

Easing the Pain

Here are a few of things you can do to make the experience easier for everyone involved.

Work Out the Anger

Work out your anger and pain with a counsellor or therapist, not with a lawyer. It may save you a great deal of money in the long run, and counsellors and therapists are better equipped to help.

Put Your Children's Needs First

Child support payments are not for the purpose of making your ex's life more comfortable. They ensure that *your* children's material needs are met and they are not being raised in a household where money problems are making their mom or dad's life unbearable at this already difficult time. If you are the spouse that is leaving the family home, call a family mediator or check on the Internet to find out what you should be paying—and pay it.

Cooperate for Tax-Planning Purposes

If you are dividing up RRSP assets, you will need a written separation agreement or a copy of your divorce decree to effect a tax-free transfer from one spouse to the other.

Your RRSP trustee (the financial institution that manages the funds) can then provide you with the required form T2220.

If you own more than one residence, you'll be pleased to know that you now have two primary residence deductions, too. If you can effect the division of assets so that one residence ends up in each of the ex-spouse's hands, you may have a substantial capital gains saving.

If you have unused RRSP contribution room and non-registered investment assets, think about using them to catch up on contribution room. You'll still divide everything, but you won't have to pay tax on the transfer.

Save on Lawyer Fees

If practical, consider hiring a family mediator rather than two lawyers.

Claim Family Property

Remember that any claim to family property must be made within six years of separation, and that you may be technically separated even if you are living in the same house.

Ask Yourself—"Do I Really Want the House?"

Don't let divorce make you house-poor—the owner of a lovely home with no money to maintain or enjoy it.

Don't assume that keeping the house is the best you can do. Remember that real estate is increasing, on average, about 2 percent per year, while your RRSP investments might be doing much better.

Definition

A **matrimonial home** is ordinarily occupied by the parties to a marriage as their family residence at the time of separation. A married couple may have more than one matrimonial home: a city home, a cottage, a ski chalet, and a condo in Florida can all be, and usually are, matrimonial homes.

Change Your Beneficiary

When it's all settled, don't forget to change your will and any beneficiary designations you may have made on your RRSPs or insurance policies.

Who Knew?

According to Statscan, a women's economic status will decrease, on average, by about 45 percent after divorce, while a man's will improve by about 72 percent. Don't let your children suffer as a result.

On Being a Single Parent

I know that when I was raising my kids in this situation, there is no way I would have bought a book on personal financial planning—or any book at all, for that matter, because books certainly weren't in the budget. I did borrow books from the library, but their titles were more likely to be *How to Make a Halloween Costume Out of Dryer Lint* or *101 Ways to Make a Pound of Hamburger into Six Nutritious Meals.*

In my business as a financial advocate and counsellor for women, however, I am seeing more and more single parents who refuse to suffer in silence, who are seeking help and becoming advocates in their own lives and those of their children.

It Can Happen to You

You never know when you're going to end up being a single parent. I'll never forget when a dear friend said to my sister and me, "I can't wait to have kids. Of course, I'd never do it like you guys, though—I could never be a single parent." My sister and I looked at each other and said in united disbelief, "Do you think we planned this?"

Depending on how you measure it, statistics tell us that between one third and one half of all marriages will fail. If you've been a single parent for a while, you could probably teach me a thing or two about saving money and making ends meet, so you can skip the next section, but if you are new to a one-income family situation, I'm hoping the following might be of help.

Your Life as You Know It Is Over

While your old life may be over, there is no reason the new one can't be better.

With my track record, it doesn't take a rocket scientist to figure out that I'd rather be happily single than unhappily married. Many Canadians, obviously, feel the same way. If you don't have children, the decisions you have to make about whether or not to try and keep working at a relationship that seems to have failed are all about you and your spouse. When you have children, it's a whole different thing.

We've all read the studies about how much better off kids are with two parents, how they do better in school and even in later life. Unfortunately, these studies compare often the children of impoverished single-parent families and the children of the more financially stable two-parent families—some of whom are even happily married.

It seems pretty clear to me that the children of happy parents will do a lot better than the children of parents who are struggling to put Kraft dinner on the table and grieving the loss of their hopes and dreams. What I'd really like to see is a study comparing the health and well-being of children from single-parent homes with that of children from two-parent homes in which the parents are hurling insults and dinner plates at each other—now that would be a study.

I'm going to assume that you're now separated, and your head is spinning. You have no idea how you're going to make it and what you're going to do. Here are some things I wish I had known.

Create a Spending Plan

Free-floating anxiety is terribly draining. Before you fall victim, sit down and figure out what you need to get by and how much income you're earning. (You can use the tables in Chapter 2.) Losing one person from the household may not make that much of a dent in your monthly expenses, but you may be surprised. For instance, when my husband and I separated, he and my teenage stepson moved into their own home. I expected my grocery bill to be approximately half of what it had been—in reality, it dropped by more than two-thirds. On the other hand, my hydro bill never dropped at all.

Even though you may be an emotional wreck (and why wouldn't you be?), this is no time to delude yourself about your financial situation. If you don't have enough income coming in to pay your bills, change is required.

Child Support

If it hasn't been offered yet, don't wait to ask for child support. It doesn't matter if your ex left you for another or if you were caught in bed with the Village People. This money is not for you—it's for your children, and they deserve it. If you are the parent who is no longer in the home, please don't be difficult—yes, you will make your ex suffer, but you are also hurting the ones who need you most right now, your kids. If you are the custodial parent, ask for money for child support from day one.

Who Knew?

Provincial statutes make no restrictions about who may apply for custody of a child. A non-parent merely has to show "sufficient interest" or be "responsible" or have "shown a settled intention to treat the child as a family member" to qualify as a custodial parent.

Table 21-1 shows a dramatically simplified look at the child support requirements for non-custodial parents with incomes between $30 000 and $70 000 in British Columbia.

Table 21-1
Child Support: One Province's Version

Gross Income Level of Non-Custodial Parent	Monthly Payment Required for One Child	Monthly Payment Required for Two Children
$30 000	$266	$446
$40 000	$343	$566
$50 000	$426	$696
$60 000	$501	$816
$70 000	$568	$920

For more information about federal guidelines on child support, you can call the federal government directly at 1-800-343-8282. You can obtain a copy of the most recent version of the guidelines over the Internet at <canada.justice.gc.ca>. You can also get a summary of current child support information at <www.mcbinch.com/family/childsupport/>, the family law Web site of the law firm of McMillan Binch. Or you can contact a family mediator or the Legal Aid Society in your area.

If You're Employed, Ask for a Raise

As a former manager, I can attest to the fact that the least compelling reason for an employer to approve a raise request is because you "need the money." As well, the time before and after a separation is likely to be one in which you are distracted and less productive at work—which makes it unlikely your employer will want to pay you more.

However, don't assume it can't work. It may be that you were due a raise two years ago and just haven't asked for it yet, or that your employer would love to increase your salary but hasn't had time to figure out what a reasonable increase would look like. (See Chapter 5, "Increasing Your Income," for suggestions on asking for a raise.)

Remember, too, that your benefit package may take on much greater significance now. Review it and think about any changes that might be beneficial.

Reduce Your Taxes at Source

When you become a single parent, your tax situation will change dramatically. The Child Tax Benefit, for instance, is based on family income, so when you go from being a two-income to a one-income family, you may very well find yourself receiving benefits you weren't entitled to before. In the meantime though, see your human resources department *immediately* to change the information on your TD1 form.

Your child, or one of your children, is now considered a spousal equivalent, reducing the amount of tax you are required to pay by about $1500 (including both federal and provincial credits). You probably need the money now—once you change your TD1 form, your employer can reduce the amount of tax withheld, increasing your net pay immediately.

Unfortunately, your Child Tax Benefit is based on your income and marital situation of the previous year, so it won't change right away, but be sure to file your income tax return as soon as possible after the year end.

Who Knew?

Adult children have an obligation to pay support to their parents in all provinces but Manitoba, Nova Scotia, Quebec, and Saskatchewan.

Moving to Crisis Control Mode

If you've done your spending plan and find that you do have enough money coming in to cover your expenses, congratulations. You can relax and get on with your new life. Don't relax too much, though—it's so easy to start spending too much, particularly on your kids, out of emotional need. Things like swimming lessons, a new TV to replace the one that moved, a new framed print to replace the wedding photo that was above the fireplace—$100 here and $400 there can add up to a credit problem in no time at all. Too many people go from a zero balance on their credit cards to their limit plus in the two months following separation.

Your lifestyle has changed. Don't be afraid to let go of the things of the past. Luxuries that you took for granted may be something you have to let go of for a while. Instead of going out for dinner, invite your friends over for a potluck. Rather than an expensive lunch out, pack some cheese, bread, and the beverage of your choice in a basket and head to the beach. Settle in for an evening with a rental movie and a big bowl of buttered popcorn rather than going to a theatre.

Deficit Spending?

If you don't have enough money coming in to live on, don't stand around waiting for the wolf to arrive at the door. Take action:

➤ If you owe money, call your creditors, first of all, and let them know that you are separated. Ask for a reduced payment schedule, and/or a month of grace while you get your financial affairs negotiated with your ex.

221

Tip

If you are in really dire straits, remember that you live in the most magnificent country in the world, with some of the best social programs. Remember all that complaining you've done about high taxes? Now it's time to get your money's worth. Call an intake officer at your Family Services Branch (they'll let you know which office to call, and you can find the phone number in the blue pages of your phone book). Tell them what your situation is, and ask if there are any emergency funds available to help. You may be eligible for day care subsidies, income subsidies, low-income housing, free counselling for you and your children, dental or medical expense assistance, and/or money for food. If there is unpaid child support to be collected, they can help you with that too.

Beware

Once you notify your bank that you've separated, the bank may feel legally obligated to freeze any joint accounts, pending receipt of a legal separation agreement. If you aren't at that stage yet, don't mention it.

➤ Cancel all unnecessary services—your cable, extra phone features that might have seemed like a good idea at the time, club memberships you no longer use, and your water cooler rental.

➤ Check your home insurance policy—with half the furnishings now in a different postal zone, you may be able to reduce your coverage. Check your deductibles now, too. You may actually want to decrease your deductibles and pay a bit more for insurance—a $500 replacement bill is a much bigger deal on one income than on two.

➤ If you have family or friends that might be able to help, do them the kindness of at least asking. Let them know that you will understand completely if they don't feel able to help.

Free Fun

Remember, you do deserve comfort, nurturing, relaxation, and good old-fashioned fun. Now is the time to network like you've never networked before. Go for some long walks around your neighbourhood, and look for community recreation centres, parks, museums, art centres, libraries, etc. Cancel the cable. Devote a couple of Saturdays to checking out all of the free or low-cost programs for kids and adults in your area. You'll meet other single parents, have the opportunity to try things you didn't have the time for before, and save money in the process.

If you can, cancel your gym membership, and join a free walking or running club instead.

Avoid Using Your Credit Cards

If you have credit cards, avoid using them. If you are thinking about separating, one of the wisest things you can do is race out and get a credit card in your own name if you don't already have one. Then, once you have the card, whatever you do—don't use it! You'll need it, of course, to help establish yourself as a distinct credit entity, separate from your spouse, but remember that it may be some time before you have more money than you do right now. Starting a new life with the burden of debt is a terrible beginning. I know.

Join, or Form, the Single Parent Paramilitia

When I was an impoverished single mom raising my son, an equal mix of embarrassment and exhaustion kept me from joining my community. Parent teacher interviews were a nightmare, and when I met neighbours and other parents, I said a brief "hello" and kept my head down. My friends were either single or married, but none of them were single with children, and I never felt comfortable talking about "my problems."

Now that my daughter and I are on our own, the richest source of support and joy in my life is my network of friends. These aren't casual friends—we have an unspoken agreement to be there for each other, and for each other's children, whenever needed. That help can range from picking up and delivering Tylenol, magazines, and juice when a bad family flu hits, to driving someone else's child to violin lessons on an early Saturday morning because their car is in the shop.

This great support system, the "single parent paramilitia," provides a deep sense of connection, and the sense of security that comes from knowing there's a community of caring friends looking after our children if ever something happens that means we can't.

The Least You Need to Know

➤ No matter how hurt, angry or devastated you are, take the high road—for your children, and for your long-term financial well-being.

➤ To save a great deal of money, get counselling from a counsellor, not a lawyer.

➤ Ask for, or offer, child support immediately upon separating. Don't make your children suffer.

➤ If ever you needed social programs, now is the time. If you find yourself in financial trouble, don't let false pride stop you from inquiring about social assistance, low-cost housing, or day care assistance.

➤ To reduce anxiety and stay out of trouble, make a spending plan sooner rather than later.

Part 6

Retirement: Will You Be Ready?

Thrift and savings are good things—good for the individual and good for the country. But there should be a balance between the needs of today and the needs of tomorrow. Canadians who believe that they need to save 18% of their earnings each and every year, or that they need to replace 70% of their employment income to escape poverty when they retire, will be unable to achieve such a balance.

—Malcolm P. Hamilton, William M. Mercer Ltd.

Retirement ... what a concept.

At the time when old age pensions and social security were introduced, a time when most North Americans still performed physical labour for a living, retirement was a way of releasing us from years of toil before our aging bodies made it too painful. Much like putting a good horse out to pasture to reward it for its years of service with good food and rest.

Retirement was a stage of life approached with both anticipation (particularly by those who did not enjoy their work) and trepidation—a kind of winding down to death. Then some marketing geniuses got a hold of an idea. What if retirement didn't have to be equated with old age—what if people, just by buying something, could retire while they were still young? What if they could retire when they were young and *wealthy enough to enjoy a luxurious life?*

In the next three chapters, we're going to take a look at retirement planning and all the myths that surround it.

Chapter 22

Preparing for Retirement

In This Chapter

➤ The changing face of retirement

➤ A closer look at the "failing" CPP program

Retirement comes faster than you think. The trouble is, none of us really think about it until it's almost too late. Here's what you could have done, if you'd been thinking, and what to do if you weren't.

Mr. Insurance Guy

Imagine being an insurance salesman in the 1960s. Every day, you go out and call on people, and your pitch is essentially, "You know, you're going to die some day, and you better get ready."

A few years pass, and if you work very hard and make death sound imminent enough, you make a good living. Then, one day, a box of brochures arrives from head office, with photos of beautiful middle-aged people waving from their sailboat.

Suddenly you are not selling death-preparedness but *life—full, rich, deep life*. Freedom 55 had arrived. No wonder it sparked our imagination, our dreams, and ... our wallets. It had to be a pretty wonderful day for Mr. Insurance Guy.

Who Knew?

"If we go by what corresponds to age 65 when social security began in 1936, the proper retirement age is now 79, given life expectancy."

—Peter Drucker, *Fortune Magazine*, September 1998.

Federal Government Plans

In the latter half of the 1950s, a very bright person in our federal government had a brilliant but rather sobering thought. Perhaps he or she had been over at the hospital maternity ward that day and realized just how many babies were being born in Canada.

Who Knew?

Life expectancy in the year 1900 was just 44 years.

In any case, someone realized there were a lot of new Canadians arriving, and just at a time when we were all beginning to live a lot longer. It was clear—something very bad was going to happen if someone didn't start paying attention to retirement planning. We therefore saw the introduction of RRSPs in 1957 and the Canada Pension Plan (almost as we know it) in the mid-1960s.

So far, we've got nothing but good news. Earlier retirements, sound universal government pensions— could it get any better?

Oh, wait—we have to add the last two human ingredients to the melting pot—fear and greed.

What Do You Need to Know About Your Retirement?

First of all, stop worrying. Really.

Over the last two decades, we've been inundated with fear-inducing propaganda about retirement. We've also been inundated with credit card applications and literally millions of advertising images of the "good life."

I'm not going to encourage you to forget that someday you won't be working anymore, and you're still going to need food, shelter, and at least a few of the luxuries we North Americans have come to rely on. We can also plan on living a long time in retirement.

For example, believe it or not, based on actuarial estimates, as a 39-year-old female exercising non-smoker with long-lived ascendants, my life expectancy is over 101 years. Assuming that things go well, if I were to "retire" at age 65, I would have to live on my savings for 36 years—almost as much time as I'd worked. That's the bad news.

The good news is that I "retired" in 1996, at age 35. Since then, I've been self-employed. At the moment, I work out of my beautiful, garden-style office overlooking the sea. I'm a late riser, so I generally return to work for a few hours after dinner, but then I sleep until about 9 a.m. each day. By 10 o'clock, I've signed on to my computer. I'm at work. I should retire from this?

Worry is not helpful.

Dimitri and Christina and Dave and Julie: A Parable

Let me share with you a tale of two households, courtesy of Malcolm Hamilton, an actuary with William M. Mercer Ltd., from an article published in *MoneySense* at <www.moneysense.ca>.

Dimitri and Christina live on a disposable income of $23 900 annually. They have a comfortable life, and travel a bit, taking one big trip every year. They live frugally, of course, but are able to give 10 percent of their income to charity, and they don't worry about retirement—because he's 75 and she's 80.

Dave and Julie, on the other hand, live on a disposable income of $24 200 per year, but they have to support their three children with it. They worry a great deal about their retirement. As a matter of fact, in a profile done on them in *The Financial Post Magazine*, financial planners told them quite baldly that they had to mend their ways or face a bleak retirement.

And Now for the Facts ...

What's unusual about this story? Nothing. Dave, Julie, Dimitri, and Christina are average Canadian citizens, as evidenced by this table published in the same article. These are *average* incomes and statistics for tax filers in 1995:

	Age 25 to 55	**Over 65**
Gross income	$29 200	$23 000
Deductions	(2 900)	(1 000)
Taxes	(7 100)	(3 400)
Net income	$19 200	$18 600

Who Knew?

According to actuary Malcolm Hamilton, government programs like the CPP and OAS are alive and well, and will provide us with enough money to support an austere but not impoverished existence when we hit 65.

Dimitri and Christina earn a total of $23 900 from Canada Pension Plan ($10 000); Old Age Security ($10 000); the Guaranteed Income Supplement ($2600); and various sales, property, and GST credits ($1300). Dave, on the other hand, would be considered a high-income earner, with a salary of $63 400 annually. By the time Dave pays his taxes ($16 300), mortgage and debt payments ($14 500), pension contributions ($6600), and work-related expenses ($1800), he is left with $24 200 to support five people, while Dimitri has $23 900 with which to support two.

I won't moralize here, but I will say this. Stop worrying. Don't buy on credit, contribute to your community, save for retirement, and stop worrying.

Beware

One-third of Canadians still smoke. We eat too much processed food, we work too hard at jobs we hate, we don't get enough sleep, and we exercise too little. It's time to divert our attention from the amassing of wealth and turn it quickly to the creation of health. If we don't, we will face a poverty that cannot be solved with dollars.

Take Care of Your Health and Be Prepared in Case It Fails

If you're concerned about Canada's health care system, or want to ensure a higher level of care than that provided by the government, consider long-term care insurance. The younger and healthier you are, of course, the less expensive it is, and if this is something you worry about, the peace of mind you buy could be a bargain.

In the meantime, know that your quality of life in retirement will be less dependent on how much money you have than on the way you *feel*. If you are chronically worried, smoking, not getting enough exercise, or otherwise not taking care of yourself, all the money in the world isn't going to make up for it.

Beware

Fifty-three percent of elderly women on their own in 1994 had incomes below Statistics Canada's Low-Income Cut-Offs. That rate of poverty was exceeded only by the poverty of women who were single-parent heads of families, of whom more than 56 percent had low incomes.

Find Work You Love

What could you do, now and when you're 75, that you love and that other people would pay you to do?

Financial freedom is not about never having to work again. Rather, it's about never having to work again *solely because you need the money.*

Whether you are 18 or 68, learn how to use computers and the Internet. The world is changing, and changing with it will keep you young, vital, and brimming with valuable skills. If you love gardening, cooking, writing, or fishing, think about ways you can share your talents and passion with other people, and perhaps make a few extra dollars in the process.

Who Knew?

"If there's one thing I agree with Malcolm Hamilton about," says economic consultant Monica Townson, "it's the need for some kind of co-ordinated strategy for the retirement-income system. There's no doubt the changes that have been proposed so far represent a piecemeal attempt to fix up different parts of the system without any concern about how the various elements interact."

North America today is perhaps the most "ageist" society in the world. We've been raised, therefore, in a culture that doesn't value experience or the wisdom of age. We tend to think of our usefulness as something that diminishes as we get older. As baby boomers age, that perspective is changing—if only because there are so very many of us to change it. The generations behind us are smaller, and though our youth should take over the world, in the way it has always been, it will the aging baby boom generation that provides support and services to our peers.

The Best Is Yet to Come

Yes, baby boomers are aging. If you read any of the demographic work done by any of the experts in this area, however, you'll find that though the early baby boomers are now reaching retirement age, the peak of the baby boom didn't occur until 1959. As a matter of fact, with immigration taken into account, there are more people in Canada right now that were born in 1961 than in any other year. That's my birth year—so I know—we are all turning 39.

Anyone older than 39 should be celebrating at this news. Because at age 39, statistically, my cohort and I are just now entering our most productive income-earning years. That's the largest segment of the population, earning the most money they'll ever earn. Barring a significant economic depression, we will pump more income tax dollars into the coffers of this nation in the next 15 to 20 years than has been seen in the history of the country.

The Canada Pension Plan: Is It on Its Last Legs?

The Canada Pension Plan is a self-funding program, which means there is no huge pool of money somewhere, out of which benefits are paid, that is getting low. Instead, CPP is funded by the premiums it collects.

Beware

If the Canada Pension Plan is under threat, it is not the threat of inadequate funding but the threat of misinformation.

If we all stopped paying our premiums today, CPP would run out of money within two or three years. The chances of us not paying our premiums, however, are pretty slim—we all look forward to receiving our pension in retirement, and the only real beneficiaries of the end of CPP would be our corporations (and their shareholders) who currently pay 50 percent of CPP benefits as employers.

Of course, the wealthiest members of our society could also divert their premiums from the public pension plan into richer private ones. In the meantime, the collapse of CPP would be devastating for the less prosperous segments of society. Luckily, unless Canadians get a lot dopier than they are, the CPP will continue, because we still have the power of the vote.

Does all this mean you can stop saving for retirement? No.

First of all, you should probably reconsider your concept of retirement. The workplace of the future may look suspiciously like your den—because it is your den. Over the last century, we have transformed from a society of labourers into a society of which it's been said that "the assets of our corporations walk out the doors each night in the heads of employees."

Now we are beginning to make the transition from corporate drones who must be supervised in cubicles in order to be made productive, to entrepreneurial contractors who are paid by the project to do work we love and are naturally talented at. Education is quickly becoming a lifetime endeavour.

When Will It All End?

Let's face it. We're not all going to be retiring at age 55, or even at 60. We won't be able to afford it anymore than we can afford to take a year or two off work now. However, over the next 25 years, we have every reason to believe that our quality of life will improve as the "time bind" is eased. Many of us will continue working well beyond what's popularly considered to be "retirement age."

Before you pick up the phone to cancel your monthly RRSP contribution, however, give some thought to exactly how many projects you'll want to take on in your 70s, 80s, and 90s—and how much competition there's going to be from younger generations.

In addition, know that the maximum CPP benefit (100 percent at age 65) for the year 2000 is $762.92. Whether you own your own home or not, that's not a lot of money to live on. My point is not that we shouldn't save and invest—my point is that we should stop worrying about it and start doing it. Fear isn't helpful.

The Least You Need to Know

➤ Think deeply about what you want your retirement to look like—it doesn't have to be about eternal sloth. If you have work you love, find ways to continue doing it at a reduced pace.

➤ CPP is only going to fail if we let it fail. Let's not.

RRSPs: What the Heck Are They?

People say they invest in their RRSP, but they really don't. They invest within it. Sound confusing? Wait till you read the rest of this chapter.

RRSPs: The Basics

An RRSP is a tax-deferral plan. Got it?

When you contribute money to an RRSP (within limits designed to keep people with too much money from tax-sheltering gobs of it), Revenue Canada says something like, "Later, dude." Though you earned the money this year, you don't have to pay tax on it until you withdraw it from the plan. That way, instead of earning, say, 10 percent on $5000 after tax, you get to earn 10 percent on $10 000 un-ravaged by tax.

Instead of paying up to 52 percent of the income you earn on the investment, you get to keep that too, allowing the magic of compound interest to do its work. When you finally withdraw the money from the plan, you're required to pay tax at the applicable rate for that year.

Things You Need to Know About Your RRSP

First, let me get one of my pet peeves off my chest. Your retirement plan and your RRSP investment are two different things—so no need to get all anxious about deciding where to invest during RRSP season. Just contribute—and decide in March or April, when you've had time to do the research.

I can't tell you how many people have told me they "invest in RRSPs." No, you don't. An RRSP is not an investment alternative, and if you're just dumping money into an "RRSP" at your bank or credit union, you are probably earning a sadly ridiculous rate of return.

Remember, you *contribute* to an RRSP; you *invest in* stocks, bonds, mutual funds, and so on. And while I'm griping, what are you doing contributing in February anyway? Get on a monthly automatic debit plan! Work dollar cost averaging into your investments, have your withholding tax reduced by your employer, never again worry about coming up with the money in RRSP season, never again stand in an RRSP line-up or deal with stressed-out financial professionals—and you can start sheltering the income on your RRSP investments earlier.

Definition

A **put option** allows the holder to sell a stock at a prescribed price within a stated time period; a **call option** allows the holder to buy a stock at a prescribed price within a stated time period.

Qualified RRSP Investments and Types of Plans

There are some investments you can hold in an RRSP or RRIF (we'll talk more about that in Chapter 24) and some things you can't. Some things make sense; some things don't.

For instance, you can't hold collectibles—art, antiques, or coins. You can't hold foreign currency. You can't hold real estate, except within a real estate investment fund (REIF) or real estate investment trust (REIT). You can hold some options (puts) but you can't hold others (calls).

Holding Your Mortgage in Your RRSP

One of the most appealing RRSP investment possibilities is that of holding one's own mortgage. The bad news is that it normally isn't a good idea.

Although Revenue Canada will allow you to invest your entire RRSP in ABC Moosepasture Mining stock, they're worried that you'll issue yourself a mortgage and then decide not to pay it back. That is, you'll take your money out of the RRSP without paying tax on it. ("Better to let them lose it all," they say.)

Therefore, if you choose to do so, you must first pay to have the mortgage insured by the Canada Mortgage and Housing Corporation, which costs anywhere from 0.5 to 4.25 percent of the entire mortgage. Then you have to have an appraisal done, and the mortgage itself has to be administered by an approved lender, generally one of Canada's banks or credit unions. You have to have a self-directed RRSP, and you'll pay an annual fee for the RRSP (usually about $125) and an additional fee for the administration of the mortgage (between $150 and $300 per year). Add on the cost of having the mortgage documents prepared by a lawyer or notary, and you've got a costly venture.

If you're thinking about this option, be sure to have a trust administrator at the financial institution calculate all of the costs you'll have over the period of the mortgage. It sounds awfully good, but you may find that you're paying $2000 or more for something that has only emotional benefits. After all, it's nice to pay yourself interest, but is it really any different from paying someone else interest and earning even better returns on other investments?

Kinds of RRSPs

There are essentially three kinds of RRSPs:

1. Managed RRSPs
2. Mutual fund RRSPs
3. Self-directed RRSPs

Managed RRSPs

If you have a managed RRSP, someone else decides where your contributions will be invested, and pays you interest on your deposits. The most common managed RRSPs are GICs and RRSP savings accounts issued by banks and credit unions.

Although you don't usually have to pay a fee for this kind of account, the financial institution does get paid by keeping whatever the difference is between what they earn investing your money and whatever it is they've agreed to pay you.

Mutual Fund RRSPs

With a mutual fund RRSP, you choose a mutual fund company, and then decide which of their funds you wish to invest in. Your contributions then become part of the mutual fund pool, and you participate in the mutual fund's profits or losses.

Until a few years ago, mutual fund RRSPs generally charged a fee in the range of $25 a year. Then someone caught on that doing so wasn't good for business. Now, RRSP clients generally pay only the same management expense costs that non-registered investors do. Remember, these RRSPs don't come with guarantees.

Self-Directed RRSPs

Entirely different from the two options previously mentioned, a self-directed RRSP is more like a closet that you can hang any qualified investment in.

The financial institution administering your RRSP does not share in your investment profits, so it charges an annual administration fee, generally in the area of $125 a year.

The benefits to you are flexibility (a much broader range of investments to choose from) and consolidation (having all of your RRSP investments at one institution, on one statement). In this way, you can move from one investment to another without having to actually transfer sums of cash from institution to institution. This is important, because it can take weeks to transfer from one RRSP plan to another.

Moreover, because the foreign content is limited to 25 percent of the book value of any particular plan (30 percent as of 2001) rather than all of your RRSPs cumulatively, a self-directed plan allows you to maximize your global investments if you so choose.

If you have more than three different RRSP accounts adding up to a total of more than $25 000, you may wish to consider a self-directed plan. Remember, with a self-directed plan, no one will make decisions for you, so you must either be a knowledgeable investor with time on your hands or have a financial advisor to assist you.

Definition

Book value is the price you paid, plus any re-invested dividends, or the price of your assets at the time you transferred them into the RRSP plus any re-invested dividends.

Market value is the current value of your assets.

Definition

For most Canadians, **earned income** is their gross salary from their job, before any deductions like income tax or Employment Insurance. If you make $40 000 a year from your job and have no other income, your earned income is $40 000.

Go for It

Every Canadian citizen with earned income should be contributing as much as possible to an RRSP. Otherwise, not only are you not saving for the future as effectively as possible, you're also paying more tax than you have to.

Even if you're in the lowest tax bracket, a $1000 contribution only costs you $740—$260 of your investment would otherwise go into the coffers of Revenue Canada. Someday, you'll have to pay that tax, but in the meantime, it's working for your benefit, not your government's.

Who Knew?

If I contributed $200 a month to an RRSP from age 39 to age 69, earned 10 percent per year on my investments, and had an effective tax rate of 40 percent, I would have a nest egg of $452 100 when I retire. If I do the same thing outside of an RRSP, I will have just $200 900.

Tip

If you are in a low income bracket but can afford to contribute to an RRSP, you may want to do so but delay claiming your deduction until your income increases. That way, the RRSP income will be sheltered from tax, compounding magic will be working on your behalf, and when your income increases, your deduction will be worth more in your pocket.

Tip

If you're one of those very lucky people who has more than $300 000 in your RRSP prior to age 55, consider hiring a fee-for-service financial planner from a reputable firm to create a retirement plan for you. At this point, there are advanced strategies that may make it advisable for you to focus on non-registered investment.

Figure 23-1 illustrates the benefits of investing inside an RRSP as opposed to outside one.

Figure 23-1
$5000 Invested Annually over 25 Years at a 10% Return

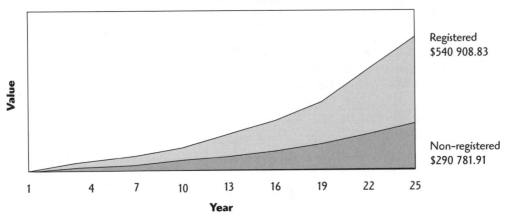

When Should I Contribute?

Unless you just happened to flip the book open at this page, you know the answer to this one—set up a pre-authorized purchase plan and contribute monthly. Not only is it the most convenient way to contribute, not only will you reap the benefits of dollar cost averaging—but you won't have to scramble around in late February arranging a loan for next year.

If you have the contribution room, consider topping up your RRSP whenever you stumble across "found" money—an inheritance, a bonus, or just a raise you weren't expecting.

Waiting until RRSP season, obviously, is the least effective method of contributing.

Contribute Early, Contribute in Kind

If you're one of the blessed few who have money actually lying around on January 1, consider contributing for that calendar year to shelter an additional 14 months of income. (But I realize that the chances of having money lying around after Christmas are about as great as those of me hooking up with Kevin Costner.) Figure 23-2 shows how 25 years of $5000 RRSP contributions at a 10 percent return can add up to different amounts depending on whether the money is invested at the beginning of the year, monthly, or as a year-end contribution.

Figure 23-2
Benefits of Early RRSP Contributions

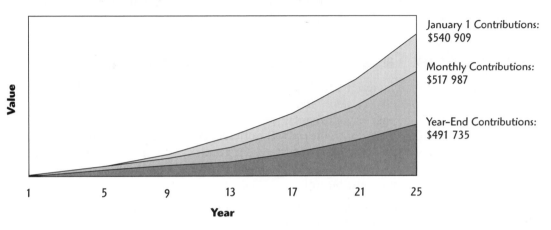

January 1 Contributions:
$540 909

Monthly Contributions:
$517 987

Year-End Contributions:
$491 735

However, if you have non-registered investments such as Canada Savings Bonds from your payroll savings plan or non-registered mutual funds, you can make an "in-kind" contribution in January and shelter the income on those investments for the whole year. ("In-kind" means that you contribute the asset itself, and receive a contribution receipt for the market value of the asset at the date of contribution, as opposed to an equivalent amount in cash.) If you are in a 50 percent tax bracket, for instance, and make a contribution of a $10 000 bond earning 5 percent in interest income, you'll save yourself a tax bill of $250 in just one year. Funky!

Beware

Another example of Revenue Canada weirdness here: if you make a contribution "in kind," it will be treated as a "deemed disposition" of the asset, as if it had been sold, and you will have to pay tax on any gain. If there has been a loss, however, according to Revenue Canada, it disappears. You aren't allowed to use it. Don't contribute assets, therefore, on which there has been a capital loss that you could otherwise use against capital gains income.

Two-hundred-and-fifty dollars should be enough of an incentive, but just in case it isn't, let's see how early contribution can add to returns over the long term. If you contribute $1000 a year for 30 years at 10 percent, you will earn an additional $6730. Even with inflation, I can't help but think that would buy a very nice holiday in Maui.

Reduce Your Taxes at Source—Employer Direct

If you are one of the many in a high tax bracket who still can't seem to find money to contribute to your RRSP, consider reducing your taxes at source by having your employer contribute part of your regular salary and/or all bonuses directly to an RRSP. That way, a $10 000 RRSP contribution will only reduce your take-home pay by $5000, a much more livable amount. Alternatively, if your employer doesn't want to play, simply make an application to Revenue Canada to have your taxes reduced at source by providing proof of your contribution.

Bottom line? The only time you should be making your RRSP contribution in January or February is when you are contributing for that calendar year, when you've received money for Christmas and want to top up last year's contribution, or when you have to borrow to contribute.

RRSP Loans—One of the Few Times It's Smart to Borrow

If you don't have the money to contribute to an RRSP, but have contribution room, taxable income, and adequate cash flow to make the payments, seriously consider an RRSP loan. It can change your life—many people I know, including myself, actually became real savers when we became borrowers. If you find it impossible to stick to a savings plan, you may find it easier to stick to a loan repayment plan and start moving in the right direction.

Shop around for the lowest rate—if you are contributing to an RRSP GIC plan, you shouldn't pay more than prime. (As I write, the prime lending rate is 7.5 percent.) Therefore, a $5000 RRSP loan would cost $375 in interest over the year, but the term it goes into should earn about 5 percent (for a one year term) or $250, meaning that the real cost of borrowing is only $125. If you're in the top tax bracket, you can expect a refund of $2500. All in all, a pretty fabulous deal. Even if you're in a 26 percent tax bracket, you are still creating a tax savings of $1300.

Most financial institutions will tell you what you can expect as a refund and then say something like "which you can then use to pay down your RRSP loan." Don't be so hasty. If you have outstanding credit card bills or other consumer debt, don't pay down your 7.5 percent RRSP loan and continue paying 18 percent interest on your Visa. Instead, apply your refund to your credit card. A caveat: If you're just going to run out and charge up a new Visa bill, don't bother. Pay down the RRSP loan, take your lumps, and continue to pay 18 percent.

One other warning—remember your loan payments. Too many people have no idea where their money goes, so they add up rent, hydro, what they think they spend on groceries, and assume the rest is available for loan payments. Well, if that were true, the money would be in your chequing account, wouldn't it? You've been spending your money on something, and it is a *huge* mistake to take on loan payments and then start charging living expenses on your credit cards.

Lifelong Learning Plan

The Lifelong Learning Plan is a relatively new program that allows RRSP holders to withdraw up to $20 000 from their RRSP plans to upgrade their education. To be eligible, you and/or your spouse must be enrolled full-time (or part-time for students who are disabled) in a qualifying program of at least three months in duration. The limit is $10 000 per year to a maximum of $20 000 over four years. Repayment required is 1/10 per year beginning in the sixth calendar year following the first withdrawal (2006 for those withdrawing in 2000), or the second consecutive year in which the student is not qualified to claim the education credit. Similar to the Home Buyer's Plan, any repayment not made as required must be declared as income for the year the payment was due.

Home Buyer's Plan

This plan allows RRSP holders to withdraw up to $20 000 from their RRSP to purchase a new home. In order to qualify, you cannot have lived in a home owned by yourself or your spouse for the past four calendar years (except for the 31 days prior to your withdrawal.) Therefore, if you were to make a withdrawal in the year 2000, you could not have lived in a home you owned after January 1, 1996. If you quality, each spouse can withdraw up to $20 000, with repayments of 1/15 per year required beginning in the third calendar year. For a year 2000 withdrawal, the first 1/15 would be due by March 1, 2003, for inclusion on your 2002 tax return.

Whether or not you avail yourself of these programs should really come down to a calculation of the costs of early withdrawal from your RRSP. Unfortunately, you and I both know that if you decide you need to upgrade your education or buy a home, a dollars-and-cents calculation is going to make a difference to about one in 100 of you. The rest of you are going to make the decision on the basis of "but that is where my money is and I need it." All the power to you. I have very mixed feelings about the home purchase, because a home is not going to make very much money for you to make up for the lost compound growth in your RRSP. An education, on the other hand, may.

Just so that you know, however—if you withdraw $20 000 from an RRSP earning 9 percent annually, and pay back the minimum amount each year over 15 years, and your RRSP continues to grow for 35 years following the withdrawal, it will cost you $173 477.82 in lost returns.

Contributions, Over-Contributions, Carry-Forwards, PAs, and PARs

The easiest way to figure out how much you can contribute to your RRSP is to dig up last year's tax assessment (the one that Revenue Canada sent you after you filed your return) and check out the number in the allowable RRSP contribution room box. This will also show you what your pension adjustment (PA) is, if you have any pension adjustment re-adjustment room as a result of leaving a pension plan, and if you have any Home Buyer's or Lifelong Learning repayments due. If you can't find your assessment, you can call the Revenue Canada hotline in your area.

At the moment, if you don't use all or any of allowable your RRSP contribution room, you can carry it forward indefinitely. Obviously, it is a better idea not to, but if you don't have the money, and can't afford RRSP loan payments, take comfort from the idea that you'll have lots of room when things turn around for you.

Your pension adjustment, if any, reflects the benefits of any company pension plan you belong to. If you leave that company, losing your pension benefits, you will now get a Pension Adjustment Reversal statement, or PAR, that gives you back some of the lost contribution room.

If you are over 18, have the money or investments lying around, and plan to leave it within your RRSP for at least 10 years, consider over-contributing. You are allowed to over-contribute up to $2000 without penalty; after that, it gets ugly, and you are charged a penalty tax of 1 percent per month on any excess.

The maximum RRSP contributions for the years 1999 to 2006 are as follows:

Year	Maximum RRSP Contributions
1999–2003	18% of earned income from prior year to a maximum of $13 500
2004	18% of earned income from prior year to a maximum of $14 500
2005	18% of earned income from prior year to a maximum of $15 500
2006	Indexed to inflation ($15 500 plus the rate of inflation)

Who Knew?

Here is a list of income that is defined as "earned" for the sake of calculating "earned income":

➤ Employment income

➤ Self-employment income after expenses and losses

➤ Rental income after expenses and losses

➤ Alimony

➤ Royalties

The following are not considered earned income:

➤ Investment income

➤ Pension income

➤ RRSP or RRIF income

Taking Money Out

When you withdraw money from your RRSP, you are robbing yourself of the benefits of tax-free compounding returns. However, sometimes necessity prevails, and an RRSP can also be an unemployment insurance policy. (Just make sure you seriously beef up your contributions when you get back to work!)

If you need to take money out, know that the withdrawals will be fully taxable as income—after all, you got a break on taxes when it went in, and you can't have it both ways. In addition, tax will be withheld by your trustee. This isn't a penalty, but rather, a prepayment, or installment, of tax you will owe on the income.

The withholding tax rates for RRSP withdrawals are as follows:

Amount	All Provinces Except Quebec	Quebec
Up to $5000	10%	25%
$5000.01 to $15 000	20%	33%
$15 000.01 and above	30%	38%

A popular strategy to minimize withholding tax has been to request three withdrawals, for instance, of $5000, rather than one of $15 000. If you need the money badly enough to take it out of your RRSP, this is a very bad idea. You are far too likely to end up owing a big ugly lump of tax in April—and have no money to pay it with. Withholding tax is a good idea. Go with it.

The Least You Need to Know

➤ Let the government participate in your financial well-being—contribute as much as you can to your RRSP.

➤ Your own mortgage may not be a cost-effective RRSP investment.

➤ Think before withdrawing money from your RRSP for any purpose.

Retirement Planning— Beyond RRSPs

If you have a steady job, you likely have a pension plan. Here's how it works, along with other plans that you might know even less about.

Registered Pension Plans

According to Statscan, just over 5 000 000 Canadians belonged to registered pension plans in 1998. Of these, 636 408 were *defined contribution plans* (in which the amount of money contributed is known but the amount of benefits to be received is not), and 4 372 867 were in *defined benefit plans* (in which the benefit is known).

If you are lucky enough to belong to a pension plan, chances are very good you'll have to contribute too, generally in the range of 5 to 10 percent of your earnings. In these days of transient employment, it is important to know that you generally can't take your pension plan with you when you go. Check with your employer to see how much of your pension is vested (that is, how much you can take with you when you go, as opposed to having it reclaimed by your employer if you leave).

Definition

A **defined contribution** plan (also known as a **money purchase plan**) is one in which only the contribution amounts are known. These are much more like an RRSP—the ultimate benefits received will be decided by both the amount of money contributed and by the returns achieved on the investments made.

If you change employers, you're usually obligated to move your vested pension funds into a locked-in retirement account (LIRA). You'll also receive what's called a pension adjustment (PA)—that is, you'll be allowed to contribute more to your RRSP to make up for the benefits that were lost to you upon leaving.

On retirement, on the other hand, you have a couple of options. You can have your pension converted into a locked-in RRIF, for example, or you can purchase an annuity.

Let's take a look at the differences between defined benefit and defined contribution plans.

Defined Benefit Plans

A defined benefit plan may be "contributory" (you contribute as well as your employer) or non-contributory (your employer pays the full shot—shockingly, these are not nearly as common).

In return for your years of service, your employer (or their pension trustee) arranges for you to receive income benefits in retirement. The amount that you receive is determined by a prescribed formula that considers your income throughout employment and the number of years of employment. For example, your pension may have an accrual rate of 2 percent. If you worked for your employer for 25 years, and your average earnings during the measured period (often an average of the last five years, or the highest five years) was $40 000, your annual benefit would be

$40 000 × 2% × 25 = $20 000

After finding out what your benefits will be, you need to know if your pension is integrated to CPP (very bad thing—it simply means you receive your pension minus whatever you receive from CPP) and whether it is indexed to inflation. Obviously, a plan that is indexed is worth significantly more than one that isn't, particularly if you plan to be long lived.

According to federal tax rules, defined pension plans can't pay more than $1722.22 for each year of employment.

Defined Contribution Plans

With a defined contribution plan, you have no idea what you're going to receive when you retire. Your employer contributes a certain percentage of your income, you probably match it, and then you generally get to decide what kinds of investments will be made with the funds. The performance of the underlying investments will determine how much money there is at retirement.

Beware

Check to see if your pension plan benefits will be "integrated" to CPP. If they are, you will receive your benefit *minus* your CPP benefits.

A defined contribution plan shifts the risk of poor investment performance from the employer to the employee. If investments don't do well within a defined benefit plan, the employer is going to have to contribute more in order to ensure you get the promised benefits. In a defined contribution plan, if the investments don't do well, you are going to have to tighten your belt—the employer is off the hook.

Deferred Profit Sharing Plans (DPSP)

A deferred profit sharing plan is different from a pension plan in that you can't contribute and your employer doesn't have to if profits are down in a particular year. Therefore, these are great to have, but think of them more as a tax-sheltered bonus plan rather than a retirement plan.

A DPSP must be paid out to the employee (or in the case of death, to the employee's estate) within 90 days of termination of employment. However, this payment can be made in equal annual or monthly payments over a maximum period of ten years, or used to purchase an annuity beginning on or before age 71, for 15 years or less.

Withdrawals from DPSPs are otherwise treated as normal employment income, unless they are transferred to an RRSP or other registered plan.

See Appendix E for a list of every Revenue Canada form and publication on retirement planning. You can drop by your nearest Revenue Canada office, give them a call at the number listed in your blue pages, or even download the forms from the CCRA site at <www.ccra-adrc.gc.ca>.

Tip

If you leave your employer, be sure to take advantage of your pension adjustment reversal if you have non-registered investments. You can contribute them "in kind" to your RRSP.

When It's Better to Invest Outside of Your RRSP

Most of us don't have to worry about this too much. However, if you're one of the lucky few who expects your annual income to be more than $53 215 in retirement, you are facing claw-backs—that is, the government is going to give you the Old Age Supplement and then take it back at tax time. Anything you take out of an RRSP or RRIF is counted as income.

As a result of the benefits of tax-sheltered compound returns, RRSPs are almost always a good thing—unless you're going to be in a higher tax bracket in retirement than you are today.

The higher you expect your income to be in retirement, the more important it is to get quality financial planning help—and the earlier the better. Remember, advice is usually worth what you pay for it, and paying sales commissions isn't the same as paying for advice. See a fee-for-service financial advisor with a reputable fee-for-service planning firm, not an investment firm.

It may be that you will be better off keeping your investment dollars outside of a registered plan so that you have the opportunity to generate tax-advantaged income (like dividends or capital gains).

Your Retirement Income

Okay. The party's over. Now you get to retire, and start living on all that money you worked so hard to collect.

First, let's decide what to do with your RRSP. You have three maturity options:

1. You can cash in the whole thing and pay tax on it. Whatever you do, don't do this.
2. You can buy an annuity.
3. You can set up a RRIF (Registered Retirement Income Fund).

Ignore the first one. It isn't really an option—unless you love paying income tax.

Once you buy an annuity, your choice is made for the rest of your life. One of the benefits of opening a RRIF, on the other hand, is that you can always buy an annuity later. As a matter of fact, after working with many retirees in their late 70s and early 80s, I believe that an annuity has much to recommend it in later years of retirement, particularly if health and energy are failing.

What Exactly Is an Annuity?

An annuity is a contract between you and the institution who writes the annuity contract. There are essentially two types of annuities—life annuities (which are issued by insurance companies) and term annuities (which are issued by both life insurance companies and other financial institutions). With a life annuity, as the name implies, payments are guaranteed for the life of the annuitant (that's you). A term annuity, also known as a "term-certain" annuity, comes with a guaranteed payment term, to age 90, for instance. If you were to die before age 90, the balance of the payments would be converted into a lump sum and paid to your estate.

Choosing an Annuity

Other choices to make when purchasing an annuity include the following:

Single or Joint Annuity

If you purchase a single annuity contract, the payments are calculated on the basis of your age and life expectancy, and the payments are guaranteed for your lifetime. (A good deal if you live for another 40 years, bad deal if you live for another 40 days). Much more popular are joint and last survivor annuities, which are purchased in the name of the annuitant and another party, generally the annuitant's spouse. Payments are then paid until the death of the second spouse, although they are reduced after the death of the first.

Guarantee Period

If you have no family to leave behind, you don't have to worry about this one. If you do, however, it may be important to you, but know that the longer the guarantee period, the smaller the payments. In the case of a single life annuity, however, this guarantee ensures that your estate will receive the equivalent of payments for a specified term (usually 5, 10, or 15 years) in the result of your early demise.

Indexing

Payments from an indexed annuity increase to help offset inflation, usually to a maximum of 4 percent per year.

Benefits of Annuities

The good news is that you know what you'll be getting. The bad news is that you have no idea how much it will be worth.

Annuities can work particularly well for those whose health does not allow them to actively manage their financial affairs. As well, where there are sufficient assets, purchasing an annuity with part of your retirement income can provide a no-stress stream of income while the balance of your assets continue to generate returns.

The Popular Choice—RRIFs

The benefit of a RRIF is that you retain the ability to manage your money and invest in a diversified portfolio of qualified holdings.

Kinds of RRIFs

RRIFs come in the same shapes and sizes as RRSPs:

1. Managed RRIFs
2. Mutual fund RRIFs
3. Self-directed RRIFs

Managed RRIFs

With a managed RRIF, someone else decides where your contributions will be invested, and pays you interest on your deposits. The most common managed RRIFs are GICs and RRIF savings accounts issued by banks and credit unions. Although you don't usually pay a fee for this kind of account, the financial institution does get paid by keeping whatever the difference is between what they earn investing your money and whatever they've agreed to pay you.

Mutual Fund RRIFs

With a mutual fund RRIF, you choose a mutual fund company, and then decide which of their funds you want to invest in. Your contributions then become part of the mutual fund pool, and you participate in the mutual funds' profits or losses. Remember, these RRIFs don't come with guarantees.

Self-Directed RRIFs

Entirely different from the two options above, a self-directed RRIF is more like a closet that you can hang any qualified investment in. The financial institution administering your RRIF does not share in your investment profits, so they charge an annual administration fee, generally in the area of $125 a year. The benefit to you is flexibility (a much broader range of investments to choose from) and consolidation (having all of your RRIF investments at one institution, on one statement). In this way, you are able to move from one investment to another without having to actually transfer sums of cash from institution to institution. This is important, because it can take weeks to transfer from one RRIF plan to another. Moreover, because foreign content is limited to

25 percent of the book value of any particular plan (30 percent starting in 2001) rather than all of your RRIFs cumulatively, a self-directed plan allows you to maximize your global investments. If you have more than three different RRIF accounts adding up to a total of more than $25 000, you may wish to consider a self-directed plan. Remember, with a self-directed plan, no one will make decisions for you, so you must either be a knowledgeable investor with time on your hands or have a financial advisor to assist you.

Making Withdrawals

With a regular RRIF, you can take out as much as you want every year (but it will be taxed as income) and you must take out a prescribed minimum payment. (See Appendix F for the exact amounts.)

If you take out more than the minimum, tax will be withheld "at source" by the RRIF trustee. This isn't a penalty—rather, it is an installment, or prepayment of tax you will owe Revenue Canada on the income. If, for some reason, you owe Revenue Canada less than the withheld amount, you will receive a refund when you file your return.

Withholding tax rates for RRIF withdrawals are as follows:

Amount	All Provinces Except Quebec	Quebec
Up to $5000	10%	25%
$5000.01 to $15 000	20%	33%
$15 000.01 and above	30%	38%

What You Can Expect to Receive from the Government

Canada Pension Plan benefit rates are indexed to inflation, so if there is a change in the Consumer Price Index, which measures the cost of living, rates are adjusted in January for the following year. Table 24-1, from HRDC, shows the maximum and the average monthly benefits for the year 2000.

Old Age Security benefit rates are reviewed quarterly. Table 24-2 shows Old Age Security rates for the year 2000.

Table 24–1
CPP Pension Rates for Year 2000

Type of Benefit	Average Maximum Monthly Benefit (June 1999)	Maximum Monthly Benefit
Disability benefit	$ 676.33	$ 917.43
Retirement pension	$ 412.27	$ 762.92
Survivor's benefit (under age 65)	$ 307.08	$ 420.80
Survivor's benefit (age 65 and over)	$ 240.29	$ 457.75
Children of Disabled Contributors benefit	$ 171.33	$ 174.07
Children of Deceased Contributors benefit	$ 171.33	$ 174.07
Combined Survivor's and Retirement benefit	$ 557.99	$ 762.92
Combined Survivor's and Disability benefit	$ 832.12	$ 917.43
Death benefit (one payment)	$2145.69	$2500.00

Source: Human Resources Development Canada.

Table 24–2
Old Age Security Payment Rates

Type of Benefit	Average Monthly Benefit (August 1999)	Maximum Monthly Benefit (April–June 2000)	Income Level Cut-off (April–June 2000)
Old Age Security Pension	$396.80	$420.34	See note*
Guaranteed Income Supplement			
• Single	$335.71	$499.55	$12 000
• Married to a non-pensioner	$303.67	$499.55	$29 088
• Married to a pensioner	$177.85	$325.39	$15 648
• Married to a Spouse's Allowance recipient	$238.45	$325.39	$29 088
Spouse's Allowance	$259.11	$745.73	$22 416
Widowed Spouse's Allowance	$443.28	$823.29	$16 440

*Pensioners with an annual income above $53 215 must repay part or all of the maximum Old Age Security amount. The repayment amounts are normally deducted from their payments before they are issued.

Source: Human Resources Development Canada.

House-Rich, Income-Poor? Think About a Reverse Mortgage

Many Canadians put all of their savings efforts into paying off their home—and then find that although they may be wealthy in assets due to the increased property values, their income level is a problem. The most obvious solution to this problem, of course, is to downsize, sell the home and move to a condo.

For most people, this solution is the most pragmatic one. You may be finding your home too big anyway, or too difficult to maintain. For others, though, quality of life is dependant on staying put for as long as possible, and for some of those people, there are reverse mortgages.

A reverse mortgage is almost like an annuity. You sign some documents and you get a monthly income payment, or alternatively, a lump sum that you can use to buy an annuity—or whatever. (The money you receive is not taxable.)

However, when you buy an annuity, you use cash, and when you arrange for a reverse mortgage, you sign over the deed to your house. As long as you live, or until the maturity of your reverse mortgage term, you will not be required to sell your house—the real downside is that, with interest, there may be no value left in your home by the time it's sold. If you or your inheritors pay off the loan, including interest, you or they get to keep the house, but otherwise it belongs to the financial institution, whether property values have gone down or doubled.

The amount you can "borrow" is generally restricted to 50 percent of the value of your property.

Get good legal and financial advice before committing yourself. If your income needs are small (but crucial), contact your municipality to see if you can defer property taxes.

Tip

From a dollars-and-cents perspective, unless you live in an area that is suffering a real estate depression, selling your home, trading down, and living on the difference is a better option than a reverse mortgage. On the other hand, if you have no heirs, or your heirs are financially self-sufficient, and you want to keep your home, a reverse mortgage may work for you.

The Least You Need to Know

➤ If you are a member of a pension plan, get the details—how much can you expect to receive, or is it a defined contribution plan?

➤ Is your pension plan indexed to inflation? Integrated with CPP?

➤ If you expect your annual income to be higher than $53 215 in retirement, seriously consider seeking the advice of a fee-for-service financial planner before making further RRSP contributions, particularly if you are over 55.

➤ Whatever you do, don't cash in your RRSP at retirement unless you love paying income tax.

Part 7

Protecting Your Assets: Risk Management and Estate Planning

All personal financial planning efforts ultimately have two objectives—to create financial well-being and to achieve peace of mind.

Risk management (otherwise known as insurance planning) helps us accomplish both. It protects us from the kinds of financial catastrophes that can devastate even the soundest financial plan, and allows us to relax in the knowledge that we've done everything possible to protect ourselves and our families against hardship.

Like life insurance, estate planning is something we do for ourselves and our own peace of mind, and for our families. Most of us aren't that keen on handing over large chunks of our assets to the government during our lifetimes; the idea of making Ottawa one of our beneficiaries at death isn't that appealing either.

Life is beautiful. And hard. We will know tragedy, grief, loss, and death. In this part of the book, however, we will learn to face the financial side of these realities with as much ease and dignity as possible.

Chapter 25

A Lot About Insuring Your Income

In This Chapter

➤ The basic principles of risk management

➤ Insuring your income—disability insurance

➤ A disability checklist

Buying insurance is similar to buying mutual funds in that in both cases, we pool our money with large numbers of other individuals. With mutual funds, of course, we hope to share profits. With insurance, we share risk. Let's find out how it works.

Insure Against Devastation, Not Inconvenience

It is almost never cost-effective to ensure the little stuff. For instance, insuring your credit card balance in case of your disability or death is rarely a good value. What if you were to pay $5 a month for insurance and get hit by a bus when you'd just paid off your card? (Although it isn't "little stuff," the same principle applies to mortgage insurance as well—you pay for insurance on the entire value of your mortgage, which then steadily declines. Better to buy term insurance to cover the mortgage, and then your family will receive whatever is left over after paying it off.)

Things like veterinary insurance, extended warranties on electronic goods, and optional coverages (known as "riders") on home or auto policies can add up quickly, and the chances of them providing real value are slim.

Now, let's look at the insurance almost everybody needs.

Beware

Are extended warranties a good deal? No. For every dollar you pay for one, the manufacturer pays about 15 cents. They are over-priced by about 700 percent.

Insuring Your Income

Your single greatest asset is your ability to earn an income. Even at an average of $40 000 a year, if you work from age 24 to age 65, you can expect to earn $1 600 000! That's the good news. The bad news is that one in eight of us can expect to be injured or seriously ill to the extent that we would qualify for long-term disability during our lifetime.

Unfortunately, because the odds of requiring disability benefits at some point are so high, so are the premiums. If you're lucky enough to work for a company that sponsors a group benefit plan, you should definitely participate if only for this reason.

Beware

If you pay your disability premiums, your benefits are tax-free. If your employer pays them, your benefits are taxable. If your employer is currently paying your premiums, ask to pay them yourself. If possible, arrange for an offsetting income increase or to have your employer pay for life insurance or medical benefits instead.

A Word on Employment Insurance

If you are employed, there is always a risk that you may become unemployed. In this, the greatest country in the world, we have Employment Insurance to make sure that day is a bad one, not an insurmountable one.

You can find all the information you need on Employment Insurance online at <www.hrdc-drhc.gc.ca/ei/common/home.shtml>.

In the meantime, know that you generally need 700 hours of employment to qualify for EI, and that the maximum benefits are 55 percent of your normal income or a maximum of $413 per week. The maximum benefit period is between 14 and 45 weeks, depending on your claim. It isn't much money, and it is a pain to get your hands on.

Who Knew?

A large group of people, like all 35 000 employees of a bank, can buy disability insurance more cheaply than a solitary, lonely, insecure, single, white, non-smoking male who likes Beethoven, red wine, and long walks in the park (like that guy looking over your shoulder while you're reading this book). Insurance companies employ hundreds of actuaries to calculate the risk involved in insuring large groups against disabling accidents. Individuals, on the other hand, have no one else to share the risk. So the cost of their disability insurance is higher. But that's still no reason not to buy it.

Know that there is a two-week waiting period (for which no benefits will be paid)—make visiting your nearest EI office to file your claim the first thing you do as an unemployed person. Don't make the mistake of assuming you'll get another job right away, even if you already have leads. If you do, you can cancel your claim; if you don't you won't lose the weeks that have passed while you waited to find out.

Despite the negative connotations associated with receiving payments from the government, remember that you've paid premiums to Employment Insurance for all of your working life—so that you won't be financially devastated by just this occurrence. File your claim.

Arranging Private Disability Plans

If the company you work for doesn't offer a group plan, you may want to begin by offering to investigate the costs of introducing one. Employers may not be willing to pay for all or even part of the premiums, but sharing risks among groups of even 10 or 15 employees may substantially reduce your costs.

If this isn't a possibility, check with any professional associations or service groups you belong to—they may offer group policies that you simply haven't heard about.

Now, just how much disability insurance will you need? Complete the exercise in Table 25-1 to find out. If you are married, you and your spouse should each do the exercise, and then decide how you would manage on only one income.

Table 25-1
Disability Needs Analysis

1. If I were unable to work, what is the least amount of income I would need to maintain my current lifestyle? (Calculate by referring to Cash Flow Statement from Chapter 2, subtracting expenses related to employment, such as office attire, transportation to and from work, lunches out, income tax, CPP, and EI.)

   A $ _____ per month

2. If I was unable to work, how much would I receive in Employment Insurance benefits? (Remember, investment income, disability pension benefits, etc., may effect this. You can get information on EI payments as they apply to your situation by calling Human Resources Canada or visiting their Web site.)

   A $ _____ per month for _____ months

3. If I were unable to work, how much would I receive in benefits from my disability insurance provider? Calculate this figure on a net basis—it is fundamental to determine whether your benefits are non-taxable (you have paid all of the premiums yourself) or taxable (your employer has paid for all or a portion of the premiums).

   A $ _____ per month for _____ months

4. How many weeks would elapse between the onset of my illness or injury and receipt of benefits from EI and/or my disability provider?

   A _____ weeks

5. Based on my cash flow expense calculation, how much money do I need in an emergency reserve fund to manage this period (between onset of unemployment and receipt of benefits)?

   A $ _____

6. How much do I currently have in an emergency reserve fund?

   A $ _____

7. If the reserve I now have is insufficient for my needs, do I have friends or relatives I could borrow from? Do I have a line of credit set up for this purpose? How much money could I access without changing my lifestyle or risking investment loss?

   A $ _____

8. Is there a difference between my long-term and short-term disability benefits? How much would I receive per month (net) if I were ill for more than a year?

   A $ _____

9. If I was severely injured or ill, and was unable to return to my career or job, would my long-term disability benefits continue until age 65? Or would they only continue if I was unable to do any kind of work (e.g., telephone soliciting, attaching mailing labels to envelopes, etc.)?

   A   ☐   Benefits would continue as long as I was unable to return to my occupation.

   ☐   Benefits would continue as long as I was unable to return to any kind of work.

Beware

Many disability insurers will insist that you apply for the Canada Pension Plan Disability benefit after a certain period. Whether you do or don't, the amount you are eligible for (a maximum of about $900 a month) will be deducted from your benefits after you've been given sufficient notice.

Shopping for the Right Policy

If you've established that the only way to have disability insurance is to buy a private policy, these are some of the factors you should consider:

1. *There are two kinds of policies—"own occupation" and "any occupation."* There are also a number of policies that begin as "own occupation" and become "any occupation" after a stated period, usually two years. "Own occupation" policies pay benefits as long as you are unable to do your job; "any occupation" policies pay benefits only if you are too disabled to do any job. Obviously, "own occupation" policies are much more expensive, but if you can afford it, you may want to spend the extra.

2. *The longer you can wait for benefits, the lower your premiums will be.* If you have an emergency reserve equal to six months net income, you can extend your waiting

time for at least that period. (Be sure to apply for Employment Insurance disability benefits as soon as you become ill or are injured.) And whatever happens, the emergency money is yours—unlike disability benefits, which will only "benefit" you if something bad happens.

3. *You'll need to decide on the duration of the policy.* Generally, disability benefits pay to age 65, but shorter terms are also available.

4. *Consider the other features of a potential policy.* You'll want to pay the extra for a policy that is "non-cancellable and guaranteed renewable." This just means that you won't be required to have further health examinations and your policy won't be cancelled by your insurer just at the time you need it. "Residual benefits" mean that you can work part-time if you're up to it, and still receive partial benefits. "Future insurability" allows you to buy more coverage without having to submit to another medical exam—unless you expect your income to rise significantly, you may want to skip this and save the additional premium. A feature you will want to look for is a cost-of-living-adjustment (sometimes referred to as a "COLA"). This ensures that your benefits will increase as the cost of living does.

Life Insurance

If there is someone who depends on you financially, you need life insurance. Unless, of course, you are one of the lucky few who will leave sufficient assets behind. The irony is that most of us don't have sufficient assets until those that depend on us most, our children, aren't dependent on us anymore.

Calculating your life insurance needs is relatively simple. You need to ask yourself the following questions:

➤ What are my financial obligations? (What do I currently owe?)

➤ If I were to die, how much would it cost to replace my income contribution to my family? (Look back at your Cash Flow Statement, and remember to subtract those employment-related expenses.)

➤ What about additional costs?

➤ How much would it cost to bring my dreams for my family into reality even if I weren't around to see it happen?

Table 25-2 shows an example life insurance needs calculation, and Table 25-3 provides a blank chart for you to fill in.

Table 25-2
Life Insurance Needs Analysis (Example)

Cost of funeral and burial expenses	$ 8000
Replacement of net income for 10 years (during which time all dependent children will reach age 21)	$300 000
Cost of a nanny for six years, minus the cost of 50% of day care (spouse pays half now)	$ 72 000
University education and/or or small business fund for child	$ 48 000
Debts that must be paid off by estate; taxes that will be triggered on my death	$ 3000
Total funds required at my death	$431 000
Subtract:	
Current group life insurance	($120 000)
Current assets and investments	($120 000)
CPP Death and Survivor Benefits	($12 000)
Required life insurance	$179 000

Table 25-3
Your Life Insurance Needs Analysis

Cost of funeral and burial expenses	$_____
Replacement of net income for _____ years (during which time all dependent children will become independent)	$_____
Any debts (mortgage, credit cards, outstanding loans)	$_____
Additional costs	$_____
University education for dependent children	$_____
Taxes that will be triggered on my death	$_____
Total funds required at my death	$_____
Subtract:	
Current group life insurance	$_____
Current private life insurance	$_____
Current assets and investments	$_____
CPP Death and Survivor Benefits	$_____
Required life insurance	$_____

Tip

Commissions paid to insurance advisors are significantly higher than those for term policies. If you've bought a whole life policy and wish you hadn't, you're free to cancel it. Just purchase term life insurance, with guaranteed renewability, before you do.

The Great Debate: Term Insurance vs. Whole Life Insurance

There continues to be great debate over the value of whole life, universal life, or variable life policies, which combine term insurance with a cash investment component, as compared to term insurance policies, which simply provide insurance. In my opinion, universal life was a valid alternative in the days when investing in anything more complex than term deposits was beyond the average Canadian investor.

These days, with a plethora of low-cost investment options at our disposal, I would recommend whole life insurance only when there are specific estate-planning objectives in mind. For instance, a whole life policy can work well to provide non-taxable benefits in order to fund tax obligations on an estate. As well, because whole life policies do provide non-taxable benefits, they provide an alternative for very conservative investors who wouldn't consider investing in equities on their own.

Go for the Term

For true life insurance needs, however, I weigh in heavily (well, as heavily as I can at 133 pounds) on the side of term insurance. As it is much, much less expensive, you can buy as much as you need without cutting into your ability to contribute to your RRSP.

Insurance advisors receive a fraction of the commission on term insurance products as compared to whole life policies—which is part of the reason that whole life policies are so much more expensive. If you're being aggressively sold whole life insurance, you'll need to consider the following:

➤ Whole life insurance provides a forced-savings/investment program. But so does an automatic monthly investment program, usually with lower costs, more flexibility, and the potential for higher returns.

➤ Whole life insurance will allow you to borrow using the cash portion of your account as collateral. But it may be much less expensive to borrow on the equity you have in your home or by using your investments as collateral.

➤ Term insurance gets more expensive as you get older, and may not even be granted if you have health problems. This is a valid concern, which is why it is important to pay a little extra for a guaranteed renewal option. Most of your insurance needs will evaporate as you get older and your asset base increases—why pay for insurance you no longer need? The corollary issue is that whole life makes it impossible for younger families to buy as much insurance as they need.

Term Insurance Features You'll Want to Buy

Premium Adjustment Periods

The longer the period your premium rate is fixed for, the more you'll pay for insurance in the early stages. Terms of 5, 10, 15, or 20 years are generally available. If your insurance needs will be the same in 20 years as they are today, you may want to pay more for a longer period. Conversely, if most of your insurance needs will disappear as your children become independent over a period of 5 or 10 years, choose a shorter period.

Beware

Many people are under the assumption that if they die, their beneficiaries will receive both the insurance death benefit and the savings portion of their whole life policies. That isn't true—the savings portion is gone.

Guaranteed Renewal Rates

As you get older, your renewal costs will rise significantly. First, use this as incentive to save aggressively and build up your asset base so you won't need insurance. In addition, check out your policy to ensure that your renewal rates are stated in your policy.

Guaranteed Renewability

This is really important—make sure you have it unless you definitely won't need life insurance when your policy expires. This option ensures you won't have to pass a medical exam to find your policy won't be renewed because of failing health—just when you need it most.

The Least You Need to Know

➤ Insure against catastrophe, not against inconvenience.

➤ If you need an income, you need disability insurance.

➤ If at all possible, arrange disability insurance through your employer or a professional, social, or civic organization you belong to.

➤ Unless you are buying life insurance to meet specific estate-planning objectives, buy term life rather than whole or universal life.

Chapter 26

A Little About Insuring Your Stuff

In This Chapter

➤ Protecting your home

➤ Protecting your visitors

➤ Protecting your car and other stuff

You get more than you think you do with some types of property insurance, although you still have to pay for it.

On the Home Front

If you own a home, and more specifically, you have a mortgage, the lender will insist that your home be ensured. Remember that you don't have to ensure the value of the land—nothing is going to happen to it (and if it does, your insurance won't cover it).

Even if you don't have a mortgage, you should insure the structure and contents of your home. If you rent, you should obtain tenant's or contents insurance, a policy that covers the contents of your home and may provide liability coverage, but does not cover the structure itself.

Home Coverage Defined

There are three basic types of home insurance coverage:

1. *Comprehensive insurance* covers both structure and contents against everything but the 362 things specifically excluded. (I'm kidding—there may actually be 400 things excluded.)

2. A *named perils policy*, which is also sometimes referred to as a standard or basic policy, insures you only against the specific risks or perils named in the policy.

3. A *broad policy* is sort of a hybrid—it provides comprehensive coverage on the building structure and named perils on the contents.

Depending on your perception of the risk, you may choose to spring for optional coverage for earthquake or sewer back-up, for instance.

Definition

Named peril insurance covers only risks that are specifically named in the policy. If it doesn't say that you're covered if your neighbour slips on the ice in your driveway, you may not be. Be very careful with this kind of policy.

What Else Does It Cover?

As well as providing funds with which to repair damage or replace contents, home insurance provides personal liability coverage. If someone is injured in your home and sues you to recover damages, your liability insurance will ensure you don't lose your home or assets as a result.

All home insurance policies have maximums for certain kinds of items, like jewellery or bicycles. If you need additional coverage, you can pay a bit more for coverage and "schedule" these specific items.

How Much Does It Cost?

The size of your premiums will depend on a number of factors, including these:

➤ The kind of policy you choose. Comprehensive is most expensive, followed by broad, followed by named peril.

Tip

Thieves sometimes strike twice, waiting for you to replace all of your stolen property and then coming back to steal the new things. This can play havoc with your insurance rates. If your home had been broken into, consider installing an alarm, putting some lights on a timer, further securing doors and windows with bars and dead bolts, or even changing your work schedule so that you come home at different times of the day.

➤ The deductible. Usually starting at about $500, deductible can range all the way to $2000. The lower the deductible, the more expensive the coverage. Think about what you can afford to replace out of your own pocket, without causing a financial crisis, and choose the highest deductible you can afford. (You are unlikely to file a claim for smaller items, anyway, knowing that your premiums can be affected.)

➤ Any claims you have made in the past. Adding insult to injury, I know—but if you've had a number of break-ins, you can count on higher insurance or, in a worst-case scenario, even a rejected application.

➤ The length of time you've been insured with a particular company.

➤ Your neighborhood. You'll pay more for living in a high-density, crime-ridden urban area, unfortunately, or in a flood zone.

➤ The value of your property.

Tip

Make sure you know what's in your home. Either take snapshots of each angle of each room or videotape your home and contents. Don't keep this record in your home—if you have a fire, it isn't going to be of much help. And while you're at it, photocopy all your identification and credit cards and keep a copy in a safe place.

Auto Insurance

It doesn't seem fair. You'll pay $400 annually for insurance on a $200 000 home, and $1400 annually for a $20 000 car. The difference, of course, is the likelihood of damages and the amount of damage you could do. (I've seen cars drive into houses, but I've never seen a house hit a car!)

Unlike home or contents insurance, which is optional unless your mortgage lender insists on it, anyone with a car on the road *must* insure. The reason, obviously, is that accidents are rarely solitary affairs. They almost always involve someone else or at least someone else's property. For that reason, the law insists that you carry enough coverage so that your insurance company will pay for damages to property and that you have personal liability coverage, as well. In all provinces except Quebec, the minimum liability coverage is $200 000; in Quebec, it's $50 000.

Don't stick with the minimum, though. If you get sued after an accident and don't have enough coverage, you could lose your assets. Therefore, be sure that you have at least as much liability coverage as you do assets.

What Else Does It Cover?

As well as liability coverage, your auto insurance may offer additional types of coverage:

➤ Comprehensive coverage. Vandalism, theft, storms, and other nasty things that may befoul your lovely vehicle. Look to the value of your car to determine the amount of your comprehensive coverage, and choose a high deductible (say, $500) if you could afford to replace your windshield or less expensive damage without making a claim.

➤ Collision. Damage caused to your car through impact with another car or solid object when you're at fault. If the other driver is at fault, his or her insurance will cover the damage. You may want to skip this if you drive a wreck. If you wouldn't spend money fixing your 1976 Ford Comet if something happened, skip the collision insurance.

➤ Accident benefits. Medical or, God forbid, funeral costs resulting from an accident.

➤ In addition, you may have underinsured motorists' coverage that will pay for medical or funeral expenses if the other driver does not have enough insurance.

How Much Does It Cost?

Your auto insurance costs will depend on your age, your sex, the area in which you live, your driving record, and the kind of car or truck your drive. To save money on your auto premiums, explore the possibility of umbrella liability coverage for both your home and auto needs, and then take only the mandatory amount of auto liability coverage required by your province. Keep your deductibles as high as you can afford—and drive safely.

The Least You Need to Know

➤ Keep your property and auto insurance low by keeping your deductibles high.

➤ Property and auto insurance cover more than just the cost of damage. They also cover your liability for injuries to other people, at least to a specified amount.

Chapter 27

You Can't Take It with You

In This Chapter

➤ When you need a will

➤ What you need to consider

➤ Clauses you may want to include

➤ Avoiding those dastardly probate fees

➤ Death and taxes—avoiding the one that you can

Once you die, you likely won't care much about what you leave behind. But your survivors sure will.

The Final Word on the Matter—Your Last Will and Testament

I'm never going to die.

What's that you say? I *am* going to die? How cruel!

Okay. I give. You're right. I am going to die. And so are you. And that, my friend, is why we both need to make a will.

When you die, your friends and family will mourn you. You don't want to add confusion, inconvenience, potential family conflict and a larger-than-necessary tax bill to their grief.

Definition

A **holographic will** is a will written in your own handwriting, dated and signed by you.

The only time you don't need a will is when you have no dependents and no assets. Once you own even a wretched old Chevy Nova or an apartment full of Value Village furniture, write up what is called a *holographic will*—a will written in your own handwriting, dated and signed by you.

As soon as you have any financial assets, of course, you need a real will. If your estate isn't large or complicated and you don't have children, you can get a perfectly decent will drawn up by a notary public.

Name a Guardian for Your Children

If you have children, you need a will to establish your wishes for guardianship in case you and your spouse die together. Don't let your last thought be, "Oh, God, I wonder who will take care of them?"

If you die without a will, your children will become wards of the Public Trustee and the Superintendent of Family and Child Services becomes guardian of your children. If relatives or friends of yours then wanted to become the children's guardian, they would have to make an application to the courts.

How Do You Choose?

How do you choose a guardian? Begin by asking yourself the following questions, and discussing them with your spouse:

1. Who would your children want to live with?

2. Do the people have the required energy? How is their health? Many of us immediately think of our parents—but would you want to be raising children at their age? If in doubt, ask. Let them know you'll understand if they don't feel up to it.

3. Do your candidates for guardian share your child-rearing values?

4. What is their current family situation? Do they have children of their own? Do they have enough time to meet the needs of their kids and yours?

5. How do their children get along with yours?

6. Have you provided sufficient insurance benefits or other assets, so the guardian you name won't also be taking on an onerous financial obligation?

7. Do you want the guardian to act as trustee of your financial estate as well?

Beware

Most people select a child's grandparents for the job of guardian. In fact, this isn't your best choice. That's because grandparents are older. If they receive guardianship of your children and then die shortly after, the children suffer. A better choice is to find a younger couple you trust. But make sure that they're up for the job.

Naming an Executor of Your Will

Most people name their spouse as an executor of their estate, or one or more of their adult children, but there are many things to consider. There's no single solution, but this is a weighty and time-consuming responsibility that should neither be given nor accepted lightly.

Your executor's duties may include:

➤ Preparing a statement of assets and liabilities

➤ Making a year-of-death RRSP contribution if your will provides that instruction (and it should)

➤ Settling all of the liabilities of your estate, including funeral costs, and dealing with creditors

➤ Submitting the will for probate

➤ Arranging the funeral

➤ Completing and submitting all insurance claims on behalf of beneficiaries or estate

➤ Distributing all assets in accordance with the will

➤ Managing all ongoing trusts, including investment and distribution

➤ Filing the final tax return, submitting taxes owing, and arranging for releases on the estate from Revenue Canada

How Do You Choose?

Begin by asking yourself these questions:

1. Does this person have the necessary business sense and experience? Good judgment, even in difficult times?

Who Knew?

The standard fee for the administrative services of the executor is approximately 4 percent of the value of the estate, providing that the assets are quickly distributable. However, if the assets are held inside a trust, then the trustee receives a care-and-management fee of approximately 0.25 percent each year based on the average market value of the estate. In addition, the trustee is usually allowed 5 percent per year of any income earned inside the trust.

2. Is this person's time flexible? Does his or her work allow for time to conduct meetings, etc.?

3. Does he or she live in an appropriate location, or will serving as an executor mean travel away from home or hours on the telephone?

4. Does this person have the social skills and emotional fortitude to deal with other family members in a time of collective grieving? Is your choice going to trigger "old wounds"—those family conflicts that go back to childhood?

Remember that you have the option of naming two executors. If your estate is financially complex, it can be beneficial to make the second executor a trustee with a financial institution who can take care of the administrative requirements.

Writing a Will

Now it's time to have your will drawn up. There are do-it-yourself wills available, but if you have significant assets or children, don't skimp here.

Many legal firms will provide you with a will preparation kit that will allow you to make all decisions in advance of meeting with a lawyer and, therefore, keep your bill to a minimum.

In addition to naming an executor and a guardian for any minor children, you'll need to think about a number of other issues.

Disposition of Property

After taking care of your dependents, this is the major function of a will. When passing on property, remember to take taxes into consideration. If you leave your $200 000 residence to one adult child, for instance, and your $200 000 RRSP to another, the second one will probably end up with not $200 000 but $100 000. When calculating fairness, use after-tax amounts.

If you have young children, think about setting up a testamentary trust (one that goes into effect after your death). One of the most devastating things that can happen to young people is to receive a large estate that they aren't ready to handle.

Definition

A **testamentary trust** is one that takes effect after your death; an **inter vivos** or **living trust** is in effect while you are alive.

Personal Effects

One of the most common sources of conflict when settling an estate is the distribution of the loved one's personal effects. When preparing your will, you don't need to list every item, but you may want to keep a list of your personal possessions and your wishes for their distribution with your will.

An alternative is to suggest to your executor that your effects be distributed according to the hockey pool method. Each family member draws a straw and then, in turn, each chooses one thing that is precious to them.

If there are some items of large value, assign a value to each item and then calculate the total for each person at the end. If the values are unfair, arrange to settle the difference in cash from the estate so that everyone is treated fairly.

It's Not Over Till It's Over

There are still more considerations involved in preparing for your demise:

➤ Life insurance. I can't imagine *not* paying the relatively small monthly amount required to leave enough money for my children to live on comfortably without me. It is only partly for them—it's really for me, and my peace of mind. I consider it a great bargain.

Definition

A **codicil** is an amendment to your will that allows you to make changes without nullifying the entire will and having to make an entirely new one. Codicils are useful if you purchase new property, for example.

Tip

Wherever possible, register assets jointly, with right of survivorship, so that ownership will pass directly to the surviving spouse without probate costs or administrative wrangling. Before doing this with any significant assets, investigate the possible tax consequence. They can be significant and sometimes nasty.

➤ Naming your spouse as beneficiary of your RRSP (or RRIF) and insurance plans, if you're married (legally or common-law). In addition, if you have children, name them as secondary beneficiaries in case you and your spouse die together. This will ensure the RRSP's tax-sheltered status can continue until the money is needed.

Tip

If you are leaving a legacy to charity, investigate the possibility of leaving assets rather than cash. The tax benefits can be significant.

Taxes

Bear in mind that all of your investments, including any vacation properties, will be treated as if they were sold when you die.

If you want an asset to pass intact to a family member, therefore, you may wish to arrange for an insurance policy to cover the cost of taxes that your death will trigger.

Power of Attorney

Power of attorney gives your spouse or another trusted person the legal authority to take care of your affairs if you are incapacitated. That means this person can sign cheques, cash in your RRSPs, and do practically anything you can do, just by signing his or her name instead of yours.

Obviously, you shouldn't make this choice too lightly. You are putting your entire well-being in this person's hands.

Beware

Be careful when choosing someone to give power of attorney. I had an acquaintance whose investment portfolio went from tens of thousands of dollars to a few thousand when she gave a boyfriend power of attorney and he tried to make some money in penny stocks on her behalf. She wasn't grateful.

Organize Your Records

I'm confident that I don't have to say this, because we covered it in Part 1, and I'm sure your records are in impeccable order by now, but leave decent records for your family.

Be considerate. Ensure that your executor knows where everything is, from your will to your latest bank statements and bills.

Tip

If you wish to leave the proceeds of an insurance policy to a charitable organization, name your estate rather than the charity as the beneficiary. That way, the charity can get the proceeds but your estate gets the charitable deduction. Otherwise, no one gets the deduction.

Who Knew?

If you are selected as someone's executor, you have to close bank accounts, terminate pension plans, apply for death benefits, notify the provincial registrar and health authorities, and submit final income tax returns. To do all this, you'll need a death certificate, which you get from the undertaker or funeral home (not the attending physician). You'll also need the person's social insurance number. (If you can't find the card, the number is indicated on the person's tax returns.)

The Last Goodbye

Prepare for your funeral and/or memorial service. Talk about it with your family and your close friends.

Do you prefer cremation or burial? Do you wish to donate your body to a university medical school? Have you discussed your choice with your family? Ensure that your organ donor card is registered and that your family knows of your wishes.

Who Knew?

Despite the good intentions indicated on an individual's driver's licence, a person can donate organs such as liver, heart or kidneys *only* if he or she is receiving life support through a ventilator at the time of death. Otherwise, the organs stop functioning and cannot be used. This eliminates most potential donors. (In Ontario, for example, only 2 percent of all deaths qualify as potential sources of organ donations, and there are only 150 donations a year.) However, any person can donate his or her body to a university teaching hospital.

Who Knew?

Do you want to be kept alive by artificial means? Do you want to be resuscitated after you've stopped breathing? Do you want to be kept alive even though you're in a coma and unlikely ever to regain full consciousness? With a living will, you can relieve your family of these agonizing decisions. A living will simply describes the level of care you want if you become terminally ill. Your lawyer can help you draft it.

You may also want a living will that decisively communicates your wishes about resuscitative medical treatment in the event of terminal illness. Canadian doctors are obliged to consider a living will as evidence of a patient's choice if the person had been conscious and competent when the living will was written.

Review Your Plan

Do an annual review of your will and other preparations for your death. Choose an anniversary date—the first week of January, or the week before your birthday. (You'll feel a lot better about reaching it when it comes.)

Review everything—it should only take a few minutes. Think about anything that has changed significantly over the last 365 days. Are the guardians you've named still healthy and willing to take on the responsibility? Married to each other?

As changes occur in your life, make changes to your estate plans and will.

Here are some clauses you may wish to consider including in your will:

➤ *Survivorship condition.* This clause prevents the unnecessary costs of probating and administering two estates in a case where you and your spouse die together, or he or she does not survive you by more than 30 days.

➤ *Tax election clause.* This simply allows your executor to administer the estate in the most tax-effective fashion.

➤ *Investment discretion clause.* Unless you insert this clause, your executor is limited to very conservative, low-return investments under the Trustee Act.

Tip

The best place to keep your will is with your lawyer. That way, in the event of your death, it can be easily retrieved. You should also keep an unsigned copy of the will in your files at home.

➤ *Discretionary encroachment clause*. Minor beneficiaries may not receive assets of the estate until they become adults. This clause will allow the executor to use assets of the estate to meet the needs of the minor children prior to their majority (the age at which they are considered adults).

➤ *Life interest in a specific asset clause*. This clause is becoming very common in the case of second marriages, and allows the testator (the person who is writing the will) to leave the income earned on an asset to his or her surviving spouse during the spouse's lifetime, while leaving the asset itself to someone else.

Estate-Planning Checklist

Here's a checklist from *Financial Serenity* that will help you address all the issues involved in making sure that your death causes as little hassle as possible for your survivors:

1. Designate a guardian and executor(s); choose financial, legal, and tax advisors.
2. Keep complete records of all financial matters and advise your family of their location.
3. Review your life insurance needs and make any necessary changes.
4. Arrange a power of attorney.
5. Arrange a living will.
6. Arrange for long-term care insurance if desired.
7. Avoid unnecessary taxes and probate fees by naming beneficiaries and holding assets jointly where possible.
8. Set up any trusts, RESPs, etc., that are required to fulfill your wishes for your inheritors.
9. Review annually and/or after any significant changes in legislation or your personal situation.
10. Discuss your wishes and arrangements with your family

What Are Probate Fees, Anyway?

Probate fees are charged by each provincial court (with the exception of Quebec) to grant "letters probate." Letters probate confirm that the court has examined the will, confirmed that it is valid, and granted the executor the right to administer the deceased's estate.

Table 27-1 shows how probate fees are applied across Canada.

Table 27-1
Probate Fees

Province/Territory	Size of Estate	Fee or Tax
British Columbia	First $10 000 $10 001–$25 000 $25 001–$50 000 Over $50 000	No fee $200 0.6% 1.4%
Alberta	First $10 000 $10 001–$1 000 000 Over $1 000 000	$25 Progressive rate to $3000 Progressive rate to $6000
Saskatchewan	All estates	0.7%
Manitoba	First $10 000 Over $10 000	$50 $50 plus 0.6%
Ontario	First $50 000 Over $50 000	$50 1.5% (yikes!)
Quebec	Notarial Wills Holograph/Witnessed	No fee Nominal fee
New Brunswick	First $5000 $5001 to $20 000 Over $20 000	$25 Progressive to $100 0.5%
Nova Scotia	First $10 000 $10 001–$200 000 Over $200 000	$75 Progressive to $800 $800 plus 0.5%
Prince Edward Island	First $10 000 $10 001–$100 000 Over $100 000	$50 Progressive to $400 0.4%
Newfoundland	All estates	$75 plus 0.5%
Yukon Territory	First $25 000 Over $25 000	No fee $140
Northwest Territories (including Nunavut)	First $500 $501–$1000 Over $1000	$8 $15 $15 plus 0.3%

Source: Trimark Investment Management.

The probate fee is calculated on the entire value of the estate, with the exception of property that is directly encumbered by debt, as in the case of a home with a mortgage on it. Otherwise, if the estate is $50 000 and the credit card bills are $50 000, probate fees will be applied as if the estate is $50 000 rather than zero.

Strategies to Reduce Probate

Here are some strategies that may help reduce probate fees. (Remember to take tax consequences into consideration before making any changes. For instance, if you transfer your family home into a joint tenancy with an adult child, half of the value of the home is no longer deemed to be a principal residence for tax purposes, and capital gains will be taxable. If in doubt, consult with an estate-planning professional.)

Tip

To reduce probate fees, hold assets jointly. Put bank accounts, investments, etc., in the name of you and your spouse or children. For obvious reasons, you should be on good terms with them. Otherwise, your assets may end up in Hawaii, along with your spouse.

➤ Name a beneficiary whenever possible. RRSPs, RRIFs, and insurance policies allow the owner to name a specific beneficiary or beneficiaries, so that these assets are not subject to probate fees.

➤ Give it away. If you are planning on leaving certain assets to certain individuals and no longer have need for their use in your lifetime, make a gift of these items now.

➤ If you have a significant assets, consult an estate-planning specialist about the possibility of setting up holding companies or testamentary trusts.

➤ Whenever possible, convert non-mortgage debt to mortgage debt. As mortgage debt is subtracted from the value of your estate before probate fees are applied. Consider increasing your mortgage on renewal to pay down other existing debts.

Death and Taxes—Avoiding the One You Can

Believe it or not, on the day that you die, Revenue Canada makes the assumption that you were busy selling all of your property. At least, that's way they choose to look at it.

All of your assets, except your principal residence, will be taxed as if they were sold. This is the dreaded "deemed disposition of property."

Let's review some of the planning techniques that may minimize the damage.

Your Home

Your primary residence is exempt from tax, but not from probate fees. Therefore, it is best to hold it jointly with your spouse so it can be excluded from your estate. If you do not have a spouse, you may want to have it registered jointly with your child or children, but be careful—this may have tax consequences during your lifetime or create tax problems for your child. Check with a tax lawyer or qualified estate planner prior to taking action.

Your RRSPs, RRIFs, or RPPs

If you are married (legally or common-law) ensure that your spouse is the named beneficiary of your plans. Be sure to also name a secondary beneficiary in case you and your spouse die together. This is particularly important if you have minor children, as it means that the registered plan can remain sheltered (through the purchase of an annuity or the purchase of an RRSP in their name), which is beneficial tax-wise and avoids probate fees.

In addition, particularly if you are in a higher tax bracket, ensure that your will has a clause allowing your executor to make an RRSP contribution for the year of your death.

Non-Registered Assets

Assets outside of your registered plans can be rolled over to your spouse with no tax consequences. (They become taxable when the last spouse dies.) However, unless the assets are owned jointly and registered correctly, they will be included in the estate and probate fees will be applicable.

Consider an Estate Freeze

If you have significant assets, you may wish to hire some estate-planning help and consider this advanced planning technique. Through the creation of a holding company or trust, your assets will be transferred into another tax entity, so that you pay capital gains taxes to the point at which the transfer is made, and your inheritors become responsible for taxes after that point. This method is particularly useful with family businesses.

Life Insurance as an Estate-Planning Tool

As life insurance is not taxable, estate planning is one of the few purposes for which whole life insurance is practical. If you have a family asset, a cottage, for example, which will become taxable on the death of the last spouse, your children may be forced to sell it in order to pay the large tax bill. If you want to keep it in the family, arrange a whole life policy to pay off the tax bill when it becomes due.

Using Trusts to Protect Your Assets

Another advanced planning strategy—if you think a trust might be of benefit, see a tax lawyer. There are two kinds of trusts, inter vivos (or living) trusts, and testamentary trusts (which come into effect upon your death). An inter vivos trust serves much the same purpose as a holding company. Assets are transferred into it, and income is paid out according to the conditions of the trust. A testamentary trust can be useful to shelter assets from tax after your death, or to help with difficult issues like blended families. For example, you may wish your current spouse to benefit from all of the income on your assets during his or her lifetime, but desire that your assets ultimately go to your children rather than your spouse's children.

Charitable Giving

Particularly if your estate is substantial, you can ensure that your estate pays significantly less tax by effectively arranging charitable donations. Donating capital gains-producing investment assets, for example, is more beneficial than donating cash. If you wish to purchase an insurance policy to benefit a charity, ensure that your estate is the beneficiary of the proceeds (which will be tax-free) rather than the charity. In this way, your executor can deliver the proceeds of the policy to the charity, but the tax deduction will benefit your estate and heirs.

The Least You Need to Know

➤ We're all going to die—be considerate and leave a will.

➤ Being named a guardian or executor is not an honour as much as it is a weighty responsibility. Think deeply before you either ask someone or accept someone else's request.

➤ Don't forget about powers of attorney and living wills.

➤ A little planning can save a great deal of money in taxes and probate fees.

The Best of the Web

If you have Internet access, check out these sites for everything from financial planning tips and online banking tools, to mortgage calculators and the latest information on government programs, insurance, and mutual funds. While most of these are Canadian sites, a few American sites have been included for their strong general coverage of topics like investment basics and managing credit crises.

Personal Financial Planning

MoneySense.ca	<www.moneysense.ca/index.html>
Sympatico Personal Finance	<www.bc.sympatico.ca/Contents/Finance/>
Canoe Money	<www.canoe.ca/Money/home.html>
Royal Bank Tools	<www.royalbank.ca/tools.html>

Banks and Banking

Consumer Affairs Financial Services Calculator	<strategis.ic.gc.ca/SSG/ca01193e.html>
Bank of Montreal	<www.bmo.com>
Bank of Nova Scotia	<www.scotiabank.com>
Canadian Imperial Bank of Commerce	<www.cibc.com>
Canadian Western Bank	<cwbank.com>
Citizens Bank of Canada	<www.citizens.com>
Laurentian Bank	<www.laurentianbank.com>
Manulife Bank	<www.manulife.com>
Manulife One	<www.manulifeone.com>
National Bank of Canada	<www.nbc.ca>
Royal Bank of Canada	<www.royalbank.com>
Toronto Dominion Bank	<www.tdbank.ca>
Canada Deposit Insurance Corporation	<www.cdic.ca>
Canadian Banker's Association	<www.cba.ca>
Canadian Banking Ombudsman	<www.bankingombudsman.com>
Office of the Superintendent of Financial Institutions	<www.osfi-bsif.gc.ca/>

Credit Cards and Credit Counselling

Deep in Debt	<www.ivillagemoneylife.com/money/life_stage/deepdebt/>
Office of Consumer Affairs	<strategis.ic.gc.ca/SSG/ca00458e.html>
Consumer Connections	<strategis.ic.gc.ca/SSG/ca00719e.html#Counselling>

Tax Issues

KPMG Canada	<www.kpmg.ca/>
TaxWeb	<www.tax.ca/>
Canadian Customs and Revenue Agency (formerly Revenue Canada)	<www.ccra-adrc.gc.ca/>

Mortgages and Home Buying

Canada Mortgage and Housing Corporation	<www.cmhc-schl.gc.ca/cmhc.html>
Home Buying	<www.bc.sympatico.ca/Contents/Finance/home.html>
The Mortgage.com	<www.themortgage.com/>
MRS Trust	<www.mrstrust.com>
Manulife One	<www.manulifeone.com>
Canada Mortgage	<www.canadamortgage.com>
The Multiple Listing Service (MLS)	<www4.mls.ca/mls/home.asp>
Remax	<www.remax.ca/>
Royal Lepage	<www.royallepage.ca/>
Lycos Real Estate	<www.lycos.com/realestate/>
Canadian Institute of Mortgage Brokers	<www.cimbl.ca>

Investing

Coffeehouse Investor	<www.coffeehouseinvestor.com>
Bylo Selhi	<www.bylo.org>
Globe Investor	<globeinvestor.com/>
Canadian Shareowners Association	<www.shareowner.ca>
Investment Dealers Association	<www.ida.ca/index.html>

Socially Responsible Investing

Ethical Funds	<www.ethicalfunds.com/index.html>
Mackenzie Financial's Universal Global Ethics Fund	<www.mackenziefinancial.com/home.html>
Citizen's Bank	<www.citizensbank.ca/investments/rrsp_info/social_investing.html>
Real Assets	<realassets.org>

Mutual Funds

The Fund Library	<www.fundlibrary.com/tfl/homepage/p_home.cfm>
Fidelity Investments	<www.fidelity.ca/>
Bylo Selhi	<www.bylo.org>
Altamira	<altamira.com/>.
TD e-funds	<www.tdefunds.com>
CIBC	<www.cibc.com/>
Sceptre Investment Counsel	<www.sceptre.ca/sceptre/wmsceptre.nsf/public/homepage>
Phillips, Hager and North	<www.phn.com/>
Bissett and Associates	<www.bissett.com/>

Insurance

Insurance Canada	<www.insurance-canada.ca/>
Canadian Life and Health Assurance Association	<www.clhia.ca>
CompCorp	<www.compcorp.ca>
Insurance Bureau of Canada	<www.ibc.ca>

RESPs and Education Planning

Revenue Canada (CCRA)	<www.ccra-adrc.gc.ca/menu/EmenuGNW.html>
Saving for an Education: RESPs 101	<search.canoe.ca/IEMoneyFeb99/ie_resps.html>
About the CESG	<www.hrdc-drhc.gc.ca/hrib/learnlit/cesg/about/about.shtml>

Retirement Planning*

Old Age Security and Canada Pension Plan	<www.hrdc-drhc.gc.ca/isp/common/home.shtml>

* See also all sites listed under "Personal Financial Planning"

Financial Dictionary

Accrued interest Interest that has been earned but not yet paid out to the investor. This interest must be declared each year as income for tax purposes, even if it has not been received.

Acquisition fee The price you pay to buy something—a sales commission.

Actuary A professional analyst who calculates mortality rates and life expectancies for insurance purposes.

Administrator The administrator of an estate is appointed by the court to handle the duties normally fulfilled by an executor when someone dies without a will or when the will fails to name an executor.

After-tax cost The cost to an investor after calculating the effect of income tax.

Amortization The process of gradually paying out debt or obligation, e.g. a mortgage, or of writing off value for tax or reporting purposes. Most commonly, for individuals, amortization refers to the period over which mortgage payments will be made.

Analyst A financial professional (usually employed by a bank, brokerage firm, or mutual fund company) who studies companies and/or markets and makes buy-and-sell recommendations. Analysts are often specialists—they focus on bonds, for instance, the auto industry, or Asian equities.

Annual report A report issued by a company to its shareholders explaining the company's operations and its financial statements for the period reported.

Annuity A contract under which assets are turned over to an institution (usually an insurance corporation) on the condition that a stream of income will be provided for a specified period. **Life annuities** pay for the lifetime of the annuitant (the person receiving the payments) and **fixed-term annuities** for a "fixed" period, generally until the annuitant reaches age 90.

Appraised Value An estimate of the potential selling price of an asset, usually property.

Assets In financial terms, anything you own that has value.

Asset allocation The planned distribution of investment assets (by percentage) into various categories (e.g., equities, bonds, and liquid investments) according to pre-determined criteria.

Averages and indices (or Stock Market Index) The DOW Jones Industrial Average (commonly known as the DOW) is one, the TSE 300 Composite Index is another. These are tools of statistical measurement, in which a basket of representative companies is used to determine the overall gain or loss of a market. In the TSE 300, for instance, the Toronto Stock Exchange's performance is measured by recording the price changes of the 300 representative companies' stocks.

Average When comparing performances of investment vehicles or categories, an average is a weighted comparison (that is, the performance of large funds or companies will affect the measurement more than that of smaller funds or companies).

Averaging down The process of buying more of a security for which the market value has declined in order to lower the average per-share or per-unit cost of the holding.

Bank rate This is the rate at which the Bank of Canada makes short-term loans to Canada's chartered banks.

Basis point Term used in reference to bond and T-bill purchases. It means, simply, 1/100 of 1 percent. Also referred to as **BPs** or **beeps**.

Bear market A term used to describe a declining market. A bearish analyst believes the market will decline.

Beneficial owner The individual or institution that really owns an asset. If Jane Jones has a self-directed RRSP with ABC Trust, Jane would be the beneficial owner, and ABC Trust would be the **registered owner**.

Beneficiary The person or persons chosen to receive the benefit of income or assets under the terms of an investment, trust, insurance policy, or estate.

Bid The price a buyer offers to pay for a trading security or asset.

Blended payment A loan payment that consists of a payment on the principal of the loan (the amount of money actually borrowed) and the interest charged on the loan.

Blue chip stocks Stocks with good investment qualities. They are usually common shares of well-established, dividend-paying companies with good earnings histories.

Board lot The minimum number of shares that may be purchased without incurring additional commission. A purchase of shares that is less than a board lot is an **odd lot**.

Bond A debt instrument issued by a government or corporation to raise working capital. A bond is a promise (or "covenant") by the issuing government or corporation to repay the principal amount on the maturity date plus interest payments on a stated schedule.

Book value Term is usually used to describe the purchase price, plus re-invested dividends, of investments within an RRSP. Book value can also be the market value at the time an asset is transferred or contributed to an RRSP.

Broker An agent who buys and sells something on behalf of a third party. Usually used in reference to an agent who buys and sells stocks, insurance products, or real estate.

Bull market The opposite of a bear market—a market in which prices are increasing.

Callable Feature of some bonds or preferred stocks that allow the issuer to redeem ("call") the bond or stock prior to the stated maturity date at a pre-stated price.

Canada Mortgage and Housing Corporation (CMHC) Crown corporation that was formed for the purpose of making home ownership available to a larger number of Canadians by administering the National Housing Act and making mortgage insurance products available.

Canadian Bond Rating Service (CBRS) An independent evaluator of creditworthiness, responsible for applying a corporate credit rating to companies. Ratings are expressed in a variety of ways, such as AAA or A1+, depending on the rating agency.

Canadian Depository Insurance Corporation (CDIC) A Crown corporation formed for the protection of investors in Canada's banks and trust companies. Under CDIC, to which all banks and trust companies pay premiums, an investor is covered to a maximum of $60 000 (on principal deposits only—interest is not included) should a member firm become bankrupt.

Canadian Investor Protection Fund (CIPF) A fund created by the stock exchanges and the Investment Dealers Association to protect investors from losses resulting from the bankruptcy of a member firm. All stock brokerage firms in Canada must belong. However, securities and mutual fund dealers are not members of the IDA, and their clients are not covered by this fund.

Canada Education Savings Grant (CESG) A grant issued by the federal government to top up education savings contributions.

Canada Pension Plan (CPP) A program funded by the premiums it collects, primarily through paycheque deductions. Everyone must pay into CPP, and may then draw from it upon retirement.

Capital cost allowance An Income Tax Act term used to describe deductions allowed from the value of certain assets, which are then treated as expenses from an individual's or company's income.

Capital gain A profit made when the selling price is higher than the purchase price of stocks, real estate, bonds, and other assets.

Capital loss The opposite of a capital gain.

Capitalization Total amount of all outstanding debt, common and preferred stock, contributed surplus, and retained earnings of a company.

Carry-forward The difference between an individual's maximum RRSP contribution limit and the amount he or she has actually contributed.

Cash account A brokerage account in which the account holder pays the full amount for any investment purchase. (The alternative is a **margin account**, which is an account that allows the holder to buy on credit within certain limitations.)

Cash flow For individuals, all income that is received in cash (or cash value) and all expenses paid in cash (or cash value). For corporations, cash flow is based on earnings before deductions such as depreciation and deferred income taxes.

Certificate of Deposit (CD) More commonly called a term deposit, this is a deposit of funds that becomes available on a stated maturity date.

Certified Financial Planner (CFP) Someone who has met the training and testing requirements of the Financial Planners Standards Council of Canada or the Canadian Institute of Financial Planning.

Closed mortgage Mortgage in which you're locked in for the full term. Terms generally range from six months to ten years, with the most common being three- and five-year terms.

Closing date When buying a home, this is the date on which the sale becomes final and the new owner gets to move in.

Codicil A written change, amendment, or addition to a will which has been properly witnessed and signed. This is often an efficient way of making a change to a will without having the entire document rewritten.

Collateral Property, securities, or assets pledged as security against a loan.

Commercial paper Short-term (less than one year), unsecured promissory notes issued by corporations to finance short-term cash flow requirements.

Commission The broker or agent's fee for buying or selling securities for a third party.

Commodity A product used for commerce that is traded on an exchange. Commodities include agricultural products (e.g., wheat and pork bellies) and natural resources (e.g., oil and gold).

Common share A type of stock that represents ownership or equity in a company. Common shares often include the right to vote in the company's affairs and entitle the shareholder to participate in a share of the company's profits, usually paid out through dividends.

Community property A legal term that describes property (assets) acquired after marriage that is jointly shared by both partners. Sometimes referred to as "family property."

Compound returns With compounding, returns (or interest) are added to the original principal of the investment. Interest is then calculated on the new amount, consisting of principal and interest. Each interest payment expands the total amount used for future calculations. Interest on debt is also compounded.

Conditional offer When buying a home, a conditional offer is one that is contingent on certain requirements. Common conditions include the completion of a satisfactory appraisal, a qualified inspection, or the sale of the buyer's current home within a certain period.

Confirmation A printed acknowledgement of a purchase or sale of stocks, bonds, or mutual fund units. These are normally mailed to an investor within 24 hours of a trade and give all the details of the purchase or sale (price, number of shares or units, and commission).

Constrained share companies These are companies whose ownership is restricted to Canadian citizens. They include banks, broadcasting and communications companies, and trust and insurance companies.

Consumer Price Index A statistical measurement of increases or decreases in the cost of living. The price of a basket of goods (housing, gas, the price of milk, etc.) is measured on a regular basis. This is generally the way that the rate of inflation is determined.

Contribution The amount you put into something, generally used in reference to an investment or savings plan such as an RESP or an RRSP.

Conventional mortgage A mortgage that does not exceed 75 percent of a property's appraised value—that is, a mortgage on a home on which the buyer has made a down payment of at least 25 percent of the value.

Convertible A feature of a security (generally a bond, debenture, or preferred share) that allows the investor to convert the asset into another asset, generally a common share, according to pre-stated conditions.

Convertible term insurance Term insurance that can be converted to a permanent or whole life policy without evidence of insurability (e.g., medical examination.).

Coupon A bond attachment that entitles the bearer to an interest payment. It can be clipped and presented to a bank on or after the maturity date. The coupon rate is the rate of interest paid on the bond. A strip bond has been stripped of its coupons and sold separately.

Covenant A promise to do something, or not to do something, as set out in a contract or bond offering. An example might be a covenant not to issue more bonds.

Current yield The annual return on an investment

Day order An order to buy or sell a security that becomes void if not filled by the end of that day.

Debenture A bond that is not backed by underlying assets.

Decreasing term insurance With this type of insurance policy, the premium remains constant while the coverage diminishes over time. Coverage begins proportionately high compared to the premium, but falls as time passes.

Deemed disposition A term used by Revenue Canada to refer to the sale of an asset, for tax purposes. This usually occurs when an asset is transferred to another individual (e.g., a spouse) or contributed or to an RRSP.

Deferred annuity Annuities for which income payments begin after a specified period, usually at a stated age.

Deferred sales charge (DSC) When you buy units of a mutual fund, the fund company may impose a commission that it pays itself, as long as you hold the investment. If you sell your units within a specified period (usually seven years) the charge is no longer deferred. It comes out of your pocket. A DSC encourages people to leave their investments for a longer period in a particular fund.

Deferred profit sharing plan (DPSP) Your employer can contribute a portion of its profits into this tax-sheltered plan for your benefit.

Defined benefit plan (DPP) A company-sponsored pension plan in which retirement benefits are determined by a complex formula based on salary and years of service. The benefits are therefore defined, and the pension holder knows or can calculate the payments in advance.

Discount The amount by which a bond or debenture sells below par or face value.

Diversification Otherwise known as "not keeping all of your eggs in one basket" when you are investing. There are many levels of diversification (e.g., by asset type, by industry, by time horizon, and by geographical location).

Distribution The payment of a dividend, income, or capital gain.

Dividend A portion of a company's (or mutual fund's) profits paid out to shareholders (or unit holders). May be paid in cash (usually the case with stock) or "in kind" (more shares or units—usually the case with mutual funds).

Dividend re-investment A process whereby dividends are paid in cash and then converted into shares or units of a company or fund (without the cash being distributed to the investor first). Some companies and most mutual funds provide this feature.

Dollar cost averaging The process of investing a specified (unchanging) amount on a regular basis. This process helps to mitigate volatility risk.

Earned income A Revenue Canada term meaning all income that is earned through employment, business, royalties, research grants, taxable alimony, maintenance and child support, net rental income, and disability pensions paid out under CPP/QPP. It does not include pension income, dividends, interest, capital gains, amounts received from an RRSP/RRIF, or severance pay.

Earnings A corporation's revenues minus the expenses incurred to create those revenues, over a stated period.

Equities The term used to describe shares issued by a company representing ownership in that company. For our purposes, it is synonymous with "stocks."

Estate All assets owned at the time of a person's death.

Estate planning Planning to transfer one's assets in an orderly manner to designated individuals, in a way that minimizes taxes, delays, fees, and potential family discord.

Excess contribution Any contribution made to an RRRSP over your maximum contribution limit.

Executor The person or institution assigned to carry out the instructions of a will and distribute the property of an estate.

Extendible bond or debenture A debt instrument granting the holder the right to extend the maturity date by a stated period.

Face value The value of a bond or debenture that appears on its "face" or the front of the certificate. This is usually the amount due on maturity.

Fixed-rate mortgage A mortgage on which the interest rate and terms will stay the same for the term of the mortgage. The alternative is a **variable rate mortgage**, for which the rate will vary according the conditions of the day.

Flow-through shares Certain losses and expenses that would normally be treated as tax deductions by a corporation or trust can be "flowed-through" or attributed to investors through these investment structures.

Front-end load Sales commission paid at the time of a mutual fund purchase. Sometimes referred to as a **sales charge** or **acquisition fee**, this fee is charged on a percentage basis ranging from 0 to 9 percent, with an average of 3 to 5 percent.

Fund family A group of mutual funds owned and managed by the same corporation. It is generally much easier and cheaper to transfer money between funds in the same family.

Future value The value of an investment at some point in the future at the current rate of return. A related term is **present value**—that is, the current value of a future amount. For example, if you invest $1000 at 10 percent interest for one year, the present value of the investment is $1000, and the future value of the investment in one year is $1100.

Futures Contracts (traded on exchanges) that allow the holder to buy or sell commodities, currencies, etc., at a stated price on a stated date.

Guaranteed Investment Certificates (GICs) Fixed-income investments issued by banks. They are guaranteed by the CDIC for up to $60 000.

Gross debt service ratio The percentage of your total earnings required to meet all payments associated with housing. (The recommended maximum is 32 percent.)

Gross Domestic Product (GDP) The value of all goods and services produced in a country in a year. This figure does not currently recognize unpaid work, such as homecare and child-rearing, but is limited to goods and services that change hands for units of value.

Gross National Product (GNP) Similar to GDP but also includes profits and interest on endeavours by Canadians living or investing abroad as well as at home.

Growth mutual fund See **growth stock**.

Growth stock A stock that's expected to grow in value more rapidly than average. In addition to their potential for rapid growth, these stocks invariably have an equal potential for volatility—rapid swings in price, both high and low. Growth mutual funds are those that invest in growth stocks.

Guaranteed income fund A mutual fund that invests in GICs and term deposits.

Guaranteed term The period during which annuity payments are guaranteed. If the annuitant dies during this period, payments will be made to the beneficiary.

Guardian A person who has been legally designated to care for the needs of a minor child or any other individual who has become incompetent to manage his or her own affairs.

Hedge A protective manoeuvre designed to limit losses. There are many ways of hedging. Diversification is a simple form of hedging that minimizes some of the risks involved in investing. By purchasing units in an equity fund and a bond fund, for example, you're hedging against a drop in the value of one or the other.

Home Buyer's Plan A plan that allows RRSP holders to withdraw up to $20 000 from their RRSP to purchase a new home. Repayments of 1/15 per year are required beginning in the third calendar year after the withdrawal.

Income bond In most cases, an income bond promises to repay the principal investment, but will pay interest income only when it is earned by the issuing corporation.

Income splitting The process of arranging income streams between spouses so that taxable income is diverted by a higher-taxed individual to a lower-taxed one.

Index A benchmark or measuring device created by tracking the performance of a group of stocks or other investments, against which the performance of other investments is measured. Examples are the S&P 500 Index, the Wiltshire 2000 Index, and the TSE 300.

Initial public offering (IPO) When a company issues stock to the public for the first time, it makes an initial public offering.

Installment receipt A stock or equity investment that allows the investor to pay in installments rather than in one lump sum.

Inter vivos trust A trust that takes effect while the person is still living. These trusts are usually created to minimize probate fees.

Intestate The state of dying without a valid will.

Intra-day tracking The charting of the movement in price of a stock or other investment within a one-day period

Investment strategy A plan to distribute investments among various asset classes and specific investments, in consideration of personal goals, time horizons, and risk tolerance.

Joint and last survivor annuity A type of annuity that provides income payments until both the annuitant and the annuitant's spouse die.

Labour sponsored venture capital corporations (LSVCCs) A type of mutual fund sponsored by labour organizations for the purpose of funding small and medium-sized businesses. As an incentive, governments offer attractive tax credits to investors.

Leverage Planning strategy that involves increasing the return (and risk) on an investment by borrowing and using the borrowed funds to invest.

Lifelong Learning Plan A program that allows RRSP holders to withdraw up to $20 000 from their RRSPs to upgrade their education. Repayment required is 1/10 per year beginning in the sixth calendar year following the withdrawal.

Liquidity Liquidity describes the ease with which an asset can be converted into cash without incurring a major delay or significant financial penalty.

Load Sales commission that is paid to somebody for selling you a fund.

Locked-in RRSP RRSP account created from pension fund money. In a locked-in self-directed RRSP, investments can be purchased or sold, but funds cannot be withdrawn or used to fund a mortgage on one's home.

Locked-in retirement account (LIRA) The equivalent of a locked-in RRSP. A registered plan that can receive pension proceeds.

Management expense ratio (MER) The total of all management fees plus other expenses, divided by the number of units in the fund.

Management fee The portion of the MER that is paid to the fund manager. It does not include the cost of administration or distribution, even though those costs are paid by the fund holders.

Margin In an account in which you borrow funds to finance a portion of your investments (a margin account), margin refers to the amount you actually own. Trading regulations determine this amount (as a percentage of the total account).

Marginal tax rate The rate at which you would be taxed on the next dollar of income.

Market order A stock market term for an order to purchase or sell securities immediately, at any price.

Money market That portion of the capital market created for the short-term borrowing and lending of funds.

Money market fund A mutual fund that invests in the money market, usually for terms of less than one year, and offers low but stable returns with low potential for volatility risk.

Mortgage-backed securities (MBS) Fixed-income instruments that are backed by a pool of mortgages insured by the Canada Mortgage and Housing Association under the National Housing Act.

Mutual fund A pooled group of investments, providing professional management and the opportunity for maximum diversification. The total value of a mutual fund is divided into "units," which are then allocated to investors based on the fund's net asset value.

Net asset value (NAV) The measure of total assets of a corporation minus total liabilities. Net asset value is sometimes referred to as **shareholders' equity**.

Net asset value per share (NAVPS) The valuation of mutual fund units, NAVPS is the measure of the total value of the assets of the fund, minus any liabilities of the fund, divided by the number of units outstanding.

No-load fund A fund sold without a sales commission.

Note A short-term debt security (usually five years or less).

Offer The price at which a holder of securities is willing to sell them. When bid meets offer, we have a **contract**.

Offering memorandum A legal document reporting the pertinent aspects of an investment, for the review of potential investors. Similar to a prospectus, but released without the same degree of scrutiny by the regulatory bodies. See also **prospectus**.

Online trading The buying or selling of investments on the Internet, generally through discount brokerages.

Open order An order that is valid until it is filled or until it is expressly cancelled by the investor.

Option An option provides the right, but not an obligation, to purchase or sell a security at the stated price within the stated period. A put option allows an investor to sell securities at a specified price on a specified date; a call option allows an investor to purchase securities at a specified price on a specified date.

Par The value for which an instrument can be redeemed. Also known as **face value**.

Penny stocks Colloquial term for stocks that trade at less than a dollar. These are generally very speculative issues traded on the resource markets (such as the VSE and ASE).

Pension adjustment (PA) The adjustment made to your RRSP maximum contribution limit, based on the combined value of your employer's contribution to your pension plan as well as your own.

Portfolio A group of investments owned by an individual or institution.

Portfolio manager The person or company responsible for investing assets and managing trading.

Portfolio tracking Monitoring the price movement of a group of investments using various analytical tools—usually done now on the Internet.

Present value The value of an investment right now, as opposed to the amount it may be worth in the future.

Price-earnings ratio Calculation used to determine whether a stock is expensive in relation to its underlying profitability. It is, quite simply, a company's earning per share divided by its share price.

Prospectus Legal document that discloses everything you need to know about a particular investment.

Real rate of return The stated return on your investment, minus tax considerations, minus the rate of inflation.

Redemption The sale of an investment or security, usually to the company that issued it. The term is most often used to refer to the redemption of mutual fund units (which are sold back to the mutual fund company, essentially) or to the redemption of a bond on maturity.

Registered education savings plan (RESP) A registered savings/investment program that accumulates funds in a tax-sheltered environment to pay for post-secondary education.

Registered pension plan (RPP) A pension plan (generally established by an employer) on behalf of its employees to provide pension income in retirement.

Registered retirement income fund (RRIF) Money transferred from an RRSP, that is similar to an RRSP, except you must withdraw a specified minimum amount every year.

Registered retirement savings plan (RRSP) A tax-deferral plan that encourages Canadians to prepare for their retirement. RRSPs allow us to defer paying income tax on a portion of our income until we withdraw the funds.

Re-investment Using dividends or income on an investment to purchase more of that investment, rather than receiving it in cash.

Renewable insurance A feature on some term insurance policies that allows the insured to renew the policy without "evidence of insurability" (e.g., medical information) at the premium rate applicable at their age.

Return The amount of income you receive from an investment

Reverse mortgage A loan against your home that is used to purchase an annuity, which then provides monthly income.

Risk In the investment industry, risk is defined as the possibility that a particular investment will not do what we expect, or hope, it will do. At its simplest, risk is the possibility of loss.

Risk tolerance Ability to cope with the possibility of loss on an investment.

Self-directed RRSP An RRSP plan in which we can hold any qualified investment. Unlike managed RRSPs, in which the manager (either the mutual fund manager or the bank, for instance) decides where our money will be invested, in a self-directed plan, we get to decide. In return, we pay an administration fee, usually between $100 and $150 per year.

Sector A defined portion of a market, industry, or economy (e.g., oil and gas sector, industrial sector, technology sector).

Securities Another term for investments or assets, such as stocks, bonds, certificates of deposit, and treasury bills.

Share Investors in public companies receive a portion of the company in return for their investment. This portion is measured in shares. For our purposes, **shares** and **stock** are synonymous.

Shareholder An investor who owns shares of a company's stock. With mutual funds, this investor is normally referred to as a unit-holder.

Speculation Purchasing an investment today in the hope that it can be sold at a higher price tomorrow.

Spousal RRSP contribution An RRSP contribution that is made (and deducted) by one spouse on behalf of the other. This is an effective income-splitting device.

Stock Partial ownership in a publicly traded company. The term is used interchangeably with **shares** and **equities**.

Stock exchange A marketplace, either real or virtual, in which shares of public companies are bought and sold.

Strip bonds Bonds that have been separated from their interest coupons. Also known as zero coupon bonds.

Tax deferral The process of postponing payment of taxes for as long as legally possible.

Tax shelter Investment vehicle that allows funds to be sheltered from taxation until the money is withdrawn.

Term insurance A kind of insurance policy that provides coverage for a stated term.

Testamentary trust A kind of trust that will come into effect after death, that is, it is set out in your will and will be implemented by your executors. See also **inter vivos trust**.

Trade The brokerage term for the purchase or sale of an investment

Treasury bill (or T-bill) Short-term government debt instrument. T-bills are very liquid as they have short maturity periods (usually 91 and 182 days), and can also be bought and sold between maturity dates. They are fully government backed, which means they are extremely safe.

Trust A legal instrument placing property or assets in the hands of a trustee (a person or institution elected to manage the assets or property and oversee its distribution to another person or persons). An RRSP is a trust, but the trusts that we normally hear referred to in regard to investment are either inter vivos (living) trusts or testamentary (after-death) trusts.

Universal life A form of whole life insurance that provides life insurance coverage and an insurance component that is indexed to money market yields. Universal life is very popular when interest rates are high.

Variable life A form of whole life insurance in which the investment portion of the plan is invested in mutual funds. These plans are more flexible and may provide higher returns than universal life policies, but are not as predictable.

Volatility The rate at which the price of an investment moves up and down—often used as a measurement of risk.

Yield The return on an investment, normally expressed as a percentage.

Discount Brokerages

	Telephone	Web Address	Basic Trade Fee
Bank of Montreal InvestorLine	1-800-387-7800	www.investorline.com	$25
CIBC Investor's Edge	1-800-567-3343	www.cibc.com	$33
CT Securities	1-800-560-6373	www.canadatrust.com	$29
Charles Schwab	1-888-597-9999	www.schwabcanada.com	$42.50
E*Trade Canada	1-888-TRADE88	www.canada.etrade.com	$27
HSBC InvestDirect	1-800-398-1180	www.hsbcinvestdirect.com	$29
National Bank InvesTel	1-800-363-3511	www.invesnet.com	$24.50
Royal Bank Action Direct	1-800-Royal83	www.actiondirect.com	$29
Scotia Discount Brokerage	1-877-536-7493	www.sdbi.com	$36
Sun Life Securities	1-800-835-0812	www.sunsecurities.com	$29
TD Waterhouse	1-800-659-7553	www.tdwaterhouse.ca	$29

The Canadian Shareowners Association's Low-Cost Investment Program

Here is a list of stocks and index funds currently available through the Canadian Shareowners Association's Low-Cost Investment Program (LCIP).

Domestic Securities

Index-Based Funds (Sponsored by the Toronto Stock Exchange)

S&P/TSE 60 Index (TSE,XIU)

Tips35 (TSE,TIP)

TIPs100 (TSE,HIP)

Companies

Aliant Inc. (TSE,AIT)

Bank of Montreal (TSE,BMO)

Bank of Nova Scotia (TSE,BNS)

Barrick Gold (TSE,ABX)

BCE Inc. (TSE,BCE)

BCT.TELUS Comm (TSE,BTS)

Bombardier "A" (TSE,BBD.A)

Canadian Pacific (TSE,CP)

CanWest Global (TSE,CGS.S)

CIBC (TSE,CM)

Cinram International (TSE,CRW)

Dorel Industries "B" (TSE,DII.B)

Fairfax Financial (TSE,FFH)

Gennum Corporation (TSE,GND)

Great-West Lifeco (TSE,GWO)

Imperial Oil (TSE,IMO)

Investors Group (TSE,IGI)

JDS Uniphase Corp. (TSE,JDU)

Loblaws Companies (TSE,L)

MDS Inc. (TSE,MDS.A)

National Bank of Canada (TSE,NA)

Nortel Networks (TSE,NT)

Power Corporation (TSE,POW)

Royal Bank (TSE,RY)

Seagram Company (TSE,VO)

Teleglobe Inc. (TSE,TGO)

Thomson Corporation (TSE,TOC)

Toronto Dominion Bank (TSE,TD)

Trimark Financial (TSE,TMF)

Unican Security Systems "A" (TSE,UCS.A)

Foreign Securities

Index-Based Funds (Sponsored by the American Stock Exchange)

DOW DIAMONDS: Dow Jones Industrial Average (AMEX,DIA)

Nasdaq-100 Index (AMEX,QQQ)

SPDRs: S&P 500 Index (AMEX,SPY)

Companies

Abbot Laboratories (NYSE,ABT)

AFLAC Inc. (NYSE,AFL)

Biomet Incorporated (NYSE,BMET)

Campbell Soup (NYSE,CPB)

Caribbean Utilities (NYSE,CUP.U)

Citigroup Inc. (NYSE,C)

Coca-Cola Company (NYSE,KO)

Colgate-Palmolive (NYSE,CL)

Concord EFS Inc. (NYSE,CEFT)

General Electric (NYSE,GE)

Gillette (NYSE,G)

Hershey Foods (NYSE,HSY)

Home Depot (NYSE,HD)

Intel (NASD,INTC)

Johnson & Johnson (NYSE,JNJ)

Kellogg Company (NYSE,K)

Lucent Technologies (NYSE,LU)

McDonald's (NYSE,MCD)

Merck & Co. (NYSE,MRK)

Microsoft (NASD,MSFT)

Motorola (NYSE,MOT)

PepsiCo (NYSE,PEP)

Sara Lee Corporation (NYSE,SLE)

Stryker Corporation (NYSE,SYK)

Synovus Financial (NYSE,SNV)

Total Systems Services (NYSE,TSS)

Wal-Mart Stores Inc. (NYSE,WMT)

Walt Disney (NYSE,DIS)

Wendy's International (NYSE,WEN)

Revenue Canada Publications

Forms

NRTA1	Authorization for Non-Resident Tax Exemption
RC96	Lifelong Learning Plan (LLP)—Request to Withdraw Funds from an RRSP
T1-OVP	1999 Individual Income Tax Return for RRSP Excess Contributions
T1-OVP Schedule	Calculating the Amount of RRSP Excess Contributions Made Before 1991 that are Subject to Tax
T746	Calculating Your Deduction for Refund of Undeducted RRSP Contributions
T1004	Applying for the Certification of a Provisional PSPA
T1006	Designating an RRSP Withdrawal as a Qualifying Withdrawal
T1007	Connected Person Information Return
T1036	Home Buyers' Plan (HBP)—Request to Withdraw Funds from an RRSP
T1043	Deduction for Excess Registered Pension Plan Transfers You Withdrew from Your RRSP or RRIF
T1090	Death of a RRIF Annuitant—Designated Benefit
T1171	Tax Withholding Waiver on Accumulated Income Payments from RESPs
T1172	Additional Tax on Accumulated Income Payments from RESPs

T2019	Death of an RRSP Annuitant—Refund of Premiums
T2030	Direct Transfer Under Subparagraph 60(l)(v)
T2078	Election Under Subsection 147(10.1) in Respect of a Single Payment Received from a Deferred Profit Sharing Plan
T2151	Direct Transfer of a Single Amount Under Subsection 147(19) or Section 147.3
T2205	Calculating Amounts from a Spousal RRSP or RRIF to Include in Income
T2220	Transfer From an RRSP or a RRIF to Another RRSP or RRIF on Marriage Breakdown
T3012A	Tax Deduction Waiver on the Refund of Your Undeducted RRSP Contributions

Guides

RC4112	Lifelong Learning Plan (LLP)
RC4135	Home Buyers' Plan (HBP)

Information Circulars

72-22	Registered Retirement Savings Plans
77-1	Deferred Profit Sharing Plans
78-18	Registered Retirement Income Funds

Information Sheet

RC4092	Registered Education Savings Plans (RESPs)

Interpretation Bulletins

IT-124	Contributions to Registered Retirement Savings Plans
IT-167	Registered Pension Plans—Employee's Contributions
IT-221	Determination of an Individual's Residence Status
IT-281	Elections on Single Payments from a Deferred Profit-Sharing Plan

IT-320	Registered Retirement Savings Plans—Qualified Investments
IT-337	Retiring Allowances
IT-363	Deferred Profit Sharing Plans—Deductibility of Employer Contributions and Taxation of Amounts Received by a Beneficiary
IT-412	Foreign Property of Registered Plans
IT-499	Superannuation or Pension Benefits
IT-500	Registered Retirement Savings Plans—Death of an Annuitant
IT-528	Transfers of Funds Between Registered Plans

RRIF Minimum Withdrawal Amounts

Age	General	Qualifying RRIF (Opened Before 1993)
71*	.0738	.0526
72	.0748	.0556
73	.0759	.0588
74	.0771	.0625
75	.0785	.0667
76	.0799	.0714
77	.0815	.0769
78	.0833	.0833
79	.0853	.0853
80	.0875	.0875
81	.0899	.0899
82	.0927	.0927
83	.0958	.0958
84	.0993	.0993
85	.1033	.1033
86	.1079	.1079
87	.1133	.1133
88	.1196	.1196

Age	General	Qualifying RRIF (Opened Before 1993)
89	.1271	.1271
90	.1362	.1362
91	.1473	.1473
92	.1612	.1612
93	.1792	.1792
94 or older	.2000	.2000

*For ages below 71, the formula is 1 ÷ (90 − age)

Index

About the Author

Lori M. Bamber has more than a decade of experience in the financial services industry, with a strong background in trust and registered plan management. Previously an executive vice-president and director of one of Canada's fastest-growing investment firms, Lori scaled back her activity some years ago to achieve a greater quality of life. A licensed financial advisor, Lori continues to offer advice through Aspen Capital Management in Vancouver.